CW00640947

PARIS

First Edition
1992

TABLE OF CONTENTS

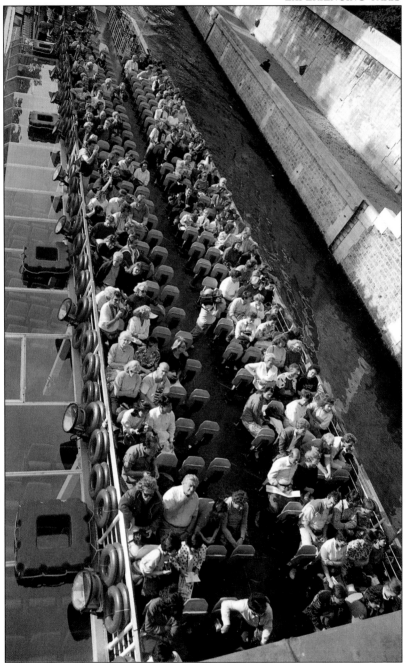

CARROUSEL DE LA TOUR EIFFEL

PARIS

– CITY OF CONTRASTS –

A strikingly attractive young woman, dressed in fine evening clothes and carefully made-up, minces heedlessly in her high heels over the legs of a ragged *clochard* curled up in search of warmth on the grating of a ventilation shaft in the Metro – this is one of the many faces of Paris. Just as the character of a capricious primaballerina is alleged to possess many scintillating sides, so do the face and heart of the metropolis on the Seine display great diversity. Paris is the city of contradictions, it is the embodiment of contrast.

The glittering affluence spread out along the stylish Avenue des Champs-Elysées between the Arc de Triomphe and the Place de la Concorde; the dirt and poverty in the quarter at the foot of Montmarte; the hustle and bustle in the underground labyrinth of the Metro stations; the whirl of student life in the Quartier Latin; the romantic tranquility of the venerable Marais district; the gigantic sky-scrapers of La Défense, and the medieval narrowness in the Sentier of the tailors – these are all just splashes of color on a palette that is as rich in nuances as the ethnic and national origins of the people who live in Paris.

Highlights of cultural life are as much a part of this city as the prostitution visible everywhere and the startlingly high rate of (petty) criminality. The most modern technology has as much impact on life in the French capital as the political

Previous pages: A chat on the banks of the Seine. History in grand style. Don't forget a tour of the Seine. View towards the east and of downtown from the Eiffel Tower. At the foot of the Eiffel Tower. Left: The "Grande Arche" in La Défense.

decisions of the president in the Elysée Palace. These opposites are reflected in an architecture that, in its diversity (from strict Classicism via playful Belle Epoque to sober high-tech constructions, is a match for the polyphony of languages heard here.

The common denominator, which ultimately unites all of these contradictions is the *savoir vivre*, both famous and notorious as a feeling for life common to the poorest and the richest in Paris. Although it does not eliminate the daily worries and rigors, it somehow makes them more bearable. This attitude is not based upon a philosophy of fatalism, but rather upon the French willingness to grant oneself even the most modest of pleasures which life has to offer.

"If only your supply of crisp baguettes and red table wine is inexhaustible, this world cannot end," is what the *clochard* wishes from his city. Yet the latter cannot furnish him with a proper roof over his head, to say nothing of a place in society. "If I could only reserve a good table in that new temple of *Haute Cuisine*, then I could also convince my banker of my plans." Such are the hopes of the dynamic but indebted young manager with the compulsive need to maintain his image.

These patterns of behavior and thought evoke a second characteristic of the French that has particularly left its mark upon Paris. Although the French are in favor of a general fundamental order, they are averse to every form of discipline. Punctuality is just as little their strong point as is perfect organization. People demanding exactness and thoroughness often run into the closed doors of museums, restaurants and other places. When the corset of constraints becomes too tight, the French tend to experience a vague loss in the quality of their lives.

In the capital city of a country with a cuisine and a wine cellar that enjoy an international reputation, this quality of life often and primarily refers to the joys of

eating. A world lies between the simple intake of food and a good meal for the French. The framework – whether at home, in the bistro, or at Maxim's – plays a subordinate role. The same rule applies everywhere: Even if there are a dozen customers waiting for a table, no waiter would ever dare to rush a guest who has not yet leisurely enjoyed the *digestif* and a postprandial cigarette.

Savoir vivre means the art of taking life as it is and getting as much out of its positive sides as possible. Financial means have only a minor influence on this French ability to enjoy life's simple (and sophisticated) pleasures. If you observe the Parisians, you will see that they are typical city dwellers with a marked tendency towards sullen, closed expressions, just like people in all other cities of the world. Yet, observe them in moments of innocent relaxation. When Monsieur

Above: Street musicians always find an audience at the Centre Pompidou. Right: Timeless elegance and art at Trocadéro.

Dupont, the frequently strained average Frenchman, sips his *express* in the café around the corner, he does so with the same relish as the fellow with the high income does with his champagne in an exclusive bar.

The disadvantages of the great metropolis on the Seine, of which the high cost of living and terrible housing shortage are cited most frequently, are accepted by its residents. A Parisian way of life singles out those who can relativize these disadvantages with a shrug of the shoulders. The reverse side of the coin is also very familiar. It is an integral part of things, just like the dents in the cars, which motorized contemporaries do their best to avoid as participants in the chaotic Parisian traffic.

One significant trait of Paris is the strong dash of charm shown by the most experienced and yet still undaunted women. And there is the coquette vanity as well, naturally. Every night, when the countless sources of light manage to magically do away with even the most

deeply entrenched wrinkles with a soft veil of illusions, the "lady" Paris becomes young again. There, where the laws of nature regarding sleep are constantly broken, in one of the innumerable restaurants or cafés full of pulsating life, even the most sober of sales representatives on a flying visit may feel the heartbeat and the fascination that have created a special position for this city.

Tourists have a tendency to fall for the Seine metropolis very quickly. Impressed by the magnificent splendor of its buildings, astonished by the high niveau of Parisian culture, delighted by the overwhelming elegance of the "beautiful people" and the chic boutiques, animated by French champagne and the colorful night-life, they experience Paris like an intoxication that tickles all of the senses at one time. However, those who stay longer find it hard to avoid the inevitable discovery of its darker sides. They will at some point lose their way in dilapidated quarters, perceive the smell of dirt and poverty, sense the rising social tensions and possibly even become the victim of a pick-pocket, car thief, or burglar. The latter unfortunately happens to each resident at least once every four years.

Still, few foreign visitors return to their native country without a certain sentimental sense of regret. Others are never able to tear themselves away again from this enchanting city. Even for those who are authorities, with extensive, not always pleasant memories of this individual and incomparable metropolis, the positive aspects usually predominate.

The cultural charisma of Paris has always extended far beyond its political significance. And the present metropolis of ten million people is considered – even if not completely without controversy – as the superb world center for top fashion, perfume, art and elegance.

It is by no means a coincidence that all of these attributes refer to the pleasant sides of life. Particularly in our age of rationalism, it is hardly possible to measure the attractive power of this city which lives out all its contrasts to the utmost.

HISTORY OF PARIS

There have been numerous theories as to the origin of the name Paris. The thirst for a mythological origin has even given rise to a connection with Paris, son of Priam, King of Troy, whose kidnapping of Helen brought about the Trojan War. What he should be doing in these remote regions is not clear, however. The more plausible assumption seems to be that the city was named after the *Parisii*, the early Celtic inhabitants of the region. The Celtic prefix of "par" stands for ship. In any case, it is certain that the Celtic river fishers from the tribe of the *Parisii* settled in the swampy river landscape of the Seine about 350 B.C. They gave their village the name *Lutuhezi* (*luth* = water, *thoueze* = middle). It was here, in 53 B.C., that Caesar called together all of the leaders of 30 Gallic tribes to the great representative assembly. One year later, the *Parisii* affiliated themselves with the Gallic rebellion against Roman dominion. However, as the rattle of weapons from Caesar's legions approached threateningly, they set fire to their wooden huts and bridges, and took to their heels. Caesar then had the new Gallo-Roman *Lutetia Parisiorum* built on the Seine island (today the Ile de la Cité) and the opposite bank.

Favorably located at an intersection of waterways and landways, the trade center grew quickly under Roman rule. The Lutetians were blessed with a forum, a theater, an arena and large public bathing facilities. A temple to Jupiter was built next to the imperial palace on the spot where the magnificent Notre-Dame is standing today.

No less than Julian Apostata, the nephew of Emperor Constantine and commander-in-chief of Gaul, praised

Left: The cathedral of Notre-Dame is inseparably tied to the history of Paris.

Lutetia for its mild winter weather, which was advantageous for wine-growing. On several occasions, the Roman general defended the town against pillaging barbarians and generously acclaimed its beauty. The Gauls thanked Julian for the protection he provided and for the love to Lutetia he had demonstrated by making him their emperor in AD 360. In this year, *Lutetia Parisiorum* appeared for the first time under the name of Paris in a council document.

In the middle of the 5th century, the *Parisii* gave way to fear and panic as the Huns under Attila pressed forward into the region close to Paris. The rich, aspiring city feared an attack, and the inhabitants wanted to get out of harm's way. But a shepherd girl named Geneviève, who was already famous locally because of her charisma and piousness, came to the aid of her fearful countrymen. Attila's hordes actually rushed by the city without even stopping. Shortly thereafter, on the Catalonian Fields, they suffered a devastating defeat. However, it was neither Geneviève's prayers, nor the intervention of the Parisians that led to their demise. It was the strength of the Roman, Burgundian and Visigothic troops under the leadership of the Roman commander Aetius, united in the fight against the Huns, that saved the day. Yet, in those times wonders were quite popular and therefore this and numerous other heroic deeds were attributed to the little shepherd girl, who later became Saint Geneviève and the patron saint of Paris. Among other things, she is said to have built a chapel for St. Denis (Dionysius) at his place of burial (the present suburb St-Denis). Denis, who was sent to convert the Gauls to Christianity, suffered a martyr's death on Montmartre. A miracle is said to have occurred here as well: According to legend, the saint was able to bend down after his decapitation, pick up his severed head and carry it 6000 paces to the plain north of the city. There he washed it under

a spring, that naturally had wondrous healing powers from that time on.

Merovingians and Carolingians

In the year 508, having conquered much of the former Roman domain of Gaul, Christian Frankish King Clovis I (founder of the Merovingian dynasty) chose Paris to be his residence. However, Clovis only seized the Roman treasury, preferring to leave the Gallo-Roman dignitaries in their offices. Latin also continued to be the primary language of the Parisians. The new realm now received the name of *Francia*, and thus the solid cornerstone of the Christian France of the Middle Ages was laid.

The city first blossomed under the Merovingians: Numerous churches were built and monasteries settled in the region, establishing a rich agricultural

Above: Charlemagne, King of the Franks (painting by Albrecht Dürer). Right: Hôtel de Cluny holds treasures of all epochs.

tradition. However, the constant division of the empire resulting from Merovingian compliance with the old Germanic law of inheritance led to bloody disputes and intrigues; in addition, there were natural catastrophes and continuing threats from the outside. The history of the city at this time reads like a ghastly thriller. The last powerful king of the Merovingians who was concerned with unity was Dagobert I (629-39), under whose rule Paris experienced a new, but unfortunately short, period of prosperity. He went down in history as *le bon roi,* the good king. The city has him to thank for its coinage and the *Foire de St.-Denis* (also known as the *Foire du Lendit*), which is still famous as a market and popular festival. The reputation of the city as a trade center was now established.

After Dagobert I, there were only mock kings who were generally referred to as *les rois fainéants* – "the lazy kings." The actual power and authority was in the hands of the palatines, the aristocratic heads of the royal household, whose power had been growing in the strife-ridden kingdom. Charles Martel was the first of the palatines to rule independently under the protection of Pope Gregory III. Martel's son, Pepin the Short, deposed the last of the Merovingians and was anointed as first Carolingian king in 754.

For Paris, however, a time of decline had now unfortunately begun. It lost its importance, since Pepin the Short was the only one of the Carolingian kings who was to keep his royal residence in the formerly blossoming city. His successor, Charlemagne moved to Aachen. Paris was put in the hands of a count.

The affluent city and above all, the rich monasteries that had become established on the right and left banks of the Seine around the Île de la Cité, were temptation enough for marauding Norsemen. Four raids drove the Parisians from the outskirts of the city onto the Ile de la Cité which had in the meantime been well for-

tified. It was Count Eudes of Paris, a member of the Capet family, who successfully withstood the 13-month siege by Norsemen in the year 885. In 888, the mighty of the empire gathered together and voted for the liberator of Paris to become king. However, the power struggles between the Carolingians and the Capetians lasted almost another 100 years until a Capetian finally ascended the throne: Hugh Capet, the great-nephew of Count Eudes.

During his reign, Paris developed quickly. Hugh Capet (987-96) made Paris his capital and bestowed upon it a certain degree of self-administration. Although he governed primarily from Orleans, the king did expand the old Gallo-Roman royal palace on the Île de la Cité. The guilds and merchants established themselves on the right bank of the Seine. The representatives of various theological systems of thought and their students settled in the houses on the left bank, leading to the founding of the first Parisian university in 1210. Paris became a center of culture and learning which would be of significance to the entire western world. Although Latin remained the language of the learned, it was the northern French *langue d'oïl* that asserted itself among the inhabitants over the *langue d'oc* spoken in the south. The former then became the basis for the modern French language.

King Philippe August (1180-1223), the founder of French unity, fortified the city with a circular wall. From this point on, a city toll was charged at the gates. The political structure of Paris altered according to the rights, which the king now granted to the economically-significant guilds and brotherhoods. They then grew and developed into an independent power. Certain representatives from their ranks were responsible for the city administration as well as for the supervision of the police and the judicial authorities. The most significant and oldest of these guilds was that of the river merchants, which had been influential since Roman times. The symbol of their guild, a ship

with the inscription *Fluctuat nec mergitur* was adopted in the city of Paris' coat of arms. In order to protect the prosperous Seine shippers, Philippe Auguste had a fortress built on the river bank from which the Louvre was later to be created.

Paris Revolts

His successor, Louis IX, had the epithet of "the Saint." This was not without good reason since he was more interested in the religious, spiritualized side of life than in the business of government. He left various sacred buildings as an expression of his piety. Less attention was paid to the needs of his people, who were afflicted with epidemics and famine.

The Hundred Years' War with England began in 1337 when the English King Edward III made claims on the French throne. Black Death brought additional suffering to the land. The dissatisfaction

Above: A side aisle of Notre-Dame. Right: Statue of the legendary Jeanne d'Arc.

of the people grew, and only one last straw was necessary to break the camel's back. This last straw was defeat at the hands of the English at Poitiers in 1356 and their taking the French King Jean le Bon (1350-1364) prisoner. The crown prince, later King Charles V, became the governor of the city of Paris.

The bourgeoisie had enjoyed new rights since 1296, enabling the guilds to send delegates to the 24-strong city council. Now, under the influence of Etienne Marcel, an affluent cloth dealer and steward of the traders' guild, the bourgeoisie revolted. Marcel demanded that the Dauphin surrender control of the administration to the estates. While prepared to compromise to some extent, the crown prince rejected such autonomy of the estates and Marcel reverted to an open attack. Charles was held prisoner in the royal palace and the Paris bourgeoisie rose up in arms. The Dauphin was, however, able to flee the bourgeoisie. This scenario appears to have been the dress rehearsal for the Great Revolution of

1789. It was not only the bourgeoisie which revolted, but also the peasants of the Île de France. Completely impoverished as a result of exploitation, the aggressive raids of the English and natural catastrophes, they rebelled under the leadership of one of their own a Jacques Bonhomme as peasants were generally referred to by their feudal masters.

Castles were stormed and the nobility hunted down. Etienne Marcel declared his solidarity with the *Jacquerie*, yet there was a lack of true support and the revolt of the peasants was then brutally crushed by a united nobility. The Parisian insurgents were also in a predicament because the Dauphin Charles had succeeded in rallying an army to march against Paris! Marcel looked for assistance to the cousin of the crown prince, Charles le Mauvais (Charles the Bad) of Navarre, who was pro-English. Just as Marcel wanted to open the city gates for the Navarrians, he was slain with a battle-ax by a group of his followers. Three days later, the crown prince entered Paris.

As Charles V, he was so marked by these events that he left the royal residence on the Île de la Cité. He also distinguished himself through frugal budgeting and a wide cultural interest. This earned him the epithet of *le Sage* (the Wise). The ensuing rule of Charles VI (1380-1422), began with a corrupt regency, which lead to tax increases. In response, the incensed Parisians plundered the arsenal, armed themselves with heavy lead mallets, and marched against the royal troops. Once again, it proved possible to restrain the seething populace. The rebellion of the *Maillotins*, so called because of the lead mallets (*maillet*) they wielded, was violently crushed and the city constitution with all the rights of the bourgeoisie was suspended.

A period of calm followed the ascendance to the throne of Charles VI, whose nickname was "le bien-aimé," the loved One. Unfortunately, his mental health suddenly vanished, leaving wide open the issue of succession. His wife, Isabelle of Bavaria, played a vital role in the fol-

23

lowing events. The interested parties for the throne were Louis d'Orléans, the king's younger brother and the queen's lover, as well as his cousin Jean sans Peur de Bourgogne. Paris became a mere plaything between the two rivaling dukedoms. In 1407, three days after the two cousins embraced each other in a touching scene, Jean sans Peur had his dangerous rival murdered and ruled from then on in Paris. But his luck did not last long: The son of the murdered Duke of Orléans, Charles d'Orléans, found help with his father-in-law, the Duke of Armagnac, and marched against Paris. Civil war became unavoidable. On the one side there were the Armagnacs, and on the other side the Burgundians. The Parisians were in the middle.

At first it appeared that the Burgundians would be victorious, even if their leader, the nominally fearless duke, was not quite as brave as his name promised. Dreading acts

Above: Francis I (1494-1547). Right: Catherine de' Medici (1519-1589).

of revenge, he is said to have built a wall around his bedroom in the middle of his palace. Another factor made matters even more complicated. Still under the reign of Charles the Mad, the slaughterer Simon Carboche had lead a band of fellow burghers in a rebellion against the king. They demanded lower taxes. This furious troop had taken the side of the Burgundians and unleashed a reign of terror in Paris. The moderate forces in the city called upon the Armagnacs for help. The fortunes of war shifted back and forth between the Armagnacs and the Burgundians. In the meantime, the people of Paris suffered famine and plague.

In 1420, the Burgundians with the help of the English, who saw the occasion to divide and conquer, were ultimately victorious in the battle. The queen had already had the farsightedness to side with the Burgundians and bestowed her favor upon the new victor. Catherine, the daughter of the king, was married to the English King Henry V and thereby endowed him with the title of heir to the

French throne. King Charles VI remained an impassive minor figure during all of these events. The Parisians longed for peace and accepted the new government.

For the Dauphin Charles – the fourth son of the mad king, whose three older brothers had died one after the other in quick succession – all hopes of the regency had disappeared. His father, now totally insane, had (at the insistence of the Burgundians and the English) signed a document which excluded his last son from accession to the throne and cast doubt upon his legitimacy. However, when Charles VI and Henry V of England both died at almost the same time (1422), the Dauphin saw that his chance had come. The English successor to the throne was still a baby and his uncle, the Duke of Bedford, ruled the occupied parts of France. Charles VII, as dauphin, had little interest in politics, preferring the indolent life of a noble with little or no responsibility. France was behind him in these difficult times, but his own mother was in the other camp, as it were. It took a woman, the Maid of Orléans, again, like Geneviève, a shepherdess, to break the spell. The legendary Jeanne d'Arc (Joan of Arc) was instrumental in raising the English siege of Orléans in 1429; she then led Charles to Reims, where he was anointed Charles VII of France. Together they tried in vain to storm Paris. Her attempt to relieve Compiègne (northeast of Paris) ended in her capture and eventual death at the stake (1431). But Joan of Arc gave France the courage to work up a new head of steam and expel the English from France by 1453 (except Calais, which they occupied until 1558). Charles VII then ruled his kingdom from Troyes. During the next 100 years, his successors followed this example.

The life of the Parisians was now initially peaceful. For a time at least, both the city and the whole country were able to recover from the bloodbath. With the Renaissance, Italian architects, poets and musicians came to the city. The university was expanded and the first printing press set up. With around 250,000 inhabitants, Paris was the largest city in Europe at the end of the 15th century. Among the first phenomena of the big city came the development of gangs. The more harmless variety, the so-called *mauvais garçons*, were mostly members of the intellectual set and students; they set out and frightened the well-behaved citizens with their pranks and preferred the brothels and public houses to their morally strict colleges. However, it was not infrequently that these "rebellious" youths went a step too far and clashed with the law to such a degree that they had to flee into the ranks of "bad company." The most famous example of such a case was the poet François Villon, who probably left behind the most impressive reflection of the morality of that time with his major work *Le Grand Testament*. After he was sentenced to ten years banishment from Paris because of the manslaughter of a priest, he was welcomed in the province by the notorious *Coquillards*, the largest band of criminals of that period. They developed *argot*, a secret language, in order to avoid giving away trade secrets to the wrong persons.

Religious Wars

Francis I (1515-1547) was among the most popular kings of France. His subjects did not blame him for his loose lifestyle, which led to his early death of syphilis. In 1525, Francis was taken prisoner at the battle of Pavia, one of many instances in his reign – a long struggle against Habsburg hegemony in Europe. The Parisians paid the ransom demanded, but did require that their king move his residence to Paris in return. Paris again became a political center under Francis I. There was a significant cultural upswing in the city during this time, especially

with the modern, breezy Renaissance style the king "brought back" from his captivity in Italy. Among the most important construction projects was the Louvre, rebuilt according to plans by the architect Lescot. In 1530, the king founded the Collège Royal de France or Collège des Trois Langues, where Greek and Hebrew (frowned upon by the university) were taught as well as Latin. What primarily distinguished the college, however, was, that the teachers were independent of the conservative, clerical university and were financed by the king.

From the 1520s onward, the Protestants had found increasing patronage among aristocratic circles. Francis I was very open-minded and not hostile towards them at first. However, under pressure from the conservative Catholic powers, which supported the crown, he soon had to take a stand against them.

Above: Is Montaigne reflecting over all the students, who passed by on the Rue Manche?
Right: Henry IV of Navarre (1553-1610).

Under his son Henry II (1547-1559), this tendency was intensified and the first persecutions took place. The *Chambre Ardente*, a special tribunal, set about trying alleged heretics and having them burned at the stake. Although the mood was tense, it was not fanatical and a limited intellectual openness remained. Rabelais was still able to publish his satirical taunts; Ronsard and Du Bellay, two of the seven poets of the *Pléiade,* were committed to breathe new life into French poetry. Up to this point, artistic expression had been reserved for the Latin language and French was looked down upon in poetry and literature.

In 1549, Henry II married Catherine de' Medici. The "true" queen, however, was his mistress Diana of Poitiers. After just 12 years of rule, Henry II was killed at a tournament (tournaments have been forbidden in France since that point in time). Shortly before his death, there had been vehement conflicts between Catholics and Huguenots, the French Protestants who had adopted Calvinism. Henry II had taken a position against the Protestants, who now saw the warning finger and the punishment of God in his sudden death. The most important figure in France during the next 30 years, which were marked by religious war, was Catherine de' Medici. After the short reign of her first son Francis II (1559-1560), she carried out governmental business as regent for her second-born, Charles IX (1560-1574).

Political tensions increased throughout the land. The Huguenots were hunted everywhere and open battles took place. Basically, however, it was not only a matter of the profession of faith but once again the issue of the French successor to the throne. The House of Valois was showing weakness: Charles IX was still a minor and after him there was his brother Henry (later Henry III) as the last successor to the throne. The Huguenot leader Henry of Navarre and the Catholic Duke of Guise were both weighing their chances of seizing the throne. However, Catherine de' Medici wanted to save it for her sons. She therefore engaged in the apparently tolerant politics of compromise, yet in reality played the two parties off against each other.

In 1572, as a sign of reconciliation, Henry of Navarre was to marry Marguerite of Valois, sister of the Catholic king. The entire Protestant nobility traveled to Paris for the occasion. Beginning on St. Bartholomew's Night (August 23), Catherine was assisted by the Catholic League and the Guises in having all of the Protestant dwellings marked with white crosses. The alarm bell rang out in the night and the mobs of city, incited by the Catholics, slaughtered the Huguenots with unimaginable cruelty – 3000 people were murdered in Paris alone.

After the death of his brother, Henry III (1574-1589) came to power. He attempted to carry on the stalling tactics of his mother, but the powerful Catholic League, supported by a large section of the population, demanded clear deci-

sions. When Henry III rejected the Catholic ultimatum that the Protestant religion be suppressed, Henry de Guise insisted that the Estates General be convened. Henry III had the Duke of Guise killed and fled to his cousin, Henry of Navarre. The two Henrys now fought side by side for Paris. In 1589, King Henry III was killed by a fanatic monk. He had already named Henry of Navarre to be his successor. But the civil war lasted another five years. Philip II of Spain had taken the side of the Catholics in order to seize the French throne for himself. But the Parisians did not want him.

"Paris Is Worth a Mass"

Henry of Navarre cruelly starved Paris through his siege. In 1724, Sauval wrote in his memoirs: "The famine of 1590 was without equal: Rats were a delicatessen which only the rich could afford. In St. Denis and Palaiseau, servants were caught in the act of eating children, and in Paris the populace ground bones from the

Cemetery of the Innocents into flour in order to bake bread with it." After he converted to Catholicism in 1594, the new king was welcomed into the city. His comment was: "Paris is worth a mass." In addition to the Edict of Nantes (1598), which guaranteed religious liberties, the city had Henry IV (1589-1610) to thank for much more; he was to become one of France's most popular kings.

The *vert galant*, as the Parisians lovingly called him because of his numerous romances, ordered public finances and repaired the economy in a short amount of time with the help of his minister Sully. By virtue of a systematic architectonically new design, "his" Paris stripped off its medieval face: Straight streets and large squares were created, the city was enlarged equally on all sides, the first apartment buildings appeared, and fountains, open squares and bridges were constructed. The first pumping station on the Seine, the Samaritaine, was developed. For two hundred years it pumped water into the city quarters on the right bank of the Seine. A *Grand Voyeur de France* supervised the cleanliness and lighting of the newly-paved streets and squares. "Every 20 paces there are lanterns hanging 20 feet high in the middle of the street on ropes stretched from house to house. During the whole winter there are thick candles burning in them from nightfall until midnight. Whoever breaks them goes to the galleys," was how Martin Lister described the appearance of the streets of Paris in 1598. The beautification and harmonization of the city's appearance was to reflect the new state concept, a rationally controlled progressiveness emanating from the capital city and the royal residence. Henry IV, who had survived 17 attempts on his life, was murdered by the fanatic Ravaillac in 1610.

Right: Louis XIV (1643-1715) with his royal court in the park at Versailles.

The Age of Absolutism

When Louis XIII (1610-1643) ascended the throne, he was just nine years old. His mother, Maria de' Medici, and a rather dubious fellow named Concini (murdered in 1617) conducted the affairs of state. In 1624, Louis XIII, having assumed power, called upon Cardinal Richelieu to be his prime minister. Maria de' Medici saw her secret dominion threatened and tried to eliminate Richelieu. But the attempt failed on the so-called *journée des dupes* (day of the dupes). The king deprived his mother of her power in favor of his prime minister, whose position of power was thereby made unassailable. The goal of the Cardinal was to curb the power of the nobility and the Protestant opposition in order to assert the unlimited power of the crown, preparing the way for the absolutist state. In foreign affairs, he wanted to establish French hegemony over her neighbours, especially over the Habsburg empire.

Under the rule of Richelieu – Louis XIII is to be regarded as no more than a puppet – the city again changed its face. The island Notre-Dame (formerly the notorious Duel Island) and the small Ile aux Vaches were combined to create the fashionable new Île Saint-Louis. In the shadow of Richelieu's palace, the aristocracy and the "chic set" settled here. The Sorbonne church was built, the Palais de Luxembourg (for Maria de' Medici) and the Palais Cardinal (today the Palais Royal). In addition to the establishment of the *Imprimerie Royal* (royal printing office), Richelieu can also be given credit for the founding of the *Académie Française*. Even today it still has the task of keeping a watchful eye on the French language.

Richelieu, Louis XIII and Maria de' Medici all died at approximately the same time. In 1643, the throne was passed onto the underaged Louis XIV (1643-1715). His mother Anne d'Au-

triche (Anne of Austria) and Cardinal Mazarin, who was not popular with the Parisians, acted as his regents during his minority. In 1648, their hard taxation policies led to the resolution by the noble's parliament limiting royal power. The people supported the nobility and took to the barricades: The *Fronde* rebellion broke out. It was to be four years before the royal military defeated the revolt, which had been weakened by the conflicting interests of its leaders. As a precaution, the royal family and Mazarin fled to St.-Germain-en-Laye.

After the death of Mazarin in 1661, Louis XIV did not appoint a new prime minister. The long-planned absolutist goal was achieved: At the head of the state was the king, accountable to neither the church nor the people. The economic foundation was provided by his finance minister Colbert, who created the first state-controlled economic system. This system helped France achieve an unassailable position of dominance over its neighboring countries.

This epoch was a Golden Age of French literature and art. In poetry and painting, the orientation was towards the classical forms of antiquity. A certain passion, drama, the triumph of virtues and the will as found in the plays of Corneille and Racine and later also in the classical poetry of Boileau, became the decisive elements.

The fright resulting from the *Fronde* rebellions – despite the concentration of power – had a sustained effect upon the king. He moved his seat of government to Versailles, where a new palace – the king's great passion – had been in construction since 1661. As regards building, Paris was not neglected, since the capital city was ultimately meant to reflect the splendor of the absolutist state. The Jardin des Tuileries, which Louis XIV had laid out by the architect Le Nôtre, had originally been created by Catherine de' Medici. It opened up on the Champs-Elysées, where Le Nôtre's work continued as far as the Rond-Point. Entire districts were re-developed, the streets il-

29

luminated, avenues, houses and palaces created in the style of French Baroque. That in the course of this redevelopment work there was occasionally some profitable land speculation was deliberately overlooked by the government since the profits ultimately benefited its own self. Neither did Louis XIV forget the veterans of his numerous wars, presenting them with the Hôtel des Invalides. Those who had money could live a pleasant life in Paris. The rest of the people were given the poorhouses, which the king had built for them. *Tout Paris* met in the literary salons that shot up out of the ground like mushrooms. People strolled along the new avenues and put in an appearance at the cafés. In the evening they sat in the *Comédie Française* which had been founded in 1680 and applauded the works of Molière (1622-1673), whose plays pulled society apart with biting wit.

Above: View of the Prefecture and Conciergerie. Right: The Ball House Oath on June 20, 1789.

All of this activity gave the king the nickname "Sun King," but that sun cost money. When Louis XV (1715-1774) ascended the throne in 1715 under the regency of Philippe II of Orléans, the debts of the country were almost twenty times as high as the annual revenue. The population was impoverished, food and housing had become scarce. Paris had almost 40,000 poor people, who lived primarily from begging. In the *Cours des Miracles*, unapproachable cul-de-sacs, which no policeman dared to enter, prostitutes, thieves and beggars attended to their business. Rousseau wrote about Paris at that time: "How disappointed I was by the city which I had imagined to be as beautiful as it was large. I entered it through the Faubourg St. Marceau and in the place of marble palaces I found only small, dirty, stinking alleys, ugly black houses, filth and poverty."

The initiatives of the regent to stabilize the national budget were quite lamentable. An example is his attempt, with the help of the Scotsman John Law, with

whom he had become acquainted at the gambling table, to create a central bank. The bank note circulation, secured by the national credit, was to increase affluence. Additional profits were to be gleaned through the colonies by the Mississippi joint-stock company. But the enterprise ended with a collapse, financially ruining thousands of people.

Participation in the Polish War of Succession (1733-1735), the Austrian War of Succession (1748) and in the Seven Years' War (1756-1763) led to the loss of territories in Canada and East India, nearly driving the country into public bankruptcy. The tax burden affected the third estate, while the nobility and the clergy enjoyed an exemption from taxes and lived in luxury. The government in the city was not conducted by the king and certainly not by the parliament, which the king had dissolved in 1771, but instead by his mistress Madame de Pompadour. However, voices critical of the *Ancien Régime* were increasingly audible. The advocates of the Enlighten-

ment and a new, liberal political science – Montesquieu, Voltaire, Rousseau and Diderot – were advancing without the slightest sign of hesitation.

The Battle for the Republic

Louis XVI (1774-1792) acceded to the throne with a desolate legacy. In a desperate attempt to stabilize national finances, the king had a toll wall built around the city. The protectionist taxes primarily affected the "little people" and triggered a storm of vehement protests. In August 1788, the liberal finance minister Necker recommended that the Estates General (delegates of the clergy, nobility and bourgeoisie from all provinces) be convoked and succeeded in ensuring that the third estate, which was the strongest in terms of numbers, have twice the number of delegates. But the privileges of the nobility, the fundamental cause of the conflict, remained. On June 20, 1789, the third estate issued the so-called tennis court oath (Serment du Jeu de Paume),

swearing that they would fight until the country had a new constitution. The dismissal of Necker added fuel to the fire of indignation. Revolution seethed in the clubs and cafés. The busts of Necker and the liberal Duke of Orléans (a cousin of Louis XVI, who later called himself Philippe Égalité) were carried through the streets in a triumphal procession. On July 9, the National Assembly declared itself to be a constitutional assembly and established its own military under the leadership of La Fayette. On July 12, 1789 the journalist Camille Desmoulins called upon the citizens from his café table to arm themselves, and the people followed him to the Hôtel des Invalides to get their weapons. On July 14, and with the cry of "A la Bastille!", about 30,000 Parisians stormed the symbol of absolutist repression and burned down the tollhouses. A short time later, the goods of the church

Above: Storming the Bastille on July 14, 1789, which started the Revolution. Right: Napoléon Bonaparte (1769-1821).

and the aristocracy which had fled were confiscated. Human rights were proclaimed. Above all, it was a matter of asserting the rights of the third estate. This goal appeared to be accomplished as the king presented himself in front of the city hall with a blue-white-red cockade and a new Convention with a constitutional monarchy was elected. Louis XVI, not one of the most savvy politicians, but by no means evil-minded, hedged. On the one hand he recognized the need for reforms, on the other hand he could not deny his position and thereby set an example for the rest of Europe. Suspicion of maintaining contacts with foreign governments and with emigré circles, and his failed flight in June 1791 only heated up the more radical forces in Paris. In July, then, a mass of people that had gathered on the Champs de Mars to draw up a petition for the king's abdication was dispersed and massacred by the National Guard. This event hardly improved the kings credibility. On September 3, the assembly voted in a new constitution granting the French people comprehensive civil rights, and the king pledged his wavering allegiance to it.

This might have settled matters, had it not been for the political clubs and groups that served as locomotives to the unleashed crowds, and to the pressure from ouside. In April 1792, Louis XVI was forced to declare war on Austria. In Paris, the situation became more tense as foreign armies neared the capital. Rumors of treason made the rounds. A Commune was declared in Paris, and on August 10, the king was forced to abdicate. Under the leadership of Marat, the incensed crowd stormed the Tuileries, threw the king into prison, and hunted every person who looked like a royalist. In September, the situation worsened. A panicked crowd – fired up it is thought by Marat – broke into the prisons and massacred aristocrats suspected of treason.

Some stability returned after the newly-elected Convention proclaimed the First Republic (September 22), two days after the army of Dumouriez and Kellermann routed the Prussians, Austria's allies, at Valmy. The next struggle took place within the Convention, where the Jacobins (named for their club) under the leadership of Robespierre gradually eliminated the moderate Girondins and centralized political power in Paris. This gruesome epoch has been named *La Terreur* for good reason. The revolutionary tribunal condemned to death the citizen Louis Capet, Louis XVI' common name, and the sentence was carried out on January 21, 1793. This in turn gave rise to royalist counteraction, which further radicalized the Jacobins. The Committee of Public Safety ordered universal compulsory military service and established prices and wages. In the place of Christianity, the Cult of Reason was adopted. Its main temple was declared to be Notre-Dame. A special revolutionary calendar was introduced. However, the Revolution soon "ate its own children": Danton,

Desmoulins, and many other activists of the revolution followed the king and the Girondins under the blade of the guillotine accused of deviating from the law. On the 9th of Thermidor (July 27, 1794), Robespierre, who had consolidated his position on the all-powerful Commitee of Public Safety by lethal purges, was deprived of his power in a surprise attack during the National Assembly and went the way of the guillotine.

A Directory consisting of five members now took over the government for five years. Yet, the end of the revolution hardly brought with it social justice: The goods which had been confiscated from the church and the aristocracy were auctioned off for ridiculously low prices and bestowed only prosperity upon the new propertied middle class. The people, bled by the revolution, lived in the same misery as before. In contrast, after the ball of terror the new bourgeoisie now danced waltzes and enjoyed itself immensely. The situation did not change as General Bonaparte, once a revolutionary activist,

overthrew the Directory in 1799 in a military coup and secured himself executive and legislative powers as the consul. Five years later, he crowned himself emperor in Notre-Dame. It was his intention that Paris, which had borne witness to the Revolution in the destruction it suffered, should now "become the most beautiful city which exists, has existed, and ever will exist." The Empire became a style that grew out of Classicism, with simple, symmetrical grandeur imitating ancient Roman forms. Politically and militarily, Napoléon also tried to imitate the Caesars, albeit with only temporary success. After the catastrophic defeat of the French in the campaign against Russia, the Allies (Prussia, Russia and Austria) marched into Paris. Napoleon had to abdicate in 1814 and was exiled to Elba. His attempt to come to power again the following year lasted only 100 days

Above: Napoléon III at a fair on the Promenade des Dames in Plombières, 1858 (E.C. Perrin). Right: Pont Alexandre III.

and was ended by his defeat at the hands of British and Prussians at Waterloo.

The Allies restored the Bourbons to the throne. With Louis XVIII, the brother of the decapitated Louis XVI, and Charles X the age of the restoration dawned. Charles X followed a reactionary course which did not even preserve the appearance of freedom and democracy. In 1830, the people stormed the Tuileries, and Charles X had to abdicate in favor of the liberal Louis Philippe. With a "Republican kiss," the Bourbon was "crowned" as sovereign of the constitutional monarchy. Under his leadership, the members of the upper bourgeoisie had a good time. The governmental motto of the new king was "enrichissez-vous" ("make yourselves wealthy"). The prosperous middle-class did not need to be encouraged twice to do so: Affluence increased, industrialization was on the march and the first trains operated. The new wealth, however, was at the expense of the "fourth estate," which came into existence in the course of industrialization. The workers lived in

inhumane conditions in new suburbs, which had been created around factories at the edges of the city. Economic downturns and a cholera epidemic further contributed to the problem. "The people complained bitterly as they saw how the rich, loaded with doctors and pharmacies, took themselves off to more healthy regions," wrote Heinrich Heine. Pressure for reforms mounted steadily throughout the 1840s, errupting finally on February 24, 1848, and once again engulfing Europe. By the end of the year, the Second Republic had been proclaimed, and the man heading it was a long-time reformer, Louis Napoléon Bonaparte, a nephew of Napoléon I. A republican at the start, he nevertheless could not hide his need for strict law and order. In the long-standing family tradition, he crowned himself Emperor Napoléon III in 1852. As a precaution, the new emperor had all of the potential rebels removed from the city, but Paris remained a reservoir of progressive powers, intensified by those seeking refuge from other countries.

Thanks to heavy subsidies and the radical architectural genius of Eugène Haussmann and Jacques Hittorf, the face of Paris changed dramatically. This was the period during which the great avenues were carved through the city, embellishing many districts and forcing the poor into the eastern part of town. These wide arteries had a military purpose as well. To enable troups quick movement through the city and to make barricades difficult to erect. The test came sooner than many expected.

In 1870, provoked by the wily Bismarck, Napoléon III was seduced into declaring war on Prussia. It turned out to be a military desaster. Prussian troops broke through the French lines at Sedan on September 4th, forcing Napoléon III to abdicate. The Third Republic was proclaimed, moving its headquarters to Bordeaux when the Prussians lay siege to Paris. On January 28, 1871, President Thiers capitulated. The city was unhappy, as it felt it had held out hunger and cold for nothing. Its National Guard, reinforced by army troups, the *fédérés,* hung on to their weapons. Thiers, with his cabinet safely installed at Versailles ordered Paris to be disarmed. And then *it* happened: The National Guard mutinied and occupied the city hall. A red flag waved above Paris. The Paris Commune, an alliance of leftist workers and bourgeoisie, proclaimed a federation of autonomous communes. On May 21, 1871, governmental troops marched on Paris and the communards were slaughtered without mercy. Paris was in flames. The last of the rebels entrenched themselves in the cemetery Père Lachaise, where they were shot on the *Mur des Fédérés.* A total of 30,000 communards were buried in a mass grave, 40,000 suspects were arrested and in part deported.

The Third Republic

Marshal MacMahon, who had distinguished himself in the suppression of the Commune, became president of the Third Republic in 1873. Even if the peace was not lasting, Paris was still initially able to glow in the splendor of the *Belle Époque.* Female legs moved to the beat of the *Cancan* in the *Moulin Rouge*, and glitter and frivolity were in demand. The first large department stores (Printemps, Samaritaine) appeared on the boulevards, the first films were shown (1896), and Paris was the metropolis of banking and capital until World War I. Three world exhibitions in quick succession (1878, 1889, 1900) endowed Paris with magnificent new buildings – the Eiffel Tower, the Grand Palais and the Petit Palais, the Alexandre III bridge and the first Métro line. Paris became a veritable world metropolis. However, not all of Paris frolicked blindly in the frenzy of pleasure-seeking into the radiant 20th century. Intellectuals (above all, Zola)

and the leftists gathered around the socialist writer Jaurès campaigned against reactionary, anti-Semitic circles that had surfaced during the Dreyfus Affair. Towards the end of the century, these right-wing forces solidified in the *Action Française.*

With World War I (1914), the *Belle Époque* was at an end. As the German troops came dangerously close to the Marne, the slogan circulated: "It is better to be shot than to retreat!". On November 11, 1918, the armistice was signed. France was victorious, but the war left over 1,500,000 dead and large parts of the north of the country devastated.

The war did not affect Paris' power to attract and inspire creative people. New movements sprang to life. Impressionism and Cubism, popular before the war, now gave way to Expressionism, Surrealism, Dadaism. The artists had now moved from Montmartre, which had become a tourist attraction in the meantime, to the Quartier Montparnasse. People swung towards the *années folles.* But artists like Cocteau, Breton and Kandinsky had all left the ivory tower of art and displayed their personal political commitment. This roster would grow during and after World War II, with the existentialists Jean-Paul Sartre, Simone de Beauvoir and Albert Camus. The world economic crisis of the 1930's resulted in unemployment, rising prices and the increased drawing power of fascist groups. In response, the socialists joined forces within the Communist Party, founded in 1920. Under the leadership of Léon Blum, this coalition, known as the *Front Populaire*, won the elections of 1936. Through the pressure of the government and a wave of strikes, wage increases, the 40-hour-week and the first employer-paid vacation plans were implemented. Still, there was a dangerous crisis under way in the popular front: The reason was Blum's refusal to support the adversaries of Franco in the Spanish Civil War.

Right: Many nostalgic memories are associated with "La Traction" by Citroën.

World War II

On May 10, 1940, German troops broke through the French line near Sedan. They marched into Paris on July 14. Marshal Pétain formed an authoritarian government in the unoccupied portions of France with its seat in Vichy; it cooperated with the Germans. Some of the French very much welcomed the German invasion with its anti-Semitic racial theory and its notion of order. Yet, many joined the Résistance, which split into two groups: the Communist Forces Françaises de l'Intérieur and the Gaullists (CFLN), followers of General de Gaulle, who built up a new army in England.

Life had also changed for the residents of Paris during the *années noires*: Swastikas waved on all of the public buildings, there were curfews and the radio spread German propaganda. More and more French were deported into German labor camps, the large-scale operations against the Jews increased, the Gestapo and the French SS interrogated and tor-

tured in their "special quarters," and hostages were shot as retaliatory measures. The resistance grew, and at night the people listened to the appeals of de Gaulle on the BBC.

On June 6, 1944, the Allies landed in Normandy. On August 25th, against Hitler's orders, General von Choltitz surrendered Paris intact to General Leclerc. One day later, de Gaulle marched in with his troops. He also took over the provisional government until the Fourth Republic was proclaimed in December of 1946. Life slowly regained its usual course, even if there was somewhat more thoughtfulness involved than before. The Existentialists met together in the "Café Flore" and the "Deux Magots". Their philosophical movement encompassed the shattered European youth far beyond the borders of their own land.

Modern Paris

The Fourth Republic had taken on a difficult heritage. The painful conse-

quences of the Second World War, and the wars in Indochina and Algeria led to an intense polarization between the Gaullists and the Communists. The majority necessary to support the governing center party was often missing, and there was a succession of rapidly-changing governments. France lost the Indochina War in 1954. In the same year, an armed uprising broke out in Algeria after a long period of unrest. An open war erupted in 1958, which led to the end of the Fourth Republic. The Fifth Republic initially persisted on a hard course but Algeria ultimately achieved its independence in 1962. In Paris, France's colonial politics led to vehement protests and agitation among the Algerians living there and the anti-colonial powers.

De Gaulle's conservative, authoritarian politics made him unpopular with some. The strong leader of the Résistance who

Above: Ceremonial changing of the guards at Élysée Palace. Right: A case of dispute during a workers' demonstration.

had been listened to with hope on the BBC in 1940 was forgotten. In 1968, Paris was the starting point for the student revolt which spread to many other countries. However, the unrest was triggered by reprisals against students who had taken part in demonstrations against the war in Vietnam. The ensuing protest actions led to conditions resembling a civil war.

Soon there was a strike of 100,000 students. Barricades were erected in the Quartier Latin, cars were burned and shop windows broken; special units brutally beat people in the crowds. The workers declared their solidarity with the movement. A short time later, ten million people went on strike in order to emphasize their demands for wage increases and better working conditions. In the violent confrontations unions and intellectuals supported those who were on strike. The national broadcasting stations were ordered to blackout all information. On May 30th, de Gaulle announced new elections. The election propaganda of the

Gaullists – anti-communist slogans and raising fears of civil war and anarchy – bore fruit: The leftists lost 94 seats in the new parliament.

The conservative consolidation of power was to continue for the next 13 years. After de Gaulle, the presidents were Georges Pompidou (1969-1974) and Giscard d'Estaing (1974-1981). In 1981, the leftist coalition won the elections and François Mitterrand became the new president. France again had a socialist government for the first time since 1936. But the euphoria at the beginning did not last.

The leftist coalition soon failed, the Communists were forced out of the government, and many of the promises made during the election landed forgotten in the file cabinets.

In 1986, the Socialists lost their majority in parliament. President Mitterand chose the conservative Gaullist Chirac, the Mayor of Paris (since 1977), to become the prime minister. The period of the *Cohabitation* then began. However, even this "forced marriage" was unable to develop appropriate solutions for the increasing social problems.

The presidential elections of 1988, brought once again a clear victory for the Socialists. The strong draw which the right-wing extremist *Front National* around Jean-Marie Le Pen had achieved, has led to a still lasting dilemma in the conservative parties.

The face of Paris has also been transformed under the changing governments since World War II. Every president apparently wanted to create a monument to himself. During the era of de Gaulle, the re-development of the Marais was started at the instigation of Culture Minister Malraux. In order to relieve the pressure on the inner city, offices were relocated to the outskirts and the skyline of La Défense rose in the west.

The quickly growing population of Paris was to be increasingly housed in

satellite cities, according to the will of the city planners. However, the largest and most controversial monument which de Gaulle had erected for himself, was the 210-meter-high Tour Montparnasse. His successor Pompidou apparently did not want to take a second place to him and immortalized himself by way of the Centre Pompidou.

The market halls which were rich in tradition, those iron pavilions built by Baltard in 1854 and which Émile Zola described as the "belly of Paris", were torn down. The new central market was evacuated to Rungis. In alliance with the Parisian Mayor Chirac, Pompidou's successor, Giscard d'Estaing, pushed the building of the Forum des Halles, which is connected with the Centre Pompidou.

Francois Mitterrand's passion is apparently museums. During the period of his government, the old Gare d'Orsay has been converted into a museum in which the art of the 19th century can be admired. The veteran Musée du Louvre is also in a state of alteration.

Rouen
Beauvais
Beauchamp
Beauv

184
A15
328
309
Saint-Br
sous-Fo

Conflans-
Sainte-Honorine
Le Plessis-
Bouchard
Eaubonne
Montmore

Maurecourt
14
Herblay
Franconville
Ermont
Soissy-sous-
Montmorency
Gros

Andrésy
192
Cormeilles-
en-Parisis
Saint-Gratien
Enghien-
les-Bains

La Frette-
sur-Seine
Sannois
14
Épinay-
sur-Seine
Montm

Achères
Maisons-
Laffitte
309
A15
328

FORÊT
Château
(Palace)
ARGEN-
TEUIL
SA
DE

308
DE
Le Mesnil-
le-Roi
Sartrou-
ville
Gennevilliers

ST. GERMAIN
308
Bezons
Villeneuve-
la-Garenne

Poissy
190
Colombes
Bois-
Colombes

184
Château du Val
(Palace)
Houilles
A86
14

13
311
192
Asnières
410
Sair
Ou

Chambourcy
Montesson
La Garenne-
Colombes
Clichy

Château
(Palace)
Le Vésinet
186
308
309
Levallois-

Saint-Germain-
en-Laye
190
186
Chatou
Courbevoie
Perret
Sacré Cœ

Fourqueux
Nanterre
190
13
Neuilly-
sur-Seine
NOR

Mareil-Marly
Croissy-
sur-Seine
Château et Musée
de Malmaison
Puteaux
ST.LAZARE
Opé

Marly-le-Roi
13
Suresnes
Arc de
Triomphe

Rouen
186
Rueil-
Malmaison
BOIS
DE
BOULOGNE
Lo

A13
Hippodrome
de Longchamp
185
Tour
Eiffel
St. Germain
des Prés

E5
321
3
PARIS

307
Saint-
Cloud
BOULOGNE-
BILLANCOURT
No
Da

Rocquencourt
Garches
307
A13
E5
MONT-
PARNASSE

A12
Le Chesnay
Sèvres
10
Issy-les-
Moulineaux
Vanves

Trianons
185
Malakoff

Château,
Musées
Montrouge
A6

Saint-Cyr-
l'École
Jardins
(Gardens)
Château
Versailles
(Palace)
118
Meudon
Châtillon
Gent

10
Chaville
BOIS
DE
Clamart
Arcueil

VERSAILLES
286
446
Viroflay
MEUDON
306
Bagneux
20
Chach

rappes
Buc
A86
Fontenay-
aux-Roses
Bourg-
la-Reine
Ro

Guyancourt
5
Aérodrome
118
Château,
Musée
Che

Montigny-
le-Bretonneux
Jouy-
en-Josas
Châtenay-
Malabry
Sceaux
186
Lar

Bièvres
BOIS DE
VERRIÈRES
Antony
Ma
de Ru

Toussus-
le-Noble
Étang
de Saclay
Igny
Verrières-
le-Buisson
Fresnes
A6
(Ma

Villiers-
le-Bâcle
446
Saclay
Vauhallan
444
20
Massy
Wissous

Cressely
Palaiseau
A10
Aéroport

GREATER PARIS
118
E5
E15
Paris - O

0   2   4   6km
Orsay
A10
Champlan
A6
Chilly Mazarin

Chartres
Orléans
Yvette
Chartres
Orléans
Corbeil-Essonn

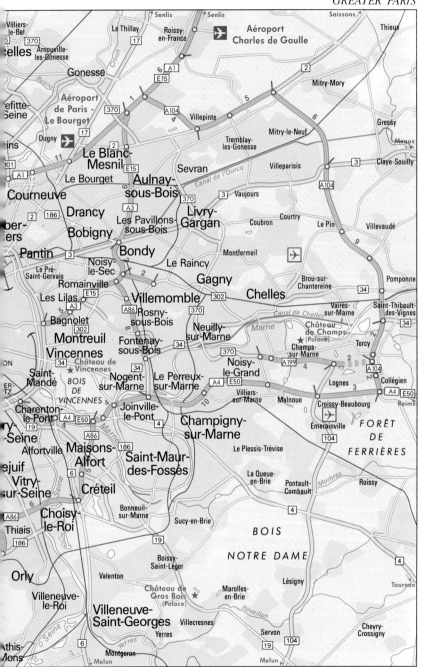

THE CITYSCAPE OF PARIS

Paris is the "navel" of the still centrally-governed France – even the building of a school in the remotest part of the country is decided here. But that is not all – it is also the economic and cultural hub of the nation. Many French have a love-hate relationship with Paris, perhaps because it reminds them of absolutist systems. Look at Paris and judge for yourself. At any rate, arriving in Paris almost always means stress, whether you arrive at one of the six train stations or have to plow through the confusion of 5000 streets in a car in order to reach your point of destination. It is loud, lively and hectic everywhere you look. The streets are congested and exhaust fumes pollute the air. You might ask yourself if this is the rush hour? Is this a chaotic quarter of

Above: View from the Eiffel Tower towards the Northwest with Chaillot Palace in the foreground, and Bois de Boulogne and La Défense in the background.

town? No! It's always like this in Paris. A comparison says it all: In Hamburg there are about two million people living on 750 sqkm, in Paris the same number of residents have to share a space of 100 square kilometers. And this applies solely outside working hours. During the day, more than a third of the over eight million people who live in the Paris suburbs additionally press into the city. The *banlieusards* also stream into the city on the weekends to go strolling or shopping.

In the Corset of the Seven Rings

The city of Paris is lined in by a 35-kilometer-long circular freeway (Ring 7), the *Boulevard Périphérique* (completed in 1973). Why is the view it offers of the city so completely ugly, no matter what section you're riding on? Paris burst its previous belt in 1924. Built in 1841 as a ring of fortification (6), it still served as a customs frontier into this century. Today, the *Boulevards Extérieurs* (they bear the names of French marshals) run in its place. Outside this ring there was a strip of about 200 meters width where building was banned. And it is there that in the past 70 years public housing has sprung up, not exactly presenting a feast for the eyes. One exception is the 16th Arrondissement, since it borders directly on the Bois de Boulogne.

You have crossed the Boulevards Extérieurs and are now working your way into the inner city. You gradually start to sniff the Paris "atmosphere." The city begins to live on the street: Bistros and stores spill over onto the sidewalks and there is lively activity everywhere.

A further ring consists of a series of boulevards (Kléber, Haussmann, Villette, Clichy, Grenelle, Belleville, etc.), which played the role of the Périphérique in the 19th century.

The customs wall constructed in 1787, the *Mur des Généraux Fermiers* (5), had to give way to the swelling city and its need for transportation routes after barely 100 years.

The ring of fortification from the 14th century (3) lies closer to the center of the city and girdles the city where today we find the Grands Boulevards (from the Opéra to the Bastille). Louis XIII expanded it in the 17th century towards the west around the Louvre (4).

In the 12th century, Philippe Auguste put up his city wall (2), the remains of which can still be seen although there are no streets following its course.

At last you land in the historical core of the city and at its first Gallo-Roman fortification from the 3rd century (1) around the Île de la Cité.

Extreme narrowness is nothing new for the metropolis. Like a corpulent matron, it burst its seams time and again. Increasing difficulty in breathing, linked with growing explosive force, had it gasping for air ever more quickly than she could loosen her belt. A brand-new belt, the circular freeway A 86 is now being completed because the Périphérique has just about suffocated our corpulent old lady.

The Suburbs

Back under absolutist rule, cities were still able to grow "wild," incorporating surrounding areas. In contrast, today almost all of the regions on the other side of the Périphérique belong to independent départements. This is the reverse side of the coin. Not even the transportation system can be controlled centrally from Paris. The city itself can no longer grow...

In order that the matron still catch a breath of air, satellite cities were built, at first in the form of giant housing developments. Because of their location, however, they were less attractive for the business community.

Because of the outrageous price increases in Paris and better transportation connections, this situation has changed. The *cités-dortoirs* (dormitory cities) have now been blessed with opportunities of employment. An increasing movement "out of Paris" has become apparent.

Between 1968 and 1975, about 200,000 inhabitants left Paris. This trend is said to have diminished; nevertheless prices in the housing market have exploded. Improved transportation possibilities and the availability of modern apartments – not even 60 percent of Parisian apartments possess a bathroom – have made the *banlieue* more attractive.

Paris and the suburbs are still a paradise for private speculators. But this shouldn't surprise anyone. It has always been obvious that the matron with her diligent manner of putting on weight would soon burst another belt. Even during the reign of the Sun King there was active speculation with land and property.

The "Cradle" of Paris

The Parisian Basin was with greatest probability already inhabited long before our chronology. It is here that the Seine, Oise, Marne and Bièvre flow together: forests, good land, a basin surrounded by

Paris in the Middle Ages

After the withdrawal of the Romans, Paris suffered. The Merovingians and Carolingians considered the city to be of secondary importance. Epidemics and famines spread there. It proved to be easy prey for the Norsemen, who "visited" it six times during the 9th century and left a trail of destruction on the banks of the Seine. The sole piece of architecture that survived this period was the Romanesque tower of the St.-Germain-des-Prés church in the 6th Arrondissement.

It was King Philippe Auguste (end of the 12th century) who first upgraded Paris. In addition to the city fortification, which served to protect the 190,000 inhabitants and the fields and meadows around he gave Paris the Louvre and new aqueducts in order to provide it with drinking water. And not only that: Paris was practically choking on its own garbage at this time, the people waded through ankle-deep dirt in the narrow alleys. The most important streets were paved and equipped with a central drainage gully. The first market hall with a roof was built in the district that is now Les Halles.

Philippe Auguste's grandson, the pious Louis IX (Saint Louis), an enthusiastic crusader and collector of relics, did little for the city itself. However, he did have such costly "caskets" built for his relics as the Sainte-Chapelle in the Palais de Justice (Île de la Cité), whose Gothic cross ribbing forms a delicate frame for the magnificent stained-glass windows. The completion (after 75 years construction) of Notre-Dame according to the plans of an unknown architect also occurred during his reign.

The medieval building has no gutters. Instead, gargoyles, waterspouts in the form of grotesque creatures spit the water onto the street. You can see several particularly effective examples on the façades of Notre-Dame.

hills with a mild climate, the Seine navigable and with access to the Sea – an ideal place to settle.

Without a doubt, the small Seine island (Île de la Cité) offered the initial and ideal protection from unwelcome intruders. However, this in no way hindered the Romans from building *Lutetia* there and on the left bank of the Seine (primarily in the current 5th Arrondissement) in 52 B.C. The Thermes de Cluny and the Arènes de Lutèce are remnants of their remarkable architectural art.

Our small island, covering 10 hectares back then (today it is 17), has changed since Roman times. In those days, the Seine flowed in a bed which was twice as wide and lapped on the shores of numerous smaller islands in addition to the Île de la Cité. The spaces between have long since been filled.

Above: This "gargouille" of Notre-Dame is probably thinking, "Paris, how you have changed!" Right: Royal grandeur at Place de la Concorde.

At the end of the 14th century, the city had 280,000 inhabitants. Under King Charles V, Paris extended considerably over the drained swampland of the *rive droite*, the right bank of the Seine. The streets were still unnamed, there was no illumination at night, and the roads were so narrow that carriages could not travel there. It was the kingdom of criminals.

Paris at the Time of the Renaissance

During the reign of King Francis at the beginning of the 16th century, a law was passed stipulating that candles must be placed in the windows at night in order to illuminate unsafe streets. Despite this, the watchmen gathered up a good dozen of murdered people every morning...

Paris was endowed with a network of broad streets and squares in the middle of the 16th century, and the first three state coaches created much excitement among the population. With Catherine de' Medici, who owned one of these carriages, the Renaissance experienced its heyday.

The Tuileries (1st Arr.) and many of the sumptuous city palaces like the Hôtel de Sévigné in the Marais (4th Arr.) were built around this time. The aristocracy preferred to move there from the dark chambers of its fortified castles.

At the end of the 17th century, Paris already had 500,000 inhabitants. Henry IV was murdered in Les Halles in 1610 as his state coach was caught in "traffic".

Paris in the Age of Absolutism

Paris changed considerably under his grandson, Louis XIV (17th century): The city walls fell, new streets with houses (Champs-Élysées, 8th Arr.) were constructed round open spaces with statues at their center (Victoire in the 2nd Arr. and Vendôme in the 8th Arr.). But for the people, Paris hardly changed at all. It is true that the streets were illuminated at night by lanterns with candles that

burned until midnight, and that the supply of water had improved. But the Parisians were only allowed one liter of water per day and per person up until the time of the Revolution. The existing underground canal system ran for several kilometers; but it primarily served those who were well-provided with water, namely the nobility and the clergy.

Under the rule of Louis XV (beginning of the 18th century), the streets finally received names, which were engraved into the walls. Apart from this occurrence, the lives of the Parisians showed no signs of change. Their city was still dirty and wretched, and it stank to high heaven. The people were exposed to famine, floods, epidemics, and the pressure of taxation by their monarch, who had to finance his wars, state buildings (Panthéon, 5th Arr.) and life of luxury.

The "open" Paris of the Sun King could not be maintained for long since the customs tax which was to be paid when entering the city could now easily be avoided.

Louis XVI gave his permission for the construction of a 23 kilometer-long toll wall, which enclosed the meanwhile 600,000 inhabitants dwelling on an area of just under 34 sqkm in 1787.

Massive Intervention in the Appearance of the City

The social upheavals of the Great Revolution did not contribute to the improvement of the quality of urban life. Even Napoléon I (beginning of the 19th century) preferred to build new monuments in the honor of his army (Arc de Triomphe and Madeleine, 8th Arr.) rather than renew the city.

The toll belt did not offer adequate military protection against attacks from the outside. But Adolphe Thiers, during his tenure as minister under Louis Philippe, had a magic formula: A new fortification ring had to be built. It was completed in 1841. The new protective wall stretched around Paris three kilometers from the old ring. However, the toll belt continued to serve as the official city boundary.

At the time of the Revolution, the villages bordering on Paris had been granted their own city administrations. Among them were, for example, Auteuil in the west, St.-Ouen in the north, Bagnolet in the east and Gentilly in the south. The new wall now cut a whole series of these in two halves. The divided villages remained independent until 1860.

Napoléon III, also called the "Operetta Emperor," served as a self-proclaimed emperor since 1852. He had high-flying plans. According to his wishes, the city was to be transformed into "the queen of the world." On his return from London, he knew what was missing: public parks and space where the public health could recover in the sun. In addition, he searched for a solution to the overburdened transportation routes. He wanted to have an adequate sewerage system laid out and the contaminated districts of the poor re-developed. He also wanted to have railroad lines laid down to carry the workers to and from the construction sites. No sooner said than done. His own master architect was Baron Haussmann, who zealously struck wide corridors through the squalid sectors, and designed English gardens (Montsouris in the 14th Arrondissement and the Buttes-Chaumont in the 19th Arrondissement). His friend Baltard erected the famous market halls: Les Halles. They were torn down in the 1960s, but the Parisians still mourn for them to this day.

The old toll belt was dismantled in 1860 and everything situated within the fortification ring incorporated into Paris. Absolutism *nouvelle vague*!

In addition, the administrative divison of the city into 20 Arrondissements that wind around the center of Paris like a snail's house was undertaken; it is still valid today. Paris meanwhile had a population of 1,600,000 and comprised an area of about 80 sqkm.

In compliance with with the wishes of Napoléon III, Haussmann changed Paris into a city which many called the "most beautiful in the world." Purists did not think much of the ostentatious architecture of this period (e.g. the Opéra Garnier, 9th Arrondissement) but even today it still characterizes the face of the city along with all the other historical monuments.

Even those rows of houses found in all of the quarters – their zinc roofs and wrought-iron parapets on high windows looking confusingly alike to newcomers – are a legacy of Haussmann. The pattern is common to both grand as well as the small style, whether lordly 300-square-meter apartments or the most shabby little flats: Spacious reception rooms border the generous entrance hall, narrow corridors lead to the kitchen and to small

Right: A nightmare even for Parisian drivers – the Place de l'Étoile.

rooms. And this principle still continues in current housing design.

The war of 1870 meant the end of the rule of the Operetta Emperor. The "wall builder" Adolphe Thiers replaced him. The Sacré-Coeur, the church of atonement in "meringue pie" style on Montmartre (in the 18th Arrondissement) commemorates the Paris Commune (1871), which he crushed. The *Belle Epoque* endowed Paris with the Eiffel Tower (7th Arrondissement) as well as the Grand Palais and the Petit Palais on the Champs-Elysées – on the occasion of the Second World Exhibition in 1889. In the meantime, the city had become the proud possessor of eight train stations, a circular railway (still used in part today by the Express-Métro RER with its Line C), the second of Europe's Métro lines and numerous department stores.

Paris Today

Styles come and go quickly in this hectic century. Yet, there have been few fundamental changes in the cityscape. Although some concrete buildings have been constructed according to Le Corbusier's space-saving model (in the 13th and 15th Arr., as well as Montparnasse), the trend was halted in the 1970's. National governments continue to erect monuments, but for the people of Paris they only trigger discussions.

Since the dark days of the Middle Ages, Paris has become a comparatively clean city. Mayor Chirac keeps his calling card in a very good condition. He was the first elected mayor in the history of the city, because up until 1977, Paris was subject to a prefect appointed by the government. One of the problems that remains for him to solve, is the city's traffic, which is at the brink of collapsing. Although relief roads are planned, experience tends to show that with an annual three percent increase in the volume of urban traffic, they will no longer be adequate by the time they are completed.

Facing that, are there any other possibilities besides moving away?

A CITY UNDER THE CITY

The underground of Paris has more holes than Swiss cheese. Métro tunnels, sewerage shafts, former gypsom quarries and the catacombs together form an extensive, chaotic, labyrinthine network of passages on three different levels, which lead down to a depth of 64 meters.

Water and Sewage

It is not at all exaggerated to speak of a city beneath the city. Even the notions Parisians have about its dimensions lag far behind reality. The best example is without a doubt the sewage system. Everyone is familiar with the Champs-Elysées. But how many people are aware that there is a second, less elegant version of the splendid avenue? It runs exactly

Above: This Métro entrance of Guimard is typical of its kind. Right: The circular stairway at the Métro station of Abbesses has been designed in its own style.

parallel and not far away at all from the famous tourist strip – a mere five meters beneath the asphalt.

In Paris, the sewerage tunnels (some up to 2.5 meters high) not only exactly follow the streets above them, but also they grace themselves with their names. The "second street network" of the Seine metropolis comprises a network amounting to 2100 km flooded with murky water. Yet, it is so generously laid out that the 663 city sewermen can wade through it upright or comfortably navigate it in rubber dinghies.

However, the sewerage system created by human hands represents only a small portion of the watery element under the city surface. A high ground-water level (minus ten meters) characterizes the Paris region and even today makes all types of excavation work rather difficult. After all, old Paris was built in a swamp region, which had numerous smaller watercourses flowing through it in addition to the Seine. The swamps were drained with time, and the water courses in the current city area were covered up along with the subsidiary branches of the Seine. It should be emphasised that they were covered up and not filled up, for the water courses of earlier times now continue to meander as underground rivers.

The Métro

When one hears "Paris under the asphalt" it is natural to think primarily of the world-famous Métro. There is actually nothing else that embodies the French capital city and its hubbub as well as the underground railroad. This means of transportation is used by 4.5 million people every day.

In its stations, however, there is music-making, buying, selling, even dealing. The official traders have their boutiques here, and the unofficial profiteers bring inexpensive fruit, watches or belts to the people. Last but not least are those countless musicians who provide for ambience with their violins, guitars and flutes as well as rounding off their own monthly incomes.

The first Métro which clattered from Vincennes to Porte Maillot on its maiden voyage in the year 1900, only travelled a 10-km route. Today the Métro together with the RER system – RER: Paris suburban fast train which also circulates underground – has 18 lines covering 301 kilometers and 315 stations.

Just as in earlier times, the Paris subway is very inexpensive to use, and there is hardly a spot in the city that cannot easily be reached by the Métro. One carnet, a booklet of ten tickets, costs 30 francs, which is around US $ 6. Unluckily, however, in the lengthy and therefore intricate tunnel network of the Métro stations, pickpockets and drug dealers thrive.

The statisticians stubbornly refuse to publicize the true extent of these criminal activities. Nevertheless, there is just as little a chance of eliminating them as

there is of getting rid of that certain and unmistakeable smell of the Métro. Travel guides prefer to praise it with the euphemistic description of the perfume of Paris. Those who constantly use it simply grumble that it stinks.

The Parisians eagerly use the Métro since only in the underground are they guaranteed quick progress through their eternally congested city. Just how unimaginable life in the capital city would be without the subway is proven by the three words with which the typical Parisian tends to describe his or her daily routine: *Métro, boulot, dodo*. In English: Métro, work, sleep.

Yet, the Métro still is not loved. That it is constantly overcrowded, dirty, inadequately illuminated and uncomfortable, is the continually recurring litany of complaints. Parisians only become conscious of what their subway means to them when a number of lines come to a standstill at the same time because of a strike or power failure. All of Paris then sinks into chaos.

Quarries and Catacombs

If, over the centuries, ancient *Lutetia* was able to grow in the constant manner it did into the Paris of today, then this was due in no small measure to the ground beneath it. From the time of the Romans and into the 19th century, it delivered the building material for houses, churches, palaces and monasteries. From the countless quarries in the current city region, the Parisians extracted not only their necessary building stones, but also loam, lime, chalk, and sand.

It was only in 1813, that the further exploitation of the last 18 (!) quarries in the city area was forbidden since the incidence of subsidence had increased threateningly over the previous 50 years. Nevertheless, the soil beneath about ten percent of the current city area has been excavated and exploited in the course of

Above: The next Métro will arrive in one minute! Right: A Parisian policeman helping with directions.

2000 years. After 1893, however, there was a systematic effort to achieve the opposite effect. Since that time, around 90 percent of the old quarries have been filled in.

However, the labyrinth consisting of more than 300 kilometers of underground tunnels which allowed access to and from the quarries was not filled up. At the end of the 18th century, the dead from the cemeteries in the middle of the city began to be transported into the tunnels and galleries. This – and not the era of pre-Christian burials – was the birth hour of the catacombs.

You can only visit a small portion of the catacombs, but essentially the intention has been to fill in this underground labyrinth. Excursions through the mazes are actually only allowed whenever employees of the post office, power company, or sewage treatment plant have to do the inevitable maintenance work.

However, particularly on the weekends, there are entire gangs that haunt the catacombs. Equipped with safety helmets and flashlights, snacks and beer, cigarettes and cassette recorders, they dive down for an exploratory expedition. The wild mud fights, followed by a cleansing bath in tunnels where larger amounts of rain water have collected, are considered to be a particularly "weird" pleasure. Sometimes even an underground rock band plays for the "cataphiles," as the odd night owls who are mostly recruited from student circles, call themselves.

Number Games

The belly of Paris has swallowed all sorts of things: 3000 kilometers of water pipes, 2320 kilometers of electrical cable lines, 330 kilometers of natural gas piping, an approximate 43 million cubic meters of cellar rooms, 2.5 million cubic meters of underground parking spaces, and 1.1 million cubic meters of underpasses or tunnels for automotive traffic.

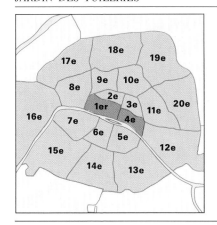

THE HISTORICAL HEART OF PARIS

JARDIN DES TUILERIES
LOUVRE
PLACE VENDÔME
LES HALLES
CENTRE POMPIDOU
MARAIS DISTRICT
ÎLE DE LA CITÉ

In the Heart of Paris

The 1st and 4th Arrondissements house the oldest and most original treasures of the city. When strolling through the narrow winding alleys, you should dip into the shady streets, with houses standing close together. You cannot help but think of the gloomy cellar of the Louvre, where the sight of the city walls and the ruins of Philippe Auguste's castle seem to turn back the wheel of time. In the Marais quarter, the venerable town houses of the 17th century cause you to pause and admire time and again.

Right next door you find showy high-tech edifices of modern times such as the Centre Pompidou or the Forum des Halles. It has only been in the past several years that they have taken over the terrain of the old market halls, much to the vexation of the purist art critics who condemn them as an "aesthetic disgrace." The controversial question is, whether modern barbarians are destroying an urban landscape, which has matured with time, or whether such developments are simply a part of architectural history?

Previous pages: Pont Neuf is actually the oldest bridge in Paris. The Louvre's magnificent façade contrasts impressively with the sleekness of the Pei-Pyramid.

This contemporary discord is revealed to us in crass vividness on the Place Igor Stravinksy between the modern Centre Pompidou and the chancel of Saint-Merri church. Gaudy colored figures frolic on the square in a water basin, designed by the daring hands of two artists. However, if the old proverb about fools and children always telling the truth is accurate, then we must admire these bold artistic sallies in form and color in the middle of the old part of the city: French children have long since taken a fancy to the unconventional water artwork.

JARDIN DES TUILERIES

The main entrance to the **Jardin des Tuileries**, which was re-designed by Pierre Le Nôtre and his grandson André after the former's death, is to be found on the Place de la Concorde. Even in recent times, many new events and incidents have happened here. Just as every king wanted to leave his impression in stone upon the city architecture, so too did François Mitterrand wish to immortalize himself and his rule: In monuments such as the enormous Arche de la Défense, the Opéra de la Bastille and, above all, the colossal Grand Louvre. In the course of rebuilding the Louvre, the Tuileries will most likely be redesigned as well.

When you enter the Tuileries from the Place de la Concorde, you will see two white marble sculptures by Antoine **Coysevox**, *Mercure* and *Renommée montée sur Pégase*. Their originals are housed in the Louvre, as are those of the powerful **Horses of Marly** (a work by Guillaume Coustou), which flank the entrance to the Champs-Élysées.

The **Jeu de Paume** museum, built in 1853, sparkles with a new luster since its renovation in June 1991. Exhibitions of modern art take place here. Its twin, the **Musée de l'Orangerie**, contains among other works of art a famous large painting by Claude Monet, the *Nymphéas*. His skilled brush kept alive the beautiful water lilies that he planted with his own hands in his spacious garden in Giverny. When the unique light from the windows above falls onto the painting, the desire to visit the original scene in Giverny will certainly be awakened within you.

The Tuileries, laid out with trees and sculptures, certainly conveys the impression of an urban art landscape. Its shady avenues lead to water basins in which small children irreverently splash around or sail their little wooden ships. There are also sail boats for rent in case you don't have one handy. This atmosphere of artistically-tamed nature is reminiscent of the strolls taken by the young Marcel Proust, who was a well-behaved child who could play for hours with Gilberte without getting dirty.

The name Tuileries is derived from the two tile factories (*tuile* = tile) that occupied this tract of land during the 16th century. Catherine de' Medici bought this piece of property, had the factories torn down and built a palace here in the proximity of the Louvre in 1564. During the Paris Commune in spring 1871, the Tuileries burned down to the foundation walls. Catherine also had the Tuileries laid out with exotic flowers and unusual trees, a pond, an aviary, an orangery, a cypress maze, a fountain, a grotto, a zoo-logical garden and a silkworm breeding house. In 1633, the aristocrat Régnard obtained permission from Louis XIII to establish a rendezvous for noblemen and noblewomen of the court here. In 1664, Colbert commissioned Le Nôtre to create the Tuileries we know today.

Charles Perrault, author of fairy tales and Colbert's first secretary, was responsible for the garden being opened up to almost all the citizens of the city. Only "soldiers, domestic servants and rabble" were denied admission. The Parisians were very pleased with their first and lovely public park. In the course of this "democratization," a pavilion was also opened up where people could buy refreshments and take a rest on the chairs.

For a long time, a deep moat bounded the park along the city walls as far as what is today the Place de la Concorde. The engineer Nicolas Bourgeois spanned it with an interesting swing bridge which was admired in 1717 by the Czar Peter the Great during his stay in Paris. He traveled through all of Europe in those days with the intention of importing the newest and best technical and artistic achievements back to his Russian kingdom. The bridge was removed in 1817, but a certain Madeleine, confectioner and inventor of the famous *madeleines* – those small sweet cakes which inspired Marcel Proust – continued to sell her baked goodies on this spot.

Famous scientists were often known to present their discoveries to the public in the park. In 1783, the physicist Alexandre Charles and his assistant Robert attempted for the first time to send a gas-filled balloon up into the air. (Allegedly) 400,000 fascinated spectators enthusiastically followed the start of the very first hydrogen balloon. Nine years later, on August 10, 1792, the royal family fled from the revolutionaries out of the Tuileries Pavilion and hid in the Salle du Manège. The building unfortunately no longer stands today. Among the recollec-

tions of this period is also the massacre of the 700 Swiss royal guard. It was in the Salle du Manège that the National Assembly met in 1789, and on September 21, 1792, proclaimed the Republic.

In the direction of the Louvre, you reach the **triumphal arch of the Carrousel**, an imitation (from the year 1808) of the arch of Septimus Severus in Rome. The intricate decoration on the monument commemorates the Napoleonic wars. During his Italian campaign, Napoléon confiscated a Corinthian quadriga from the 5th century B.C. in Venice. After it was returned to Venice in 1815, it was replaced by a copy.

LOUVRE

The **Louvre** consists of a number of pavilions that are grouped around inner courtyards. Built in different stages of

Above: A fair in the Jardin des Tuileries.
Right: The art treasures in the Louvre are between 100 and 4000 years old.

construction, every new or converted annex recalls the work of a particular king. The first Louvre was a fortification constructed under Philippe Auguste in 1190. It was actually the fulfillment of an old Parisian wish: The Parisians had, for long, demanded that a fortification be built after the city was invaded by fierce Norsemen.

The structure consisted at that time solely of a battlement and a keep, the dungeon, whose foundations can still be viewed today under the Cour Carrée. Philippe Auguste housed his archives in the 32-meter-high dungeon. Philippe le Bel (the Fair) kept his state treasury, his arsenal and sometimes also his most important political prisoners safe here. Francis I had the grim tower razed.

The hall of King Louis the Saint under the Louvre is now open to the public for viewing. In the very low room with its richly-decorated capitals, you can vividly imagine the lively atmosphere present at royal audiences in former times.

Charles V had a second fortification wall built around the city, through which the Louvre lost its previous protective function. In 1360, the king retreated from the hectic activity of his official residence in the Hôtel Saint-Pol, to the old, still sparsely-furnished Louvre in order to read and relax in peace and tranquility.

If you want to re-experience the entire splendor of the medieval Louvre, read *The Duc de Berry's Book of Hours*. For a long time, art historians considered it to be an exaggerated, idealized description, but the latest research confirms that the royal residence actually must have been comparable to a fairy-tale castle.

One and half centuries later, Francis I had the wide, sweeping avenue laid out from the Louvre in the direction of the present Arc de Triomphe and La Défense as a splendid approach route to the city palace. He had the dilapidated Louvre extended and further fortification work was begun. This endeavor stretched out over

300 years, and had the overall effect of making the mighty building uglier instead of more beautiful.

The stately premises continued their decline during the reign of Henry IV. At the end of the 16th century, he had his deer-breeding farm housed in the Louvre.

The famous **colonnade** of Claude Perrault was started in the 17th century under Louis XIV. It was not finished until the year 1811, together with the Cour Carrée.

The Louvre of the 20th century, with the famous **glass pyramid** by the Japanese sculptor I. M. Pei, and charming water basins, once again projects a special harmony. Whether you like the façades of the Louvre or not, its true luster develops when you pass through the entrance in the pyramid to the interior. In 1981, in the course of a gigantic re-designing project for the "new Louvre," the Ministry of Finance moved out of the former Richelieu wing. Numerous fresh archaeological excavations were then undertaken, the new entrance through the glass pyramid was created and façades and the inside of the court.

According to those responsible for the project *Grand Louvre*, the exhibition areas in the interior are to be completely re-designed and doubled in size by 1996. The exhibitions are to be re-grouped and the numerous treasures, which have been stored in giant magazines up until now, will be made accessible to the public for the first time. The seven departments of the museum will then exhibit a total of 28,000 objects.

If you have the time, you can start with the art of antiquity and become acquainted with the Louvre in an engrossing walk through the centuries. You will then also discover numerous interesting works of non-European primitive art.

Alternatively, it is possible to join a guided tour (offered in various languages) and have the most famous works on display explained to you within one or two hours. Brochures and the times of the tours are posted in all languages at the entrance of the Louvre.

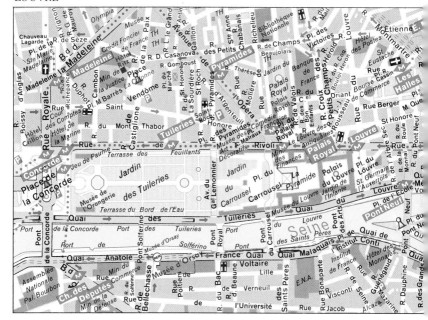

At the eastern exit of the Louvre, you can cross the Place du Louvre. There you catch a glimpse of the **Saint-Germain-l'Auxerrois** church, which appears to be still waiting for the royal family to come to services. It is dedicated to Saint Germain, Bishop of Auxerre at the end of the 7th century. Although it was completely destroyed by the Vikings, the church was later reconstructed. In the following centuries, it was continually extended and renovated in all types of styles.

As an aside, the bells which rang out in the bloody massacre of Protestants on St Bartholomew's, the night of August 23, 1572, are still hanging there in the graceful medieval church tower dating from the 12th century.

During the Revolution, the church served the lowly function of a barn and then later had a stint as a printing shop. Before it was returned to its original religious purpose, it was the scene of a demonstration by a crowd opposing King Charles X in 1831, after which it had to be rebuilt again. A series of bestially looking stone sculptures were created in memory of this uprising.

One anecdote relating to this church tells how, in 1848, an unusual funeral ceremony was attended by all the "ordinary people" of the area. A worker had stolen diamonds, swallowed and then finally spat them up again. His crime had its own deadly consequences: The diamonds slit open the man's stomach. Nevertheless, he was buried in the cemetery here with an extraordinary amount of pomp and ceremony.

Directly next to the church, a Merovingian grave with a sarcophagus made of a three-ton monolith, now displayed in the Musée Cluny, was discovered in the 19th century.

Palais Royal

After a stroll through the Rue de L'Arbre-Sec, where those who died of the plague in 1553 were thrown into a trench, and through the Rue Saint-Honoré, you reach the **Palais Royal**.

firework display on the occasion of Marie Antoinette's wedding to the Dauphin. A few decades later, the revolutionaries, who were intent on eliminating all royalist monuments from the face of the earth, removed Louis XIV's statue, dubbed the plaza Place de la Revolution, and set up their guillotine on it. Louis XVI, Marie Antoinette and 1119 other people lost their lives here, among them Charlotte Corday, Danton, Philippe Égalité and Robespierre. In order to help these bloody events on their way to oblivion, the Directory renamed the square *Place de la Concorde* in 1795.

Its beauty can be better appreciated at night, since then the traffic lets up a bit and the illumination system bathes it in a magical light. If indulging in a taxi tour of the city, one must pass by here before midnight – because after that the lights are extinguished and the square sinks into darkness.

Standing in the center of the plaza is the **Obelisk of Luxor**. This pink granite monolith is 23 m high and weighs 220 tons. It is 3300 years old and ornamented with hieroglyphics exalting the reign of Ramesses II. The obelisk was presented as a gift to Charles X by the Egyptian viceroy Mohamed Ali in 1829. The monument was installed here under the rule of Louis Philippe who, bearing in mind the destruction caused during the recent upheavals, was pleased to have found a non-political monument. So that future generations would be reminded of the effort it required to erect this colossus here, the procedure, including all of the mechanical devices that were necessary, was portrayed on the pedestal.

Before the corners of the Place de la Concorde were decorated with statues in 1836, entire families resided in the future pedestals, beneath roofs pieced together from whatever boards were available. These peculiar tenants also planted vegetables and fruits in the ditches surrounding the square. One fellow named Joseph Thurot even set up a snack booth, that also sold lemonade. Of course, today these shelters have disappeared, and the vacated

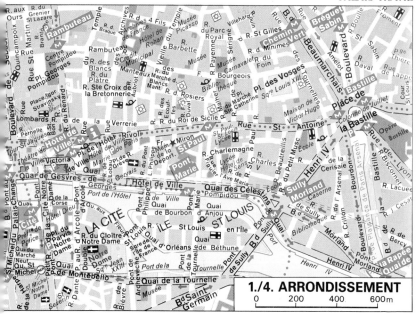

1./4. ARRONDISSEMENT

0   200   400   600m

This was the city palace of Cardinal Richelieu, who wanted to live close to Louis XIII. It was built upon the demolished ruins of 3rd-century public Roman baths, which had been destroyed by the invading Vikings.

When Louis XIII died, his widow Anne of Austria took leave of the Louvre along with their two sons, the future Sun King and the Duc d'Orléans, and took up residence in the Palais Royal, which she had inherited from her spouse. Her confidant Cardinal Mazarin lived right next door in the Hôtel Tubœuf. The houses were connected by a garden.

Could it have been because the revolts of the *Fronde* forced the royal family to flee the Palais Royal on two occasions? Or was it because Louis XIV almost drowned in a pond in the lush garden as a child? For whatever reason, the young prince absolutely insisted upon moving back to the protection of the Louvre when he was 14 years old. He later moved to his pet project Versailles, which supports the first hypothesis.

As the ruling king, Louis XIV lodged his mistress, Mademoiselle de la Vallière in a wing of the Palais Royal, the Hôtel Brion. Here she gave birth to two sons, both of whom died young.

The Palais Royal was given as a whole to the Duc d'Orléans, whose son became regent for the underaged Louis XV. His grandson Philippe d'Orléans, who was later known as Philippe Egalité, had galleries built on the three garden sides in 1780. This fundamentally changed the structure of the building. Plagued by debts, he rented the 60 pavilions to traders, who operated their sales stands on the garden side. The sight of the back portion with its piles of garbage was naturally a thorn in the side of the adjacent well-to-do residents. But their complaints were futile. D'Orléans led an extravagant life. After the performances in the newly-constructed Théâtre Royal, he invited his royal retinue to extravegent costume parties and orgiastic balls in the Grand Palais. The arcades with their busy bookstores, cafés, gambling dens and restau-

rants were also the haunt of the simple people, including dubious mountebanks, magicians and prostitutes, which did not exactly contribute to the improvement of the area's reputation.

The Great Revolution was not long in coming. The revolutionaries held their speeches from the terraces of this district; one of the insurgents was the young Camille Desmoulins. It is said that they went as far as taking the leaves from the trees of the Palais garden for their revolutionary cockades.

After the Revolution, Louis Philippe, the somewhat tamer son of the revolutionary Philippe Égalité and the new owner of the property, drove off the ladies of the night and had the gambling dens closed. The dignity and grandeur of the palace was then restored.

The Palais Royal was plundered on two further occasions: during the Revolution of 1848, and at the time of the upris-

Above: A refreshing romance in the park at the Palais Royal.

ing of the Commune. In modern times, it has been renovated and serves the city council as a meeting place. Its current cold, unfriendly atmosphere is in crass contrast to the turbulent life of the 18th century. In our day, there are only the magnificent columns by Daniel Buren to conjure up the images of this past.

The gardens were laid out at the edge of the former city forest of Rouvray, of which at the present time only the Bois de Boulogne remains. Traversed by lonely footpaths, the lovely old garden was taken to heart by the 18th-century philosopher Denis Diderot who then wrote: "Whether it rains or the sun shines, I love to walk through the garden of the Palais Royal at five o'clock in the afternoon."

You now enter the **Rue de Rivoli**. Under the arcades there are tourist boutiques to rummage through; that is, if you like the somewhat old-fashioned souvenirs such as colorful scarves and T-shirts with Paris imprints on them. However, you will also find some interesting art galleries and luxury boutiques here.

Turn right into the **Rue Castiglione**, where the convent of the *Feuillants* used to be located. The club of the *Feuillants*, whose chairman was La Fayette (who led the storm on the Bastille), was closed in 1790. The building itself was torn down in 1804 to make room for the Rue Castiglione, Rue de Rivoli and Rue de Mont-Thabor.

PLACE VENDÔME

The most elegant jewelry stores of Paris and the incomparably fashionable Hotel Ritz stand on the **Place Vendôme**. Desert sheiks and international millionaires meet here at this stylish site. Together with the *haute couture*, jewellers have made a sizeable contribution to the world-wide renown of French elegance.

In the 17th century, Louis XIV gave his architects Mansart and Boffrand the task of designing a square plaza around his equestrian statue. On the day of its dedication in 1699, gigantic sheets with house façades painted on them concealed the still yawning gaps along the surrounding streets. Modern Paris has revived this means of disguising construction sites.

Louvois, the superintendent of all the builders, praised the plan since it would relieve the traffic in the adjacent streets. Even back then, there was congestion – a deplorable malady, which has not been dealt with adequately to date. The area also proved to be a true goldmine for cunning real-estate agents, who were also already represented back then.

The square was first called Place Louis-le-Grand, then later the Place de Piques. During the Great Revolution, the equestrian statue was removed. The middle of the square is now decorated with the **Vendôme column**, a copy of the Trajan column in Rome, and built in honor of Napoléon. It was cast from the bronze of 250 cannons captured from the Austrians and the Russians in the battle of Austerlitz. The ground relief shows battle scenes from the campaign of 1805. The statue of Napoléon in the costume of a Roman emperor, which you can see today, replaced an older sculpture which showed the ruler in civilian dress. The latter figure was toppled from its pedestal by the insurgents of the Commune. Among them was also Gustave Courbet, the president of the *Commission des Beaux-Arts* at that time. He had the column put back in place, paying for it from his own pocket in 1873. This gesture made him the laughing stock of the people. After six years of prison, Courbet emigrated to Switzerland where he died a lonely death at 58 years of age.

You can reach the **Saint-Roch** church by way of the Rue Saint-Honoré. This building in classical style is almost as high as the more famous Notre-Dame. Stop a while in front of the remarkable façade with its Corinthian columns. Within its walls, the Scottish financial expert Law converted to Catholicism. However, this was not an act of inner conviction, but rather only for the practical purpose of acquiring the position of a general inspector in France during the regency of Louis XV. The name of God in the Hebrew language is etched into the altar.

Still on the Rue Saint-Honoré, at the Place André Malraux, you will find yourself exactly there where one entered Paris through the old city gate of Saint-Honoré at the time of Charles V' s city walls. The **Comédie Française**, long the absolute synonym for French language and culture, has been situated here since 1790. Although the "style of the Comédie Française" is still referred to today, in the meantime people have also become open to the more modern productions. Since the time of Napoléon I, the actors, no matter if they were students or professionals, have possessed rights similar to those of civil servants with fixed pensions. This is quite impressive considering the fact that before the Great Revolu-

tion most actors hardly enjoyed any civil rights at all.

LES HALLES

From the Rue Saint-Honoré, you turn left into a maze of narrow alleys, into the **Rue des Bons-Enfants**, where you reach the historic market district. Unfortunately, through the years it has begun to lose its popular old charm. Many years before this pleasant shopping district was established, it was known in Paris as the dirty quarter of the poor people and the clochards.

Today, in contrast, the uppercrust of Parisian society meets here at the **Café Costes** or in the **Père Tranquille**. Untiring skateboard riders glide around the **Fontaine des Innocents**, while the masses shove their way through the **Forum des Halles**.

Above: Place Vendôme under renovation.
Right: The Forum des Halles. Far right: View from Centre Pompidou.

The history of the great market halls goes far back in time. Louis VI bought the *petits champs,* the fields after which a street is still named today, from the bishop of that period. In 1135, the king inaugurated the first open air public market here. When the market was closed down in 1969, it had already reached the proud and unparalleled age of more than 800 years of commercial service.

Back then, the property was in the alluvial region of the Seine and by no means safe from floods. The first buildings were erected in 1183 in order to protect the sales people from inclement weather. A wall was built to discourage night-time thieves. The long period of peace under the dominion of Philippe Auguste made further expansion and growing prosperity possible. A third hall was added in 1263, and three further halls were built within a short period of time thereafter.

Fruit, vegetables, fresh and pickled fish, tanned hides, ropes and leather goods exuded the greatest variety of smells. Patrick Süskind very vividly described these sensory impressions in his novel *Perfume.* To get an approximate idea of the distinctive aroma of the area, one must just imagine the fishmonger gutting and scaling his fish in the street. The Rue Verderet was called *Merderet* (this translates roughly as "little shit") at that time, which alluded to this smell.

Death, which was and is at home just a few steps further down the road at the **Cimetière des Innocents**, was also a part of this little world. The merchants who sold shrouds and the writers who wrote eulogies set up their small businesses between graves that had hardly been covered – an extension, as it were, of the busy commercial district.

The cemetery thanked its existence to the ancient Roman custom of burying the dead along the streets. At first, the graves were placed on the road to Saint-Denis, but the cemetery grew so quickly that Philippe Auguste had it surrounded with

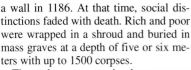

a wall in 1186. At that time, social distinctions faded with death. Rich and poor were wrapped in a shroud and buried in mass graves at a depth of five or six meters with up to 1500 corpses.

The only structures in the cemetery were a clerical hall, an obelisk which served as a lantern and several chapels for very rich people. In addition, arcades were constructed, in which the remains from dug-up mass graves were deposited.

Artists decorated the arcades, of which an alabaster skeleton still preserved at the Louvre today bears witness. We know that there was a fresco consisting of a series of pictures on 30 panels. These portrayed a *danse macabre* and the power that death has over human beings. This work, created in 1424, was destroyed in 1669 together with the charnel house. Fortunately, the painters had produced several versions on wooden panels which have been preserved.

The market halls were destroyed during the Hundred Years War, but rebuilt under Francis I and his son Henry II.

Many revolts, of which the *Fronde* (1649-1653) was one of the most important, arose here in the heart of the city. Despite this, the traders remained among themselves. Begun under Napoléon I and continued by Baltard under Napoléon III, the renovation of the Halles district was not finished until 1936.

In the late sixties, the twelve halls were demolished and the market moved to the Parisian suburb of Rungis. On the spot where the clochards had tramped about in the hopes of making a good catch, a new temple to consumerism, with gigantic proportions, rose into the heights: the modern **Forum des Halles**.

On five spacious and bright sales levels, all wishes of the modern consumer can be fulfilled: Reading (you can buy books), listening (you can buy records and cassettes), seeing (in the theaters, movies and museums), renewing one's wardrobe, and eating. The customers flock here from all over Paris and the suburbs. It is more pleasant strolling through the Forum during the week since

the Parisians primarily visit it on Saturdays. It is best to start out your exploratory tour of the enormous building in the second basement. Here you will be greeted by a marble Pygmalion created by the contemporary Portuguese artist Julia Silva.

Also take a look at the **Musée Grévin**. This wax museum, which has another subsiduary (the original) on the Boulevard Montmartre, is a unique tourist attraction. The picture-and-sound presentations experienced here can sweep you away to the *Belle Époque*. On the same level you will also find the **Musée de l' Holographie**, which magically attracts not only the fans of holograms and three-dimensional portrayals of all varieties.

A newly-expanded level between the old stock exchange and Saint-Eustache Church contains a large swimming pool

Above: "Ecoute", de Millers sculpture in front of the church Saint-Eustache. Right: Fountain of Innocents – formerly the center of an extensive cemetery.

with a luxurious tropical garden and glass pyramids towering above it, a sports ground, a billiard room, a concert hall in which mainly jazz is played, a discothèque, a videothèque and a movie theater. There are naturally a great many boutiques for you to browse and shop in as well.

In front of the **Saint-Eustache** church, a labyrinthine asphalted plaza frames an enormous sculpture of Burgundy sandstone. Created by the artist Henri de Miller, *Écoute* ("listen") is more than just a head supported by a hand: The sculpture radiates that repose and harmony longed for by hectic city dwellers.

You can find your own repose and time for contemplation in Saint-Eustache. Its decorative Renaissance interior is quite enchanting and presents a fascinating contrast to the Gothic architecture of the exterior of the building. The construction of the building was started in 1214. The church was first dedicated to Saint Agnes, but later to the patron saint of hunters. Saint Eustache was a Roman soldier who converted to Christianity after encountering a wild stag with a cross shining between its antlers. On the façade of the transept you will discover a sculpture that portrays the head of that stag.

Since the church soon proved to be too small for the number of parishioners, expansion began in 1732. This work was completed in 1754 when the original façade was replaced by a classical column façade. Famous French personalities, such as Molière and the Marquise de Pompadour, are immortalized upon it. The lady had been married to several other men before she was „discovered" by Louis XV and later "passed on" Mirabeau (father of the famous Honoré de Mirabeau) and the composer Rameau. The spirit of the latter probably keeps his watchful eye over the parsonage. Its organ is now played by Jean Guillou, who, like his eminent predecessor, understands how to compose contemporary music for this instrument as well.

Be sure to view the gracefully built rotunda, the **Bourse du Commerce** while sauntering through the streets around the gardens of Les Halles. The **Hôtel de Nesle** once stood on this spot, the last domicile of Blanche de Castille, the mother of Saint Louis. After losing at a gambling game, Louis II of Orléans had the house turned into an unusual convent for "fallen" girls. Catherine de' Medici lodged them elsewhere and furnished herself a comfortable town house here, where she thought herself to be safe from the gloomy prophecy predicting that she would die "close to Saint-Germain." She ultimately did not breathe her last here in the Hôtel de la Reine, but rather in Blois after she had received last rites at the hands of a priest who bore the name of Julien de Saint-Germain.

In 1748, the palace was destroyed down to one last column, which a rich curio-dealer by the name of Petit de Bachaumont resold to the city of Paris. The column, with which Catherine de' Med-

ici's astrologers allegedly observed the heavens, was situated in the interior of the house, not far from the private chambers of the queen, who was counseled in secrecy.

An astrological column? A monument to the memory of Catherine de' Medici's deceased husband Henry II? No one knows for sure what the purpose of this column was. This will probably remain a secret for all time. The veil of history conceals the true use and purpose of this strange object.

A circular structure replaced the palace in 1765. It served as a warehouse for wheat. In 1889, the rotunda in which the stock exchange is housed today, finally took its place.

If you return to the **Place des Innocents**, behind the Forum you will see a wonderful carousel with wooden horses that turn in a circle to the sound of old-fashioned fairground music. This place is a popular meeting point for people walking their dogs, for young skateboard riders, but unfortunately also for dealers.

In the middle of the Place des Innocents is a fascinating fountain which Jean Goujon completed in 1549. Back then it stood at the corner of the Rue Saint-Denis and Rue Berger. When it became necessary to relocate it here, a further face needed to be added to it. However, in order to maintain the suspense, we will not disclose to you whose face was added. The prostitutes, who in the Middle Ages plied their trade around the Saint-Merri church, had to give up their traditional territory in Les Halles and move to the Rue Saint-Denis.

Before you cross the Boulevard Sébastopol, take a look at the little **Saint-Leut Saint-Gilles** church on the boulevard. The pillars of its stays are found in the interior of the church, which is an unusual approach. It originated in the 12th century and survived many alterations before being reconstructed in its original form by Baltard in 1858.

Above: Centre Pompidou is a bustling place any time of day.

CENTRE POMPIDOU

In order to reach the pedestrian zone around the Centre Pompidou again, cross the Boulevard Sébastopol and follow the **Rue Aubry**, a small street that is lined with the most peculiar curiosity shops. Here you can find the craziest earrings, the most unusual second-hand goods, or other aesthetic gadgets. You should give the cold shoulder to the fast-food places and grant yourself a sumptuous Greek sandwich in the Rue Saint-Martin.

Even if you are already familiar with the **Centre Pompidou** from postcards, you will be astonished at the sight of the giant puzzle of colorful pipes that wind upwards towards the heavens in the old heart of the city.

Already back in 1927, Le Corbusier dreamed of building a "museum of unlimited ideas" here, to be dedicated to the 20th century. But it was only in 1963 that André Malraux, the minister of culture at that time, was successful in officially announcing the large-scale project. Two years later, the death of Le Corbusier sent the plans in another direction.

Yet, Le Corbusier's ideas had taken on a life of their own. Georges Pompidou, incumbent president of the Republic and well-known as a lover of poetry, wanted to finally make this dream become a Parisian reality. And with the wide spectrum of sculpture, cinema, music, literature, and paedagogical center, the place became an aesthetic playground for all imaginable expectations and interests.

The Centre Pompidou was erected according to the principles of "flexibility, durability, and tenacity." The building is supported by 84 beams with a weight of 74 tons each; every storey has a surface of 7500 sqm. It opened its doors in 1977.

The eye-catching colors on its exterior are to reflect diverse functions. The red markings represent the transportation of people and goods, the yellow ones are electrical circuits, green symbolizes the transportation of water, and all white parts hold the building together. This appears to be a logical system, doesn't it?

On the esplanade, a clock shows you how fast time passes by. It tells how many seconds still divide us from the year 2000. Your reflectiveness is then just as quickly dissipated by the entertainers who frolic on the plaza as soon as the slightest ray of sunshine appears. These troubadours of the 20th century are familiar with almost all of the arts. Among them are fakirs, mime artists, dancers, street musicians with their hurdy-gurdies, story-tellers, portrait painters, acrobats, card-trickers and, naturally, *chanson*-singers with their guitars. Police patrols often inconspicuously join the crowd in order to keep a watchful eye on this "hotbed of vice." Hidden away on the plaza is also the unostentatious, reconstructed studio of the sculptor Brancusi.

Even if the sun is shining, you should still visit the **Musée d'Art Moderne**, covering the time period from 1905 until today in the interior of the Centre Pom-

pidou. Here you will also find an enormous library, an inviting cafeteria and many halls with art exhibitions.

Before you leave the "Beaubourg", give some attention to the artful contrast between the chancel of the Saint-Merri church and the fountain by Jean Tinguely and Niki de Saint-Phalle on the **Place Igor Stravinsky**.

The themes from the Russian musician's works such as *The Firebird, Petrushka* and *The Rite of Spring* are taken up by the eccentric figures and mobiles, which turn with the wind. Among the musicians of our time who have emerged from this spirit, Pierre Boulez, the director of the ICRAM, can be mentioned in primary position. His music, though unusual and difficult, has gradually come to be accepted.

The **Rue Saint-Martin** is one of the oldest in the city of Paris (next to the Rue Saint-Jacques). Even when Paris was still called *Lutetia,* this street led in a northerly direction to the abbey Saint-Martin. Located close to Les Halles, it quickly became an important trade route. In our day, Rue Saint-Martin has the appearance of a play street with permanent parties.

Standing in the shadow of the houses around it, the **Saint-Merri** church can also tell an eventful history. A small chapel of Saint-Pierre-des-Bois, in which the miracle-making monk Médéric d'Autun was buried around AD 700, was located here before the church.

Since the saint appeared to work wonders even after his death, Gozlin, the Bishop of Paris, wanted to have a more appropriate house of God built for him. Saint-Merri is a diminutive of Médéric. The church was reconstructed twice, once in the 13th century and at the time of Francis I in flamboyant late-Gothic style. The jube was later destroyed, and in the 18th century the Gothic windows were even replaced by plain glass windows! All that is then left of the original is the bell, but it is still the oldest one in Paris.

Situated in the vicinity of the **Rue des Lombards**, the place of worship became the parish church of the merchants from Genoa, Florence and Venice, who had settled on the little street during the time of Philippe Auguste. These prosperous residents were certainly more generous in their contributions to the church than they were in giving alms to the poor. Their donations were mostly in the form of works of art that have, in the meantime, became quite valuable.

Unluckily, the affluence of the church also attracted many thieves, who were apparently less god-fearing. And in a special register, a priest listed some of the names of local prostitutes; in 1387 he succeeded in rooting out and eliminating harlotry around the church.

The surrounding traders, however, were not at all happy with this development since they had lost those customers who were most willing to buy. Saint

Above: St. Jacques Tower. Right: Hôtel de Ville – presently the mayor's office.

Louis, France's very pious king, who reigned from 1226 to 1270, described them as "crazy" or „obsessed with their own body". They were organized into a „sisterhood" of 5000 - 6000 women with their own rules and privileges.

The streets **Rue Flamel** and **Rue Pernelle** recall the benefactors of the parish **Saint-Jacques-la-Boucherie**. Of this church only the tower remains. At the time of Saint Louis there was a large butcher shop next to it, which was originally built in 1060. Nicolas Flamel and his wife Pernelle, a generous middle-class couple, financed the construction of the side portal of the church and charitably opened the doors of their house in Rue Montmorency to all of the poor. The passionate writer, who also moonlighted as an alchemist, is said to have performed that mysterious feat: turning crude metal into gold. In 1756, three centuries after Flamel's death, the new owner had the house destroyed in order to search for the treasure supposedly buried here along with the philosopher's stone. The house was finally completely torn down in 1852, but the secret was never aired. In our day, the Métro line 1 irreverently races on rubber tyres through the former cellar of Monsieur Flamel.

The church also preserved its share of memories when it was destroyed in 1797. However, the bell tower from the 16th century survived and was purchased by the city of Paris in 1836. Pascal carried out his experiments here, as is still obvious in the interior. Covered with the black dust of pollution, it still has an uncanny effect even today with its height of 158 m. The place where the church of Saint-Jacques once stood has a very special atmosphere indeed.

If you wander along the **Boulevard Sébastopol** in the direction of the Seine, you will be surprised by the generous space and harmony of the **Place du Châtelet**, which is bordered by two imposing theaters. The Châtelet, a fortress,

once stood here in the middle of winding streets. On January 26, 1855 the hanged corpse of Gérard de Nerval was found in the neighboring Rue de la Vieille Lanterne. This place is marked by a plaque at the artists' entrance of the Théâtre du Châtelet.

The square itself was first created in the 19th century when the medieval fortress had been destroyed. Built under Louis VI (known as the Fat) in 1130, the Châtelet was feared by everyone who attempted to approach it.

When the new city walls were erected by Philippe Auguste in 1190, it lost its function as a protective structure but continued to be used as a courtroom, a forbidding prison and morgue. It is certain that cruel scenes of torture took place within its walls during the Middle Ages.

Around the gruesome building, from which the screams of the mistreated regularly echoed, daily life continued in its usual routine. Parisians purchased meat in the Halles and fish in the Rue Pierre-à-Poisson, where the Théâtre du Châtelet

stands today. Or they visited the cattle market, which was situated nearby on the Quai de la Mégisserie.

Built by Davioud in 1862, the **Théâtre du Châtelet** is today a concert hall. Directly across from it, the **Théâtre de la Ville** – previously the Théâtre Sarah Bernhardt – is a mecca for ballet fans. Both theaters are centers for the pulsating cultural life of Paris. Because of the reasonable price of subscriptions, there is also a young public in regular attendance. In the pleasant atmosphere of the impressive halls it is easy to enjoy theater and dance in a relaxed mood.

On the way to the **Hôtel de Ville**, you pass the **Quai de la Mégisserie**. It is mainly the hearts of children which are thrilled by the doves, kittens, puppies, baby chicks and other small animals.

The location of the Hôtel de Ville used to be a large free tract of land which led down to the Seine. In 1141, Louis VII sold this piece of land on the right bank *(la grève)* to the guild of shippers that carried out its prosperous trade on the

Seine, Marne, Oise and Yonne rivers. However, the harbor of Landry on the Île de la Cité soon became too small for the booming business and a new installation was planned on the right bank. Since sailors in search of a job loitered here on the *grève,* the modern French *faire la grève* came to mean the voluntary cessation of work, that is, to go on strike.

It was only in 1357 that the prefect Etienne Marcel set up a city hall on the **Place de Grève** in a house decorated with columns (the Maison-aux-Piliers). It was renovated in Renaissance style from 1533 to 1628 and burned down to the foundations on May 24, 1871 during the final days of the Commune. During the Revolution it was one of the most important political centers. After seizing the Bastille, the people stormed over to it and killed the prefect Flesselles.

The absolutist monarchy fell on that fateful day, July 14. A national revolutionary guard was created under general La Fayette, who added the royal white to the French flag with the colors of blue and red. This is how the tri-colored flag of France was created. Before the guillotine stood on the Place de la Concorde, the heads of criminals rolled on the Place de Grève. It was also here that Danton, Marat and Robespierre incited the crowds of people with their speeches.

During the revolution of 1848, a provisional government, which had come together in the city hall, drove off Louis Philippe. Still in the name of the Revolution, 20,000 people lost their lives in the uprisings of the Paris Commune here. The city hall went up in flames illuminating the skyline. The current building was then constructed in the elegant, majestic neo-Gothic style prevalent at the turn of the century.

From 1310 to 1830, the outsiders and outcasts of society were pilloried and flogged on the public square. You can read about this in Victor Hugo's *Notre-Dame de Paris* as follows:

"The Place de Grève had always been a gloomy place; so, too, its old dark city hall which Dominique Boccador replaced with the Maison-aux-Piliers. Death was constantly present here through the gallows and the pillories standing in the middle of the square and the criminal court and the manacks, as they were called in those days. This fatal place magically attracted the glances."

Before the condemned was handed over to the executioner, he was allowed one last prayer at the foot of the large cross. Henry IV later had it replaced by a fountain, to the regret of the Parisians. They had scratched the high-water levels of the Seine into the cross.

Before you traverse the Rue Lobeau, you reach the little **Place Saint-Gervais**, which lies in the shadow of a "patchwork" church. First built under the Merovingian King Clovis, the church was devoted to the martyrs Gervais and Protais, two brothers executed by the Roman Emperor Nero. In the 13th century, the church was torn down and built anew. Only the early-Gothic spire of the church remained when the church was redesigned in Gothic flamboyant style in 1494. Since the work dragged on, taste and style had changed by the time the entrance façade was finally completed in 1616: The trend was toward classical antiquity during that period and that is why you now enter the church through Greek columns. Voltaire sang the praises of the beauty of this church, Madame de Sévigné married here, and all of Paris was proud of its lovely new house of worship.

MARAIS DISTRICT

If you now stroll over the Rue de Rivoli, you will come to the middle of the Marais district. There is always some-

Right: Rue des Rosiers has always been the heart of the Jewish Quarter.

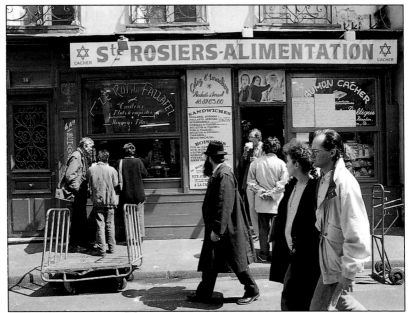

thing happening here day or night, and the masses of people are made up of all skin colors and social classes. The *nouveaux riches* and the monied aristocracy live in their expensive, renovated apartments. Artists and other creative people set splashes of color. And there has also been a small Jewish community living here since the Middle Ages.

For some years now, an effort has been made to restore the dilapidated quarter. The old-established residents do not have the resources to do so themselves. The main concern was for the town houses of the 17th and 18th centuries that were in such a deplorable state that they were scheduled to be torn down. However, in 1964, the Minister of Culture at that time, André Malraux, supported a complete renovation and declared the entire quarter to be a „historical monument."

The Marais district was soon upgraded: The prosperous people bought houses, and new shops and stores were opened. Restorers found plenty of work. The bars attracted the homosexual scene,

and galleries and art dealer's shops were happy to rake in the profits. Back when Paris was still called *Lutetia*, the Marais was a barren swamp area on the shores of the Seine. The **Rue Saint-Antoine**, which led from Paris to Melun, was already built in an elevated position during Roman times in order to protect it from flooding. In the 13th century, the Knights Templar took possession of the tract and built a fortress in the proximity of the Place de la République. Settlers soon took up residence there.

Further in the south, near the **Rue Ferdinand Duval**, an important Jewish community established itself. Today, there are still many Jews living in a thriving community there. There are synagogues and *kosher* butcher shops; sidewalk stands sell *falafel* sandwiches and restaurants tantalize with the specialties of the Middle East, as well as the cuisine of Eastern Europe, North Africa and Turkey.

Culinary diversity was not as important during the Middle Ages, when the district was still situated outside the city

walls. It was only under the sovereignty of Charles V that it was included as a part of the city within the second ring wall.

Positioned between the two walls, the Marais was soon considered to be chic by the rich. Even Charles V took up residence here in his Palais Saint-Pol (later destroyed by Francis I). He moved to this palace between the Seine and the Rue Saint-Antoine after the uprising of February 22, 1358, led by the Parisian prefect Etienne Marcel, had driven him from the Palais de la Cité. His son Charles VI died alone and mentally deranged in Saint-Pol. Henry IV finally had the work of the Templars resumed, and the swamps were dried out for the most part.

If you turn into the Rue Geoffroy l'Asnier at the Saint-Gervais church, you will find the **Mémorial de la Déportation**, a memorial to the deportation of the French Jews during the last war. The way

Above: An oasis in the Marais district – Place des Vosges. Right: In a colonnade café at Place des Vosges.

through the Rue Figuier leads to the lovely **Hôtel de Sens.** Paris has only been a bishop's see since 1622; its archbishop resided in Sens up to that point in time. However, the clerical dignitaries soon preferred the city to life in the country and constructed this palace from 1475 to 1519. It was soon considered to be one of the loveliest of the town.

In 1558, the Council of Sens condemned the heresy of Martin Luther. Among the famous residents of the palace was Cardinal de Pellevé. After he had stood in the service of Charles IX, he could not get over the fact that Henry IV, a protestant of all things, had ascended to the throne. The cardinal died, a disappointed and bitter man, in this house on March 22, 1594, the day of Henry IV's march into Paris.

Afterwards, the unfaithful wife of Henry IV, Marguerite de Navarre, took refuge in the Hôtel de Sens. A freight-forwarding business occupied the premises in later times, and then a manufacturer of preserves. Today it houses the **Forney li-**

brary, which specializes in applied arts and artistic handiwork. Do not forget to take a look at the inner courtyard and the reading room of the library, which has been outstandingly restored.

If you go through the labyrinth of the crooked streets and alleys and look at the trim town houses of the 17th and 18th centuries, you will discover the true face of this district.

Soon you will reach the **Place des Vosges**. Parisians are almost unanimous in the opinion that this square is the most beautiful in their city. It lies there harmonious, green and sunny, and invites one to take a rest on a park bench or in one of the cafés. In the **Musée Victor Hugo**, those interested in literature will find drawings, private mementos, and also the spiritualistic table of the writer, who lived here 1832 - 1848.

The history of the square is one of destruction. Henry II died in the Hôtel des Tournelles after he had injured himself in a tournament. His wife, Catherine de' Medici, then had the house torn down.

Afterwards, there were horse markets that took place periodically on the property. Henry IV had the first public apartment houses built here, but they were so expensive that only rich citizens could afford them and not the workers from the surrounding silk factories. In 1800, the Place Royale was given its present name Place des Vosges in honor of the French département with the highest tax yield.

There is, naturally enough, an exciting story full of intrigues involving the struggle for love, power and money woven around each of the houses in this old quarter between the 1st, 3rd and 4th Arrondissements. Only few of these houses can be visited. However, you can take a look at the **Hôtel de Sully** (Rue du Faubourg Saint-Antoine nr. 62), where the *Caisse Nationale des Monuments Historiques* (information office for historic monuments and sale of publications) is situated today.

The Marais brings the old Paris of copperplate engravings to mind and has remained a living part of the Middle Ages,

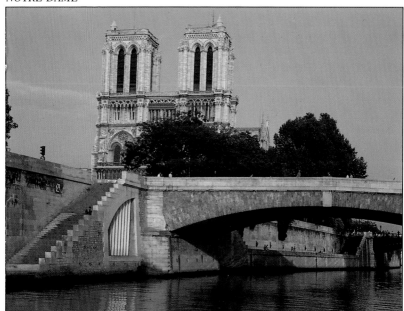

just like the Île de la Cité. And this is probably the most engaging attraction of Paris: In the middle of its vibrating modern life you can sense the existence of thousands of people who once lived here and left their traces behind them. Paris is known as a city in which even the stones spark with life.

ÎLE DE LA CITÉ

The city has a ship in its coat of arms. And just like a ship, the **Île de la Cité** anchors in the Seine. Since Roman times the administrative center of the whole of France has been located here.

When you have crossed the Pont d'Arcole, you will find yourself in the tourist center of the city. The countless boutiques with T-shirts and souvenirs will make you unmistakably aware of this long before you catch your first glimpse of **Notre-Dame**. In front of Notre-Dame

Above: Located at the center of the city, Notre-Dame impressively stands out.

cathedral, a stone with the kilometer zero on it is used as the starting-point for all distances to Paris. Try to imagine the enormous effect which the magnificently balanced façade of the cathedral must have had on the people in the Middle Ages. The foundation stone of this most famous church in Paris, if not the world, was laid in 1163. 170 years later, years in which the Gothic style was emerging from the Romanesque, it was consecrated.

As early as the year 30, Roman seamen erected a temple in honor of Jupiter on this spot. Its foundations have been discovered under the church. Five semi-precious stones decorated with reliefs as well as Latin inscriptions and the busts of people and gods are today displayed in the Musée de Cluny (on the left bank) and are probably among the oldest artefacts found in Paris. The stone heads portray Roman as well as Gallic deities – evidence of the coexistence of the two ancient cultures and religions.

Under the crypt (entrance on the Rue de la Cité), Gallo-Roman walls, fragments of defensive walls of early imperial times, ruins of Roman and medieval houses, as well as graves from the 17th century were found in 1965 during excavations for an underground parking lot. Once again the construction workers had to hand over their terrain to the archaeologists and the museums.

In 528, Childerich I, a son of Clovis I, and King of France, had churches of Saint Stephen and Saint Mary built upon the demolished heathen temple. Both were destroyed by the Vikings in 857.

The construction of a new cathedral – one equal to the Saint-Denis Basilica – was decided upon by Bishop Maurice de Sully in 1160. Generous contributions by the parishioners supported this plan, which not even the admonishing ascetic sermons of Saint Bernard, a Benedictine monk, could put a stop to.

Located in the heart of the city, this church is more than just a house of God. Saint Louis kept here what was thought to be Christ's crown of thorns when it was brought back by the crusaders. Philippe le Bel opened the first meeting of the Estates General here in 1302. Kings were crowned. Joan of Arc was canonized here in 1920, nearly 500 years after her martyrdom. In contrast, revolutionaries wanted to destroy the cathedral. As the king's statues were struck from the façade and smashed on the pavement, they would have loved to have seen the entire church razed to the ground.

In the Middle Ages, religion all too frequently embellished itself with wastefulness and dissipation. Extravagant mystery plays often took place in front of the theatrical façade of the church, holding entire masses of people in their spell. The pen of Victor Hugo resurrected the atmosphere of these days gone by. However, he also described the decline of the building:

„But just as splendid as its old beauty may appear to be, one should still be sad about the pitiable state in which the

church finds itself, how many diverse alterations it has been subject to by ignorant people and which wounds time has dealt it."

Thanks to generous donations, it was soon possible to renovate the building. The famous Viollet-le-Duc was inspired by the spirit of the Gothic statues and consciously let them flow into the architecture of the 19th century.

Among the people's pleasures of the Middle Ages were the fools' festivals, which were observed until some time in the 16th century. The priests organized them and even the kings were present at them. The more or less clothed penitents walked through the city in long processions at Christmas, Easter and Pentecost. The people of Paris lined the streets and applauded when the penitents flagellated themselves.

Afterwards, a „Bishop of Fools" was elected in the church. He then celebrated a mass and „blessed" his parishioners with words which were hardly understandable. The air heavy with incense, his assistants consumed blood sausage or did a suggestive dance in front of mocking priests who were dressed in women's clothing and wore grotesque masks. For another four days, the priests and fools enjoyed free lodging while they got drunk and visited the „little women of Paris." However, the law soon put an end to these depraved activities.

Today in Notre-Dame there is a considerably more tranquil and worldly public function which takes place every week. Admission to the concerts on Sundays at 5:00 p.m. is free.

Where once a house took in foundlings, the **Hôtel-Dieu** was constructed in Florentine style close to the end of the 19th century. It opens up to a wonderful inner courtyard. You can view it free of charge.

Historical documents appear to prove that Maurice de Sully set about building the hospital for the poor at the same time

as Notre-Dame. It is without a doubt that the bishop wanted to counter his expensive and ambitious building plans, which met with disapproval from Saint Bernard, with a charitable and altruistic work. And when the Hôtel-Dieu burst into flames on December 30, 1772, the afflicted found refuge within the walls of Notre-Dame for two days.

There were naturally also moving love stories in the Middle Ages. One of the most famous and tragic tells of Abélard and Héloïse: The canon Fulbert lived between the Rue de Chanoisse and the Rue de la Seine with his beautiful niece Héloïse. She and her private tutor, the young scholar, poet and musician Abélard, fell in love with each other. When it happened that she was expecting a baby, she declined marriage in order not to be detrimental to his career. Fulbert then had Abélard arrested and castrated. The

Above: A bird's-eye view of history. Right: Gothic splendor in brilliant colors at Sainte-Chapelle.

lovers interpreted this as a a sign – or a warning? – from God and each of them retreated separately into a monastery. Their mortal remains were later buried either together or separately a number of times until they finally received a joint grave at the Père-Lachaise cemetery.

At the tip of the island, on the **Square de l'Île de France**, a simple, poignant monument reminds us of the deportation of Jews under the Fascist rule; it is not far from a cathedral where Monseigneur Lustiger, a converted Jew, was cardinal.

Heading in the direction of the Palace of Justice, the flower market on the **Place Louis Lépine** is one place to call a brief halt. During the days of the week, it is radiant with a gaudy burst of flowers, rain or shine. On Sundays, it becomes a delightful bird market, if one happens not to mind the dubious kindness of holding birds in cages. Just like Notre-Dame, the site of the **Palais de Justice** was already an administrative and judicial center long ago, in fact during Roman times already. The Merovingian kings continued this

tradition and built a palace here, in which Clovis died. This is where the Meroving-ians and Carolingians stayed when they came to Paris.

Louis IX, also called Saint Louis, lived in this palace and had the **Sainte-Chapelle** added to it. The place remained a royal residence until Etienne Marcel and his insurgents drove Charles V out of it. The parliamentarians appointed by the king later met here. They were ousted in turn by revolutionaries.

During the *Ancien Régime,* the **Con-ciergerie** was a prison in which famous prisoners like Ravaillac, who murdered Henry IV, Cartouche the bandit, and Madame de Brinvilliers, a most no-torious poisoner, served time or waited for thier death sentences to be carried out. The oldest tower originated in the year 1250 and was not called the torture tower without reason. During the Revolution, Marie-Antoinette and her royal retinue, Danton, Marat, Saint-Just and many others were held here. About 2600 pris-oners left the Conciergerie in order to

mount the scaffold on the Place de la Concorde. Men and women were sepa-rated, but were able to speak to each other and touch hands. How many hopeless sparks of love probably ignited here in the face of death one can only speculate.

There are guided tours around the Con-ciergerie and Sainte-Chapelle. The latter was constructed as a place worthy to house a reliquary with Christ's crown of thorns and a relic of the Cross. In addi-tion, it also safeguards holy objects such as the purple mantle, the reeds, the cross of victory and the blood of Christ, as well as the milk and hair of Mary.

Until 1770, there was an exorcism ceremony here during the night of Good Friday every year. Critical minds rid-iculed it as a hypocritical spectacle with hired actors who were to keep alive the belief in the power of the relics.

In 1793, the chapel served the Jacobins as a prison for the Girondins; the latter sang and drank night after night until they were delivered to the executioner one morning.

The Sainte-Chapelle was often renovated in the course of time, yet retained its Gothic character. Its 15-meter-high windows with 1134 scenes depicting God's saving grace are unique.

The **Pont-Neuf**, the oldest bridge in Paris, leads across a trench which separated the Île de la Cité from two smaller islands, the Jewish and Patriarch islands. Henry III had it filled up and the islands connected with each other.

Île Saint-Louis

This small island, which the **Pont Saint-Louis** connects with its bigger sister, the Île de la Cité, is a peaceful oasis in the middle of the city.

It is considered a privilege to live here. Students of the Sorbonne, who prefer the spring sun to the gloomy libraries, like to go for strolls here. And Parisians, in search of culinary delights, stand in line

Above: The Île Saint-Louis beckons dog and master in the early morning hours.

in front of **Chez Bertillon** for its excellent ice-cream, especially its sherbet. Like the Marais, the narrow alleys feature numerous 17-century houses.

During the Middle Ages, the Île Saint-Louis consisted of two islands: the Île de la Vache ("cow island"), where cows actually grazed, and the larger Île de Notre-Dame, which belonged to the canons of Notre-Dame. It is said that devils and imps did their foul work here at night.

Against the will of the canons, Louis XIII had the canal between the two islands filled in. The place turned into a showpiece. Louis and François le Vau earned a fortune here by building town houses for aristocrats and other wealthy citizens of the 17th century.

Restif de la Bretonne, that dignified writer of the Enlightenment, also left his mark here. He had the habit of scratching Latin professions of love into the house walls. Many of them have disappeared, but with some luck during your excursion on the island you may find one or the other of these ancient grafittis.

1st AND 4th ARRONDISSEMENT
Accommodation

LUXURY: **Inter-Continental Paris**, 3, rue de Castiglione, Tel: 44 77 11 11. **Hôtel du Jeu de Paume**, 54, rue Saint-Louis-en-l'Ile, Tel: 43 26 14 18. *MODERATE:* **Hôtel du Louvre**, pl. André Malraux, Tel: 42 61 56 01. **Le Compostelle**, 31, rue du Roi de Sicile, Tel: 42 78 59 99. **Hôtel des Ducs de Bourgogne**, Tel: 42 33 95 64. **Hôtel Saint-Roch**, 25, rue Saint-Roch, Tel: 42 60 17 91. **Hôtel Saint-Louis**, 75, rue Saint-Louis-en-l'Ile, Tel: 46 34 04 80. *BUDGET:* **Hôtel Sansonnet**, 48, rue de la Verrerie, Tel: 48 87 96 14.
YOUNG TRAVELERS' GUESTHOUSE: Opposite the Centre Georges Pompidou, Tel: 42 77 87 80. *YOUNG TRAVELERS' HOTELS* (rooms with 4-6 beds): **Le Maubuisson**, 12, rue des Barres, Tel: 42 72 72 09. **Le Fauconnier**, 11, rue du Fauconnier, Tel: 42 74 23 45. **Le Fourcy**, 6, rue Fourcy, Tel: 42 74 23 45.

Restaurants / Nightlife

Le Soufflé, 36, rue du Mont-Thabor, Tel: 42 60 27 19, good French cuisine. **L'Alsace aux Halles**, 16, rue Coquillère, Tel: 42 36 74 24, open 11.00 a.m.-midnight, snacks, seafood. **Au Diable des Lombards**, 64, rue des Lombards, Tel: 42 33 81 84, open 11.00 a.m.-1.00 a.m., good French and American dishes. **La Lieutenance**, 24, rue Chanoinesse, Tel: 43 54 91 36, elegant French cuisine. **Nos Ancêtres les Gaulois**, 39, rue Saint-Louis-en-l'Ile, Tel: 46 33 66 07, open 7.00 p.m.-1.30 a.m., specialities from the charcoal grill. **Aquarius**, 54, rue Sainte-Croix-de-la-Brétonnerie, Tel: 48 87 48 71, open 12.00 noon-9.45 p.m., vegetarian restaurant.
Au Duc des Lombards, 42, rue des Lombards, Tel: 42 36 51 13, jazz from 11.00 p.m. **Guinness-Tavern**, 31, rue des Lombards, Tel: 42 33 26 45, country and rock music, 9.00 p.m.-6.00 a.m. **La Scala**, 188, rue de Rivoli, Tel: 46 61 64 00, Métro Concorde, gigantic disco from 10.00 p.m. **Les Trottoirs de Buenos Aires**, 37, rue des Lombards, Tel: 42 33 58 37, Métro Chatelet, Argentinian music, Tango.

Museums

Musée National du Louvre, 9.00 a.m-6.00 p.m., Mon and Wed open until 9.45 p.m., closed Tue. Tel: 40 20 50 50. **Musée des Arts de la Mode**, 109, rue de Rivoli, Tel: 42 60 32 14, Mon–Sat 12.30-6.00 p.m. Sun 11.00 a.m.-6.00 p.m., closed Tue. **Musée des Arts Décoratifs**, 107, rue de Rivoli, Wed–Sat 12.30-6.00 p.m., Sun 11.00 a.m.-6.00 p.m. **Orangerie des Tuileries** and **Jeu de Paume**, Place de la Concorde, daily 9.45 a.m.-5.15 p.m., closed Tue. **Conciergerie**, 1, quai de l'Horloge, June, July, August 9.30 a.m.-

6.30 p.m., September, April and May 9.30 a.m.-6.00 p.m., October until end of March 10.00 a.m.-4.30 p.m., closed on public holidays. **Sainte-Chapelle**, bd. du Palais, Oct 10–March 31 daily 10.00 a.m.-5.00 p.m., April 1–Sept 30 daily 9.30 a.m.-6.30 p.m.
Notre-Dame Cathedral daily from 8.00 a.m.-7.00 p.m., cathedral spire in summer 9.30 a.m.-12.00 noon and 2.00-6.00 p.m., in winter 10.00 a.m.-5.00 p.m., closed on public holidays. Crypt with excavations April 1–Sept 30 open daily 10.00 a.m.-5.30 p.m., Oct 1–March 31 daily 10.00 a.m.-5.00 p.m. **Hôtel de Sully** (town palace of the aristocracy), 62, rue Saint-Antoine, Tel: 44 61 20 00, open 9.00 a.m.-7.00 p.m. **Maison de Victor Hugo**, 6, pl. des Vosges, Tel: 42 72 10 16, daily 10.00 a.m.-5.40 p.m., closed Mon. **Musée des Médailles et Antiques**, Bibliothèque Nationale, 58, rue Richelieu, Mon–Sat 1.00-5.00 p.m., Sun 12.00 noon-6.00 p.m. **Centre Georges Pompidou** with **Musée National d'Art Moderne** (4th floor), rue Rambuteau, Tel: 42 77 12 33, daily 12.00 noon-10.00 p.m., Sat, Sun 10.00 a.m.-10.00 p.m., closed Tue.

Shopping

FNAC , bookstore with a large selection of international literature, records, hifi etc., Forum des Halles, 1, rue Pierre Lescot. **Forum des Halles** with 280 shops: Métro rue de Rivoli.

Sightseeing / Leisure

Parc Océanique Cousteau, Forum des Halles (3rd basement floor), Tel: 40 26 13 78. Métro Porte du Jour or Porte du Louvre, Tue and Thur 10.00 a.m.-4.00 p.m., Wed, Fri, Sat and Sun 10.00 a.m.-5.30 p.m.
Tuileries (gardens, rue de Rivoli). **Palais Royal** (once cardinal Richelieu's town palace, rue de Valois). **Tour Saint-Jacques** (rue de Rivoli). Romantic old squares are the **Square du Vert-Galant** and **Square de l'Ile de France** (Ile de la Cité), **Square Charlemagne** (rue Charlemagne) and the **Place des Vosges** in the Marais quarter. **Flower Market** on pl. Louis Lépine daily 9.00 a.m.-7.00 p.m., except Sundays, when the bird market takes place. **Round trips by boat** from the Pont-Neuf bridge, square du Vert-Galant.

Post / Police / Exchange

Post Offices, 1st Arr.: 52, rue du Louvre, Tel: 40 28 20 00 (open 24 hours daily). 8, rue Molière. 90, rue Saint-Denis. 9, rue des Halles. **4th Arr.:** 12, rue Castex. 1, bd. du Palais. 10, rue de Moussy. Pl. de l'Hôtel de Ville.
Police: 1st Arr.: Pl. du Marché Saint-Honoré. **4th Arr.:** 34, rue de Rivoli. **Foreign Exchange:** **CIC**, rue Saint-Martin (Centre Georges Pompidou), open 12.00 noon-7.00 p.m.

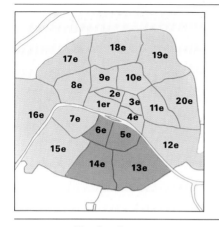

THE BRAIN OF PARIS

**PANTHÉON
QUARTIER LATIN
SAINT-GERMAIN-DES-PRÉS
RIVE GAUCHE
13th ARRONDISSEMENT
CHINATOWN
AROUND PORT ROYAL**

**The Southeast
5th, 6th, 13th, 14th Arrondissement**

If the old market halls in the center of the city were considered to be the belly of Paris, the southeast can then certainly be called the brain of the city.

This is the famous Paris of Abélard and Héloïse, Thomas Aquinas, Erasmus of Rotterdam and Ignatius of Loyola, that of Gertrude Stein and Ernest Hemingway, Jean-Paul Sartre and Simone de Beauvoir. It is the home of the Sorbonne, the Collège de France, the École Normale Supérieure, the École de Médicine and the Faculty of Law, to name just a few centers of learning.

Here, the Existentialists discussed matters until their heads were hot in the street cafés of the large boulevards, and the student revolts of May 1968 also mostly took place here.

The city districts which we now visit have been able to retain their charm through the years of changes. Here the visitor will sense their originality more in the smaller crooked streets than in the monumental buildings and the large boulevards.

Previous pages: Jardin du Luxembourg and Palace. Left: View from the Luxembourg Gardens of the Panthéon's majestic dome.

In addition to satisfying historical interest, a stroll in this quarter is also considerable fun because of the very many boutiques and galleries.

While it is best to explore the 13th and 14th Arrondissements by car or with the Métro, the very concentrated and historical 5th and 6th Arrondissements can be explored on foot.

For this reason, we want to suggest a number of walks. However, not everything that is worth seeing can be mentioned in such a tour of the sights. If you go through the city with open eyes, you will discover much more than can possibly be described here.

PANTHÉON

The first stroll, for example, could lead you to the **Mont Sainte-Geneviève** and thereby to one of the most famous monuments in Paris, the Panthéon. *Mont* is equivalent to "mountain" in French, but here we will only climb the "highest" hill of the left bank.

Just 60 meters high, this elevated area is named after the patron saint of Paris, Sainte Geneviève. Her prayers are said to have saved the city when it was threatened and sieged by Attila, the king of the Huns, and his army in 451. The church named after this saint, which was built at

85

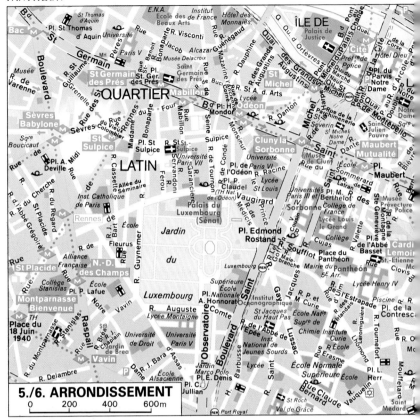

5./6. ARRONDISSEMENT
0   200   400   600m

the top of the hill, later became somewhat run down. It was Louis XV who, in the 18th century, ordered the construction of a new church to be built as a vow of thankfulness after his recovery from a serious illness.

The building, known today as the **Panthéon**, a unique combination of primarily neo-classical architecture, was completed exactly in the year of the French Revolution, after over 30 years of building time. The new house of God could hardly have been further from its original purpose when the revolutionaries turned it into a memorial to the heroes of the nation. Because of this, two years after its completion the church was already the secular counterpart of the Saint-Denis basilica in

the northern part of Paris, where the kings had their last resting place.

In 1871, the Panthéon was used temporarily as the headquarters of the Paris Commune. Then, for a period of time, it was again a church. Since the burial of Victor Hugo in 1885, it has again become a mausoleum for the great figures of the *Grande Nation*. Voltaire and Rousseau have also been lying in the enormous Panthéon ever since the Revolution. Later, about 60 other leading French figures were also buried in the crypt, which stretches beneath the entire building. Among them are politicians such as Raymond Poincaré; the inventor of *Braille*, Louise Braille; and Jean Moulin, a leader of the Resistance.

demonstrated the rotation of the earth on its axis.

The numerous paintings, the most famous of which recount the life of Sainte Geneviève as seen through the eyes of the painter Puvis de Chavannes, were not yet there at that time. They originated during the last quarter of the 19th century.

The Panthéon makes the greatest impression on the observer if viewed from a distance. One particularly lovely perspective of it can be glimpsed from the **Rue Soufflot**, when coming from the Boulevard Saint-Michel.

On the ring-like street which circles the Panthéon you will also find the **City Hall** (*Mairie*) of the 5th arrondissement, the Faculty of Law (*Faculté de Droit*) of the University of Paris and the **Bibliothèque Sainte-Geneviève**. In the entrance hall of the latter, there is, among other things, a statue of Ulrich Gering, the printer from Mainz (Germany) who installed the first printing press in France in the Sorbonne in the middle of the 15th century. The library contains half a million books as well as thousands of hand-written manuscripts. Only those who are in possession of a library card are allowed to enter the Bibliothèque Sainte-Geneviève.

Where the library now stands was once the location of the **Collège Montaigu**, built in the 14th century. Such famous scholars as Erasmus of Rotterdam, the Protestant reformer John Calvin and Ignatius of Loyola, founder of the Jesuit order, studied there. The college was famous for the excellent achievements of its graduates, but also notorious because of its strict discipline and the extremely difficult living conditions. The students slept on hard floors and shared their lice-filled home with hungry rats.

The **Saint-Étienne-du-Mont** church is a short walk away from the Panthéon. It is primarily worth seeing because of its very successful mixture of design elements in the interior. Construction of the building was started in 1492 and only

When François Mitterrand was elected to be the first Socialist president of the Fifth Republic, his first act in office took place at the Panthéon, where he laid down a rose, symbol of the Socialist Party, at the tomb of Jean Jaurès, the Socialist leader who was murdered in 1914.

The interior of the building, the floor plan of which has the form of a cross with a length of 110 m and a breadth of 85 m, is primarily impressive because of its size. Readers of Umberto Eco's *Foucault's Pendulum* will perhaps be interested to know that it was the dome with its height of 85 m, which inspired the physicist Léon Foucault to carry out his first experiments with the pendulum in the middle of the last century. With it, he

ended 130 years later with the completion of the façade. The architectural style accordingly also reflects the development of Gothic into the Renaissance. The gallery, or jube, which is the elevated tribune between the choir and the nave, is a rarity; those in other Parisian churches were unfortunately destroyed in the 18th century.

On the way back through the Rue Soufflot, the visitor can take the route to the **Sorbonne** along the Rue Victor Cousin. This is the most famous symbol of French scholarly tradition and the oldest university in Europe, according to its own claims. The history of the university extends back to the time of the 12th century. The institution which was named after Louis IX's father confessor was founded as a theological seminary in the middle of the 13th century.

The **Church of the Sorbonne**, built in Baroque style in the 17th century, is only

Above: A late afternoon at the Sorbonne.
Right: Marie de Medici's palace in the Jardin du Luxembourg.

open today for exhibitions and other cultural events. It was built as the burial church of Cardinal Richelieu who, as one of the patrons of the university, had the medieval buildings replaced by new ones during the 17th century. As one of the greatest and most powerful of France, he was also the model for the figure of the gray eminence in Alexandre Dumas' *The Three Musketeers*.

The church is the only structure originating during the time of Richelieu which still stands on the grounds of the university. The complex of buildings erected under his jurisdiction was torn down at the end of the 19th century. The building created at that time (it has been expanded again in the meantime) stretched almost 250 m in a north-south direction and thus became the largest structure in Paris during the 19th century.

Behind the Sorbonne is the **Collège de France**, which can be accessed from the Place Marcelin-Berthelot. It was founded in the 16th century at the suggestion of the humanist Guillaume Budé, who, in the spirit of the age, wanted to provide an alternative to the Sorbonne, which at that time was intolerant and strictly theological in orientation. His patron, King Francis I, gave his blessing for the *Collège Royal de France*. The institution lost its royal title during the Revolution and with time became the generally accessible temple of scholarship, which it still is today.

The current appearance of the Collège dates back to the 18th century, when the buildings were adapted to the requirements of the times. From 1935 on, further lecture halls were added in the course of a modernization program. Among its most famous professors we find, for example, the philosophers Roland Barthes and Raymond Aron, as well as the composer and conductor Pierre Boulez, to cite just a few names from this century. The program for the courses of the college is posted at the entrance.

Also behind the Sorbonne, right next to the Collège de France, is the **Lycée Louis Le Grand**, whose history can be traced back into the 16th century. It used to be the Jesuit institute, the Collège de Clermont. Its list of alumni includes such fellows as Maximilien de Robespierre, Eugène Delacroix and Victor Hugo.

QUARTIER LATIN

Some of the nooks and crannies of Paris are enchanting because of their charm, their harmony and peace. Walking around without any particular aim, one can suddenly find oneself in an oasis that dispels the hectic pace of the surrounding big city. Two such idyllic places are in the area around Saint-Sulpice and the lovely Jardin du Luxembourg.

Start at the **Place Saint-Sulpice**, one of the prettiest spots in Paris and named after the church that stands upon it. This residential area is one of the most expensive in Paris, but a visitor stressed by the big city will soon understand why the

more solvent Parisians like to move to this area. The murmur of the high fountain built in 1844, the benches beneath the chestnut trees, also the people sauntering by on their way to enjoy a sandwich from the *traiteur* on the corner of the **Rue du Vieux Colombier** or to feed the pigeons: This all makes the feeling of life in the big city more human. The harmoniously designed square is surrounded by expensive fashion boutiques and the central offices of publishing companies.

The square is dominated by the towers of the **Église Saint-Sulpice**. The layout and dimensions of this church are similar to those of the older Notre-Dame.

There was a house of God for the community of Saint-Germain-des-Prés here during the Middle Ages. With the increasing population, however, a larger church became necessary and the construction of the current building was started in 1646. But the church could first be consecrated in 1745 since the work had to be interrupted for 40 years at one time because of a lack of money. This is

why, as was often in case, many architects worked on the church, each leaving his own special mark. Among the most attractive aspects of the interior are the fine murals in the first chapel to the right of the entrance, whose execution was supervised by Eugène Delacroix.

From the Place Saint-Sulpice, the visitor can then either choose the path through the tranquil little Allée du Séminaire straight to the Jardin du Luxembourg or take a small detour through the Rue Saint-Sulpice to the **Théâtre National de l'Odéon**. The latter can be seen in a charming perspective from the square that lies in front of it.

Through the small Rue Rotrou, the visitor then reaches the other place of promised peace, the **Jardin du Luxembourg**. The well-known **Fontaine de Médicis**, which was first created in 1620 and received its current form during the

Above: Lie back and dream – though it is just a few steps back to the Sorbonne.
Right: The Quartier Latin by night.

19th century, stands right next to the entrance if you are coming from the Rue de Vaugirard.

Chairs and benches await those taking a walk and at one of the reflecting ponds, little model sailboats can be rented for the children to sail. French mothers love to walk through this park with their presentable children.

Tourists will discover this to be a tranquil place to take a rest, look at the numerous sculptures on display, and enjoy a bit of the Parisian way of life.

The palace at the north end of the gardens was built during the 17th century at the order of Maria de' Medici, the widow of Henry IV and mother of Louis XIII. The **Palais du Luxembourg** was designed to remind her of her Italian origins and therefore adhered to numerous stylistic elements from her home country.

Some of the paintings for the palace commissioned from Rubens hang today in the Médici gallery in the Louvre. The works by Delacroix, which were created in the beginning of the 19th century can

still be admired here in the reading room of the library.

At the end of the 18th century, in the wake of the Revolution, the Palais functioned as a prison. Later it was the seat of the Directory and of the Consulate under Napoléon Bonaparte, and still later on, that of the French Senate. Occupied by the German air force during World War Two, the palace now again serves the French Senate. For this reason, visits are only possible on the first Sunday of each month.

Hôtel de Cluny

Your initial impression of the famous Quartier Latin will probably first appear to be a chaotic confusion of fast-food parlors and stands, motorcycle parking spaces, and a Babylonian variety of languages. Whereas Latin was the predominant means of communication in this student district as of the early Middle Ages, today the dominant sound is an unconcerted cacophony of languages and dialects coming from the students and visitors from all nations on earth.

In the pedestrian zone to the east of the **Boulevard Saint-Michel**, the century-old history of this part of the city meets up with the modern forms of student life. North African, Vietnamese and Greek restaurants also make their contribution to the somewhat chaotic appearance of the Quartier Latin.

On the intersection of the Boulevards Saint-Germain and Saint-Michel is the **Hôtel de Cluny**. This venerable building is considered by many experts to be the loveliest example of extant French medieval architecture.

The former Paris residence of the abbots of Cluny is today a museum, which is worth a visit primarily because of its tapestries. Outstanding among these are the wall hangings with unicorn motifs (for example, the *Dame à la Licorne* – Lady with the Unicorn), which hang together in a round hall. Created towards the end of the 15th century, they symbolize the *Five Senses*. After the visitor's

first astonished glance at these fantastic horned creatures, the information presented by the museum reveals the rich and enigmatic backgound of these works. They originally came from the former royal, and now state-owned, tapestry manufactory of the Gobelins (named after the family of dyers who founded it); the workshop is located south of the Quartier Latin.

The Cluny museum still features structural remains from Gallo-Roman times when thermal baths were installed here; archaeological finds are exhibited.

If you now cross the Boulevard Saint-Germain into the pedestrian zone, you will reach the **Rue de la Parchemenerie**. Across from the Canadian book store there, you will find one of the oldest houses in Paris. Afterwards, you can turn to the left (Rue des Prêtres) in order to get

Above: The Gothic church Saint-Séverin.
Right: Waiting for the rush of customers. Far right: At Café de Flore it goes – to see and to be seen.

a glimpse of the **Saint-Severin** church. The church was named after the hermit who lived there in the 6th century. The present building was started in the 13th century and is characteristic of the transition from Romanesque to Gothic style. During the Revolution the Sans-culottes turned the dignified old structure into an arsenal. Restoration of the interior began in the 19th century.

When you leave the church, turn to the right into the Rue Saint-Severin and then cross the Rue Saint-Jacques where the traffic, racing up from the Île de la Cité can be murderous at times. You will then reach one of the most graceful little churches in Paris: the church of **Saint-Julien-le-Pauvre**.

Built at approximately the same time as neighboring Notre-Dame, it is also one of the city's oldest churches. Used as a storage hall following the Revolution, it remained empty for a long time afterwards. About 100 years ago, it was renovated in order to serve the people as a chapel. Its altar wall is worth the visit.

From the little plaza to the north of the church, **Square René Viviani**, the visitor is given an attractive view of Notre-Dame across one arm of the Seine.

SAINT-GERMAIN-DES-PRÉS

If you meanwhile have come to the conclusion that a stroll through the city primarily leads you from one church to the next, you should now take heart again. Paris does have an incredible variety of other sights to offer the visitor along the way.

Although we do suggest that you still visit the oldest church in Paris, Saint-Germain-des-Prés, you can first take a breather and relax in one of the most famous cafés in the Seine city, the **Deux Magots**. The café is also called the "Two Wise Men," which is the insignia of a department store previously located here. It stands at the edge of the square in front of the church and can be just as easily reached as the latter from the Métro station of Saint-Germain-des-Prés.

Although the interior of the café with its wood carvings is an impressive sight indeed, the connoisseur sits down at one of the tables outside (weather permiting of course), where city life can be observed as it passes by. If you are interested in recent history, you may remember that the Existentialist philosopher and intellectual father of the later student unrest, Jean-Paul Sartre, held court here during the 1950's and the 1960's.

If you are not comfortable in the surroundings of the Deux Magots, you can find a seat at the **Café de Flore**, known as the meeting place of the Existentialists in earlier days. It is just one house further down the street. On the tables there are large plates with croissants and jam waiting for the guests every morning.

The history of the church of **Saint-Germain-des-Prés** on the other side of the square extends back into the 6th century. *Prés* is the French for meadows: The church used to be located beyond the limits of the city but the latter continually grew and finally closed in around it. Like

other churches, it was destroyed in the 9th century by marauding Vikings (according to the legend, the wood torn out of the churches was used to repair their ships). At the turn of the millennium, the building was reconstructed and extended. Up to 10,000 people are alleged to have lived within the narrow walls that surrounded the church itself and later also the Benedictine abbey attached to it.

As seen in other churches of the area, the gradual transition from the heavier Romanesque to the more airy Gothic style can also be spotted here. At the time of the Revolution, the building was utilized for the production of nitric acid. It was later again restored to its original purpose as a church. One of the smaller chapels, the chapel decorated with a modern statue of the saint Germanus, still shows quite clearly the original design elements of the building. Visitors to the

Above: The former haunt of the existentialists – the Deux Magots. Right: It seems to be shortly before closing time.

church are greeted in a friendly manner at the entrance with information sheets in English as well as other languages.

The walk can be continued down the **Rue Bonaparte** to the quay of the Seine, which is given the name of **Quai Malaquais** at this site. The academy of fine arts, the **École des Beaux-Arts** is to your left. It is possible to visit it if you ask at the adjoining bookstore at Quai Malaquais nr. 13.

It is also worth taking a stroll in the quarter around this great center of artistic learning, the aura of which appears to shine into the surrounding streets. The artistic climate of the neighborhood appears to have developed over a long period of time. For hundreds of years, painters and poets have chosen to settle in these surroundings. Today they can no longer afford to.

It is still possible to view the studio and apartment of Eugène Delacroix at the **Place Furstemberg**, a tiny island in the middle of a small street by the same name. Both are open daily except on

Tuesdays from 9.45 a.m. to 1.00 p.m. and 2.00 to 5.15 p.m. If you are not aware of who this painter was, probably the most internationally famous of Delacroix's paintings is *La Liberté guidant le peuple de Paris*, a crowd scene in which liberty – portrayed as a women, her breasts bared – brandishes the flag of the Revolution.

The square has the loveliest effect in May when the paulownia trees planted there are in full bloom with tender lilac blossoms.

Close to the École des Beaux-Arts, in the Rue Bonaparte nr. 5, is the house in which the Impressionist painter Edouard Manet was born in the year 1832. The German composer Richard Wagner lived in the Rue Jacob nr. 14 for some months in 1841 and 1842, and the poet Racine spent some years of his life in the Rue Visconti nr. 24.

If you continue your stroll from the Saint-Germain church through the Rue Bonaparte to the Seine and turn right instead of left to the art academy, you will find numerous *bouquinistes* at the Quai Malaquais. In the afternoon, they open the flaps of their little crate stores set up against the wall cornice and offer a surprising number of interesting used books for sale.

There are many other well-known buildings and monuments to visit in this part of the city. Among them are the **Institut de France**, home of five academies including the famous **Académie Française**. Traditionally, the academy which Richelieu founded in 1635 to cultivate and preserve the French language comprises 40 members from the fields of literature, the military and the diplomatic service among others. They are usually male (the late writer Marguerite Yourcenar being a notable exception), and some of their decisions concerning the French language are either hair-raising or simply a sanctioning of popular usage.

Bibliophile visitors will be delighted by the **Bibliothèque Mazarin**, which is housed here. It contains about half a million of printed works, almost half of them originating in the 16th to 18th centuries.

The library was initially the private collection of Cardinal Mazarin, the regent during the minority of Louis XIV. However, in the year 1643, i.e. during his lifetime, it was made available to the public and is therefore also the oldest public library in all of France. The two-storied reading room cultivates the traditions of past centuries through its furnishings with precious parquet, wood paneling and sculptures. In addition, the visitor also has a good perspective of the interior of the buildings of the Institut de France from its windows. The library can be viewed without charge Monday to Friday from 10 a.m. to 6 p.m. During summer, it is closed from August 1st to 15th for the vacation.

The chapel belonging to the Institut de France can also be viewed on a guided tour on Saturday and Sunday afternoons. The concierge can provide you with ap-

Above: Boutiques offer a wide-range of articles. Right: Tidiness is important here, too.

propriate information as to the exact times.

On the shore of the Seine, a few hundred meters further on, the pedestrian comes across the **Hôtel de la Monnaie**, the Parisian coinminting institution (Quai de Conti nr. 11). Except on Mondays, you can visit its museum daily from 1 - 6 p.m. and Wednesdays until 9 p.m.

In addition to the commemorative coins and modern metal sculptures that are available in the adjoining boutique just around the corner at the Rue Guénégaud nr. 2, you can also find such small items as key chains or decorative coins, which can serve as souvenirs.

Also suitable as presents are the often humorous objects primarily for the home from modern designers offered a few steps further at *Axis* in the Rue Guénégaud nr. 18. The branch of the store in the Rue de Charonne (11th Arrondissement) sells articles ranging from modern tableware to T-shirts.

Like many streets in the neighborhood, such as the Rue Bonaparte and the Rue Jacob, there are also numerous galleries and some individual antique stores which have become established here. Gothic wooden sculptures can be found as well as avant-garde paintings. Lithographs are also sold at affordable prices. For example, the Breheret gallery at Quai Malaquais nr. 9 offers numerous prints with typical Parisian motifs.

In addition to its artistic ambience, the district around Saint-Germain is well-known for its many boutiques. However, the small stores are no longer as original as they were some years ago. The high rents have unfortunately driven young designers out of the area. The current stores and boutiques primarily feature established fashion designers or brand names.

Le Shopping, as the French like to call it, can still be a lot of fun, however, since a dash of Parisian flash continues to be in evidence here. A good starting point is

the **Boulevard Saint-Germain**. Starting at the church and moving in the direction of the **Boulevard Saint-Michel**, you will find many stores, primarily of men's fashions. The smaller boutiques that have remained are mainly to be found in the side-streets to the right and left of the much-traveled boulevard. They are located, for example, in the Rue du Four or the Rue du Cherche-Midi. Some of the larger couturier establishments are located in the Rue Bonaparte.

The boutique *Souleiado* in the Rue de Seine nr. 78 offers a more native flair in scarves and clothing articles with traditional folkloric patterns from southern France. On the **Rue Saint-André-des-Arts**, almost at the point where it intersects with the Rue Dauphin, is the start of a small shopping passageway by the name of **Commerce Saint-André**.

By way of a gate entrance, one reaches the small, enchanting **Cour de Rohan**, a remnant which carries the visitor back into earlier centuries. Not far from the Cour, at the Rue de l'Ancienne Comédie

nr. 13, is the **Procope**, dating back to revolutionary times. This makes it the oldest café in the whole of France. For some years now it has been a restaurant offering a small lunch menu at affordable prices.

Gourmets who enjoy taking a shopping stroll through the markets will have an adventure, too. A look at some of the traditional grocery stores in the **Rue de Buci** and the **Rue de Seine** will tantalize your appetite. Moreover, it is not far to one of the few enclosed market halls of Paris, the **Marché Saint-Germain** in the Rue Mabillon.

Saint-Germain also has much to offer those who are still not too tired from the long march on Parisian asphalt to gain an impression of the night-life in Paris. In the bars and clubs of some of the hotels in the district there are jazz bands or blues bands that start performing at 8 or 9 p.m. Among them are the *Latitudes* in the Rue St.-Benoit nr. 7-11, *La Montana* a few steps further in the same street at nr. 28, and *La Villa* in the Rue Jacob nr. 29.

RIVE GAUCHE

La Rive Gauche, the left bank of the Seine, exudes the air of literary history and is a paradise for those who love books. Not only the giants of French literature from Racine to Camus, but also the "lost generation" of American authors who lived in Paris between the two world wars fell under the spell of the intellectual ambience of the Quartier Latin and Saint-Germain-des-Près. And there were many others.

Those thirsty for knowledge can poke around in the countless hidden bookstores with their wealth of specialist literature. The palette offered ranges from navigation to black magic.

Or you can put aside the map of the city and go on an unplanned exploratory expedition along the quays on both sides of the Seine near Notre-Dame. Here you

Above: Relaxing on the quays of the Seine. Right: What about a browsing through the street sellers books?

can browse at the *bouquinistes*' stands. The green boxes where they display their wares are a bonanza for everything: from last month's copy of *Playboy* to a coveted first edition of a Corneille drama.

A pleasant walk can also be enjoyed along the Seine shore from the Institut du Monde Arabe to Notre-Dame. Along the way, the visitor will pass *bouquinistes* and house boats and can take a short break in the botanical gardens, the Jardin des Plantes.

The **Institut du Monde Arabe** at Quai Saint Bernard nr. 23, founded in 1987, is worth a visit not only because of its exhibitions providing a look at cultures, which otherwise are less accessible to the average traveller, but also because of the building itself. The architect Jean Nouvel created translucent ornaments, which can be adjusted according to how the sun shines into the glass façade on the south side of the building. Depending upon how the light falls, the façade, which has an oriental look, can be transformed. In the museum of the institute there is a per-

manent collection and frequently changing special exhibitions. In addition, you
will find a bookstore with an adjacent gift
shop. Gazing out from the roof terrace of
the building, the visitor is greeted by an
inviting view along the Seine to Notre-
Dame.

You can enjoy this view from other
perspectives of the Quai as well. From
there you can also take a trip to the little
zoo in the Jardin des Plantes. To do so,
turn right in front of the Institut in the
direction of Gare d'Austerlitz.

If you follow the Quai in this direction,
you will reach one of the most interesting
parks in Paris. The city administration
commissioned the design of this section
of the left bank of the Seine as an open-
air museum for modern sculpture at the
beginning of the 1980's. In the park
which was laid out there – and dedicated
in part to the chanson-singer Tino Rossi –
the sculptures of numerous modern artists are on display. Among them are
works by Ossip Zadkine who died in
1967. His works are otherwise exhibited

in a museum set up in his former residence in the Rue d'Assas nr. 100 (6th Arrondissement).

In the park, benches and sheltered
coves along the Seine invite you to stay
for a while. The walk then leads you
under the stone Seine bridges and past
some of the picturesque house boats an-
chored on the quay. More bouquinistes
have their crate stores set up against the
walls along the **Quai de la Tournelle** and
the **Quai de Montebello**. Most of them
open up in the late afternoon, some of
them only in the early evening in summer. On the quay beneath Notre-Dame
there is also a landing pier for the
bateaubus, the boat-buses which travel
on the Seine.

From Jardin des Plantes to the Rue Mouffetard

This initerary, which leads a little way
away from the well-beaten tourist trails,
starts at the **Jardin des Plantes**, the
botanical gardens.

99

The garden and its museums are under the guardianship of the National Museum of Natural History. They profit from the long and great tradition of French inventors, scientists and biologists such as Lamarck, Cuvier, Becquerel and Buffon. The names of the streets around and in the garden reflect this little bit of French scientific history.

The garden not only offers adults a feast for their eyes with its flowers, blossoming bushes and trees but is also an adventurous experience for children of all ages. Close to the main entrance and across from the Métro station Gare d'Austerlitz, there is the **Palaeontological Museum**. The exhibition of comparative anatomy is one of its most interesting because of the painstaking reconstruction of various dinosaurs (open from 10 a.m. to 5 p.m.).

Above: Relaxation for young and old in the Jardin des Plantes. Right: The Arènes de Lutèce lie hidden between narrow streets.

On the other side of the park, there is an intricate maze of hedges and bushes on a hill; this is an adventure playground for both young and not so young anymore. On the side of the hill that faces the Seine, the cedar of Lebanon planted in 1734 stretches its branches into the sky. Next to the labyrinth, children will find a playground with sandboxes and a slide in the form of a *stegosaurus*. But the animal park is probably the place that most attracts children. This small zoo was set up after the French Revolution using animals from the royal menagerie in Versailles. In the smallest amount of space, the zoo presents an astonishing variety of animals: birds, apes, reptiles, lions, tigers (open from 9 a.m. to 5.30 p.m.).

The park offers further attractions in its museums of mineralogy and entomology (open during the same hours as the Palaeontological Museum); there is also an extensive greenhouse featuring a lot of exotic plants (1 to 5 p.m.), an open-air alpine garden and a botanical nursery with 10,000 different species.

The various museums and the winter garden are closed on Tuesdays, and the botanical hothouse is closed on Saturdays, Sundays and public holidays. For some inexplicable reason (though the Finance Ministry might be able to provide an explanation), there is no general ticket available for the entire grounds. The visitor has to pay a steep entrance fee for each of the individual attractions (but children under five years of age have free admission). You should also be aware that the entrance times and prices tend to change with discouraging regularity.

Behind the Jardin des Plantes, the Parisian **Mosque** is on the Rue Geoffroy-Saint-Hilaire. Its tall minaret, dazzling white walls and colorful ridge tiles give the impression of a fata morgana from the Orient. However, the mosque was actually constructed at the beginning of this century as the first Islamic house of prayer of its sort in France.

Its library also serves as the Moslem registry office. Actress Rita Hayworth and the Aga Khan are said to have married here. The building can be viewed on a guided tour.

Because of its large steam bath, the mosque is also popular among non-Moslem Parisians. The entrance days for men and women alternate on a daily basis. The experience of spending several hours in this *hamam*, with a massage and a sweet mint tea in the Moorish café, is almost like an escapist and sensual journey into the seventh heaven.

If we follow the Rue Geoffroy-Saint-Hilaire to the point where it becomes the Rue Linné (both of them named after famous naturalists), we reach a small street, which winds along a pretty park on the left-hand side. Trim apartment houses line the other side.

The park comprises the **Arènes de Lutèce**, the Roman *Arena Lutetia.* It is the remnants of a Roman arena, which was destroyed in the 3rd century and lay buried and forgotten from that time until road builders discovered it in 1869. Although it does not belong on the „hit list" of famous Roman theaters, it is still one

of the two most important Gallo-Roman ruins of Paris. (The other is the Cluny baths, also in the 5th Arrondissement). The arena originally accommodated up to 17,000 spectators and offered gladiator fights as well as theatrical performances on its program. However, the remnants which you can see are partially only reconstructions.

Let us interrupt the walk at the Place Monge Métro station. If you still have some extra energy, you can continue across the Rue Monge and the Rue Rollin or the Rue Lacépède up to the Place de la Contrescape. This picturesque confusion of buildings flows into the famous **Rue Mouffetard**. In the mornings this street is particularly bustling when the stands and stores offer vegetables and fish in extraordinary abundance. You can satisfy your appetite almost around the clock there. Take a glance at the store signs, many of which (like the one at house

Above: Early morning in a housing area designed by Le Corbusier.

number 122, for example) are remarkable works of art.

At the foot of the Rue Mouffetard, you will see the **Saint-Médard** church, which was started in the 15th century but only completed in the 17th century. The Renaissance influence can be particularly clearly seen in the dimensions of the sanctuary. Before you reach Saint-Médard, cross the **Rue de l'Arbalète**. The famous sculptor Auguste Rodin was born in house nr. 3 of this street.

13th ARRONDISSEMENT

Compared to others, the 13th Arrondissement offers the visitor little in the way of exceptional attractions. As in the 14th Arrondissement, a generally middle-class population lives there.

Yet, you will still discover some points that glitter even after you have experienced the fireworks of other parts of Paris. For example, there is the **Gobelin Manufactory** in the Avenue des Gobelins nr. 42.

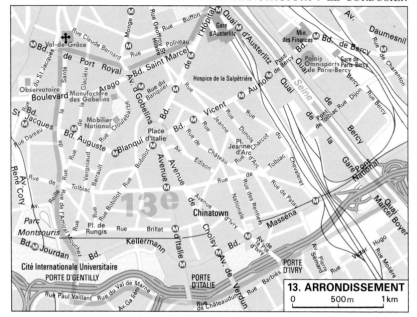

Its establishment extends far back into the 15th century, but its sustained reputation began when Colbert, finance minister of Louis XIV, elevated it to the position of royal manufactory in 1667 with the aim of creating employment.

This government-controled economic measure had an effect which has continued until recent times. In 1981, Mitterrand actually based his reasoning for nationalization of the key industries and banks upon Colbert's royal control of tapestry production. The Gobelin workshop is still operated today. Visitors are admitted on Wednesday, Thursday and Friday between 2 p.m. and 4 p.m.

Behind the Gobelin Manufactory there is another sight well worth seeing, one which is hardly familiar to the general public, the national furniture institute (**Mobilier National**). This is where cabinetmakers learned their craft and developed the intricate styles from Louis XIV onward.

Today, this building serves as storage space and restoration workshop for the considerable – and notable – amount of old furniture, which is in the possession of the state. This includes the complete furniture inventory of the Louvre and various decorative items of value in ministerial offices.

Unfortunately, these treasures cannot be viewed. Visitors have to be satisfied with standing in front of the iron gate imagining what goes on within.

Fans of the architecture of **Le Corbusier** will find various buildings of his throughout the 13th and 14th Arrondissements. The French-Swiss Le Corbusier settled in Paris in 1917 in order to come to grips with Cubism in both painting and thought. He developed theories about the city of the future and its architectural elements including interior design.

Among the most conspicuous of his buildings is the headquarters of the **Salvation Army** close to the Quai de la Gare at nr.12, Rue Cantagreland. The building was painted in luminous primary colors to accentuate Le Corbusier's style.

Not far away, you will find an apartment building in the Boulevard Massena nr. 128, which already shows the ravages of time, but is still typical of Le Corbusier's architecture. Further to the south in the **Cité Universitaire**, he designed the Swiss and Brazilian pavilions as parts of the student residential complex.

The Cité itself was commissioned after World War One as accommodation for foreign students. It was to portray a miniature world community, expressed architecturally through foreign elements in the student halls.

Close to the Cité, the house of the painter Ozenfant in the Avenue Reille nr. 53 is another of Le Corbusier's designs. This well-preserved building has been supplemented by the works of subsequent architects, who made the effort to maintain visual harmony with Le Corbusier's style.

Above: Two totally different cultures meet in Chinatown. Right: Market life in Chinatown.

You now find yourself close to the **Parc Montsouris**. It was designed according to plans by Baron Haussmann and inaugurated by Emperor Napoléon III in 1869. This little folly of sorts has artificial grottos and cascades, the typical stylistic elements of the horticultural art of those times. There is also a miniature imitation of the *Bardo*, the summer palace of the Bey of Tunis, built for the World Exhibition of 1867.

CHINATOWN

The French are foreigners in their own country when they enter the Golden Triangle. This district in the 13th Arrondissement, lying between the Avenue de Choisy, the Avenue d'Ivry and a part of the Boulevard Massena, is firmly in Asiatic hands. This can be particularly emphasized in the case of the economy that flourishes there.

One anecdote shows the transformation: In 1958 a Frenchman strolled along the Champs-Élysées with an Asian friend. There they encountered a group of Asians – Japanese, according to the Chinese. In response to his companion's astonished question as to how the Chinese man could so quickly determine their nationality, the Asian replied: "I know all of the Asians who live in Paris."

Today, however, there are approximately 300,000 Asians in Paris according to cautious estimations. About 70 percent of them are Chinese or Southeast Asians of Chinese descent. Their largest colony, in the 13th Arrondissement (at the same time the biggest Chinatown in Europe), is the homeland for about one-third of them.

The macabre rumor of "eternal life" in Chinatown persists doggedly. Death notices are not registered. According to gossip, the public officials are not to become aware of the death of any Asian. The latter's papers then serve to help an illegal immigrant since they can assist the for-

eigner in building a new, legal existence. Chinatown is actually the starting point for many newcomers in the Seine metropolis. Most of them first find refuge here: with family, with friends, with employers. If they are successful in climbing socially, then they usually leave this "revolving door" in order to settle in "better areas" of the city.

Everyday Life: 16 Hours of Work

The Asians are reluctant to be a financial burden to their hosts. With determination they quickly find a job working for their countrymen who are already established. In the process, it is irrelevant if they are considerably overqualified for this "slavery." Their own credit system, *tontine* by name, helps the Asians to become economically independent. A number of people join together in a financing group and each of them pays certain sum into a common pot. Who may take capital from this fund is decided according to the drawing of lots. The prompt repayment

of this credit is considered to be a matter of trust. Contracts do not exist.

Contacts with French neighbors are pursued only up to a certain extent. Despite their efforts to live well together with the "natives," it is important to the Asians that they remain among themselves and continue to maintain their languages and culture. Even in their new homeland, they are successful in preserving the traditions of their strictly hierarchical family structure. The crime rate is low and their own system of order functions. Asian secretiveness prohibits any information regarding what extent the *Triads*, secret Asiatic societies similar to the Mafia, have their hand in this.

Dragons Between High-Rise Buildings

Within a period of a few years, refugees from Southeast Asia have succeeded in placing their stamp upon the district. They provide colorful life between the gray, tall concrete buildings. At every turn there are little restaurants that

105

will tempt you with specialties from Vietnam or Thailand, with sweet-and-sour soups, fish dishes, or glazed duck. Neon advertising as well as the menus are decorated with Asiatic characters.

Old women in dark-blue pants and colorfully embroidered Chinese jackets hurry to do their shopping: The grocery dealers have their displays constructed outside of their stores and sell fresh soya sprouts, which are cultivated in an old warehouse around the corner. Or they offer carefully composed mixtures of spices, which the unschooled nose of a European cannot define. Some steps further on, there is the smell of sesame oil, plum wine and scented rice; sentimental light music echoes from some of the hairdressers' shops or a videothèque, whose display windows are plastered with Kung-Fu cassettes.

Once a year „the gods are loose" in Chinatown, when colorful dragons with

Above: At the Cimetière Montparnasse, with the Tour Montparnasse in the background.

wild and fiery looks parade through the streets as the Asians celebrate their New Year's festivities. Countless firecrackers then explode, rice rains from the hea–vens, and best wishes are offered for the coming year. It's a spectacle that fascinates increasingly more French, but in which they only take part as onlookers.

AROUND PORT ROYAL

On our walk through the 14th Arrondissement, we also encounter several places which will possibly stimulate us to think about life and death.

We begin at the edge of the 5th Arrondissement, to the east beyond the intersection of the Boulevards Saint-Michel and Port Royal, near the **Val-de-Grâce Church** at nr. 277-279 Rue Saint-Jacques. This impressive Baroque building with its front facing the street is among the most splendid churches in France. It was designed by the architect Viollet-Le-Duc. The high altar was given a canopy based on Bernini's baldachin over the

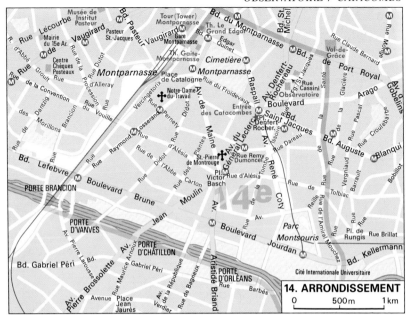

14. ARRONDISSEMENT

0   500 m   1 km

tomb of St. Peter's, Rome. You can view the church from 10 a.m. to 5 p.m. A monastery is also connected to the church building. However, the abbey constructed in the 17th century today serves as a military academy and army hospital.

If you now cross the Boulevard Port Royal, turn right from the Rue du Faubourg-Saint-Jacques into the Rue Cassini. A picturesque avenue leads to the Paris observatory, the **Observatoire**. „Star-gazers" should be sure to obtain permission ahead of time to take part in the guided tour on every first Saturday of the month at 2.30 p.m. This can be obtained from the secretariat (Avenue de l'Observatoire nr. 61, 75014 Paris). The building was planned by Colbert and erected in the second half of the 17th century. The Paris meridian, which runs through its middle, was the starting line for the longitudinal division of the world until it was replaced by the Greenwich line in the late 19th century.

If you now continue further along the Rue Cassini, we recommend that you turn left into the **Avenue Denfert Rochereau** in order to reach the square of the same name. It is easily recognized because of the giant bronze lion in the middle of it. The entrance to the **Catacombs**, one of the most fantastic sights to see in Paris, is on the square. Admission is daily (except Mondays) from 2 p.m. to 4 p.m. and additionally on the weekends from 9 a.m. to 11 a.m. Only those who are of a solid physical and mental constitution should risk this tour. In addition to the strenuous climbing up and down the winding stairs, there is a hike of about a mile which leads through the tunnels and along the niches of this underground city. You come back to the light of day in the Rue Rémy Dumoncel.

If you are in a mood of thoughtfulness about the transitoriness of existence, you should subsequently visit the **Cimetière Montparnasse**, which is close by. From the Place Denfert Rochereau, you can reach the back entrance after about 200 m via the Rue Froidevaux. Or you can turn to the north in order to reach the cemetery

through the main entrance on the Boulevard Edgar Quinet. This potter's field is not among the most impressive in Paris, yet Charles Baudelaire, César Franck and Guy de Maupassant do lie buried here; the graves of Simone Signoret and Serge Gainsbourg are also to be found in this cemetery.

Among the most interesting churches in Paris is the **Notre-Dame-du-Travail** (built between 1899-1901). The exterior has the same look as the countless neo-Gothic stone churches, which can be seen everywhere in Paris. However, in the interior you will find an impressive iron frame construction which is both sweepingly elegant as well as sturdy. It is a courageous attempt to reconcile the religious tradition of Christianity with the Industrial Revolution. The church lies directly to the south of the tower of Montparnasse in the Rue Vercingétorix nr. 59.

Above: Montparnasse can be leisurely enjoyed even in the smallest nook.

5th ARRONDISSEMENT
Accommodation
MODERATE: **Claude Bernard**, bd. St.-Michel, Tel: 43 54 21 39. **Hôtel Minerve,** rue des Écoles, Tel: 43 26 81 89. **Grand Hôtel St.-Michel**, rue Cujas, opposite the Sorbonne (university), Tel: 46 33 33 02, Métro St.-Michel.

Restaurants / Nightlife
Although the Latin Quarter is liberally dotted with restaurants, the prices tend to be more overwhelming than the quality of the food.

Chez Toutone, 5, rue Pontoise, traditional cuisine. **Le Coupe-Chou**, 11, rue Lanneau. **Brasserie La Gueuze**, 19, rue Soufflot, dishes from northern France.

Aux Trois Maillets, 56, rue Galande, Tel: 43 54 00 79, Métro Maubert Mutualité, Piano Bar, closed Sun, Tue. **Caveau de la Huchette**, 5, rue de la Huchette, Tel: 43 26 65 05, famous jazz cellar, from 9.30 p.m. **Le Caveau des Oubliettes**, 11, rue St.-Julien-le-Pauvre, Tel: 43 54 94 97, Métro St.-Michel, troubadour-chansons in Gothic vaults. **Paradis Latin**, 28, rue du Cardinal Lemoine, Tel: 43 25 28 28, one of the nicest variety theaters, from 10.00 p.m.

Museums
Musée de Cluny, tapestries, Roman baths, medieval art, Métro St.-Michel, 6, pl. Paul Painlevé, Tel: 43 25 62 00, in summer 9.30 a.m.-5.15 p.m., in winter 9.30 a.m.-12.30 p.m. and 2.00-5.15 p.m., closed Tue. **Panthéon**, neoclassicist mausoleum, pl. du Panthéon, Métro Luxembourg and Cardinal-Lemoine, in summer 10.00 a.m.-6.00 p.m., in winter 10.00 a.m. and 2.00-5.30 p.m. **Institut du Monde Arabe**, rue des Fossés Saint-Bernard, Tel: 40 51 38 38, open 1.00-8.00 p.m., closed Mon. **Institut Océanographique**, 195, rue St.-Jacques. **Sculpture en Plein Air**, open-air museum, modern sculpture, quai St.-Bernard. **Histoire Naturelle,** Jardin des Plantes, 57 rue Cuvier, Métro Monge, open 1.30-5.00 p.m., closed Tue.

Sightseeing / Leisure
Arènes de Lutèce, Roman arena, Métro Monge. **Jardin des Plantes**, zoo, park, 57, rue Cuvier, Métro Austerlitz. **Sorbonne**, university, church, Métro Luxembourg and St.-Michel. **Shakespeare and Company**, 37, rue de la Bucherie, Métro Maubert. Legendary English language bookshop, once frequented by Ernest Hemingway. Owner Sylvia Bach first published James Joyce's Ulysses. Lively **Market** along the Rue Mouffetard, Métro Cardinal-Lemoine.

Post / Pharmacy
Post Office: 2, rue des Écoles. **Pharmacy** (with emergency service): see 6th Arrondissement.

Tourist Information / Police
Town Hall and **Police Station**: 1, rue Soufflot.

6th ARRONDISSEMENT
Accommodation
MODERATE: **Jardin de Bréa**, 14, rue Bréa, Tel: 43 25 44 41. **Welcome Hotel**, 66, rue de Seine, Tel: 46 34 24 80.
BUDGET: **Delhy's Hotel**, 22, rue de l'Hirondelle, Tel: 46 26 58 25, Métro St.-Michel.

Restaurants / Cafés
Le Procope, 13, rue de l'Ancienne-Comédie, elegant restaurant, one of the oldest in Paris. **La Fourchette en Habit**, 75, rue du Cherche Midi, fish. **La Houlotte**, 29, rue Dauphine, multilingual service, French cuisine. **Le Bilboquet**, rue St.-Benoît, jazz from 7.30 p.m.-3.00 a.m.
Aux Deux Magots, 170, bd. Saint-Germain, Métro St.-Germain-des-Prés. This café used to be Jean Paul Sartre's favorite. A bit further on is the **Café de Flore**, 172, bd. Saint-Germain, another famous meeting place of the existentialist scene.

Museums / Culture
Musée Eugène Delacroix, 6, place de Furstemberg, 9.45 a.m.-5.15 p.m., closed Tue. **Histoire de la Médecine,** 12, rue de l'École de Médecine. **Institut d'Architecture**, 6, rue de Tournon. **Hôtel de Monnaie**, coin collection and mint**,** 11, quai de Conti. **Musée Ossip Zadkine**, sculpture, 100 bis, rue d'Assas. **École des Beaux-Arts**, art college, 17, quai Malaquais.

Sightseeing / Leisure
St.-Germain-des-Prés (boutiques, bistros, cinemas, churches). **Jardin du Luxembourg** (park, exhibitions in the Palais du Luxembourg).
Markets: Rue de Buci and rue de Seine. Marché Saint-Germain. Market hall in the rue Mabillon (daily) and market along the bd. Raspail.
Shopping: Elegant boutiques on the bd. St.-Germain and in the surrounding streets. **FNAC**, books and reservations for special events etc., rue de Rennes, near the Tour-Montparnasse.

Post / Pharmacy
Main Post Office: 111, rue de Sèvres. **Pharmacy** (with emergency service)**:** Drugstore, bd. St. Germain (corner rue de Rennes), Métro St.-Germain-des-Prés.

Tourist Information / Police
Town Hall, Police Station: 78, rue Bonaparte.

13th ARRONDISSEMENT
Accommodation
MODERATE: **Mercure Paris-Tolbiac**, 21, rue de Tolbiac, Tel: 45 84 61 61. **Grand Hôtel Jeanne D'Arc**, 43, bd. St.-Marcel, multilingual service, Tel: 47 07 43 17.

BUDGET: **Victoria Hôtel**, 47, rue Bobillot, place d'Italie, quiet, Tel: 45 80 59 88. **Lebrun**, 33, rue Lebrun, Tel: 47 07 97 02.

Restaurants
Les Marronniers, 53 bis, bd. Arago, elegant, fish dishes. **Chez Grand-mère**, 92, rue Broca , Métro Gobelins, near the rue Mouffetard, good traditional food, closed Sat and Sun. **Auberge Etchegorry**, 41, rue Croulebarbe, Métro Gobelins, traditional French cuisine.

Museum
Musée des Gobelins, 42, av. des Gobelins.

Sightseeing / Leisure
Chinatown: Métro Chevaleret. **Market:** Auguste Blanqui, place d'Italie, Tue, Fri and Sun. **Shopping:** Place and Avenue d'Italie (shopping center) and in Chinatown.

Post / Pharmacy
Main Post Office: 23, av. d'Italie. **Pharmacy** (with emergency service): 61, av. d'Italie.

Tourist Information / Police
Town Hall and **Police Station**: 1, place d'Italie.

14th ARRONDISSEMENT
Accommodation
MODERATE: **Hôtel du Maine**, 16, rue Maison-Dieu, Montparnasse, Tel: 43 22 00 67. **Le Moniage Guillaume**, 88, rue de la Tombe-Issoire, Porte d'Orléans, Tel: 43 27 09 88.
BUDGET: **Hôtel de Blois**, 5, rue des Plantes, near Montparnasse, Tel: 45 40 99 48.

Restaurants
La Maison du Cantal, 82, bd. de Montparnasse, specialities from the Auvergne, music. **Auberge de l'Argoat**, 27, av. Reille, Montsouris, fish dishes. **La Guérite du Saint-Amour**, 209, bd. Raspail, French cuisine. **Le Zeyer**, 234, av. du Maine, Métro Alésia, inexpensive brasserie.

Sightseeing / Leisure
Catacombes: Place Denfert-Rochereau, Tue–Fri 2.00-4.00 p.m., Sat and Sun 9.00-11.00 a.m. and 2.00-4.00 p.m. **Observatoire** (observatory): Avenue de l'Observatoire 61, guided tours on the 1st Saturday of the month at 2.30 p.m. **Cimetière du Montparnasse**: Métro Montparnasse, the last resting place of many famous (or forgotten) artists. **Market**: Rue d'Alésia, behind Ste.-Anne, Wed and Sat. **Shopping:** Along the rues d'Alésia, Denfert-Rochereau and Montparnasse.

Post / Pharmacy
Main Post Office: 15 bis, av. Général Leclerc, Métro Denfert-Rochereau. **Pharmacy** (with emergency service): 106, bd. de Montparnasse.

Tourist Information / Police
Town Hall and **Police Station**: 2, pl. Ferdinand-Brunot, Métro Mouton-Duvernier.

EIFFEL TOWER

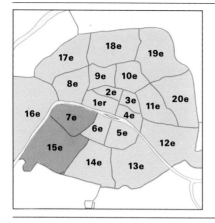

QUIET SQUARES
AND GREAT
HEIGHTS

MONTPARNASSE

PARKS QUARTER

EIFFEL TOWER

CITY PALACES

MUSÉE D'ORSAY

In the sedate, bourgeois world of the 7th arrondissement there are numerous ministries, the parliament, and embassies. All of them are located in splendid town houses, which the impoverished aristocracy had to sell. The people live in seclusion behind the façades and walls in this residential and administrative quarter. The Ministry of Foreign Affairs also insulates itself behind the gold-plated, wrought-iron gates on the Quai d'Orsay.

In contrast, the 15th arrondissement on the other side of the Boulevard de Grenelle, which was first incorporated in 1860, has maintained its bustling atmosphere in narrow village-like streets. It has the Paris of the 20th century to thank for its charming squares and wide avenues, which invite one to stroll along them. With 260,000 inhabitants, it is the largest district in Paris, and it is a quarter where many parks are found.

MONTPARNASSE

Even today the theaters in the **Rue de la Gaîté** are always full, and the charm of legendary places such as **Le Sélect**, **Le**

Previous Pages: What a contrast between the skyscapers in the 15th Arr. and the Seine's promenade! Left: The symbol of all symbols in Paris – the Eiffel Tower.

Dôme, **La Coupole**, and the **Closerie des Lilas** has survived. Painting courses and art academies – and even the occasional old studios – can still be found here. And beneath the 210-meter-high office tower, the **Tour Montparnasse** – its 57th storey is the second highest vantage point in Paris –, there is lively activity until deep into the night at the intersection of the 14th, 15th and 6th Arrondissements.

The artistic roots of the Montparnasse quarter extend far back into time. Already in the 17th century, students roamed through this hilly, meadow landscape while reciting verses. The area was first called *Mont* ("mountain"), and *Parnasse* (after the Greek mountain Parnassus, sacred to the Muses) was added to it.

In the 20th century, several modern artists fled from the famous studio house of Montmartre, the *Bateau-Lavoir* (washhouse), to the very cheap accommodations available in Montparnasse. Modigliani, Chagall, Apollinaire, Zadkine and Foujita met in the legendary cafés: in La Rotonde and the others already mentioned above. Later, Bourdelle, Picasso, Derain, Kessel, Cocteau, Max Jacob, Hemingway, Stravinsky and many others also joined in.

On the way to the **Cimetière de Montparnasse**, the last resting place for a great

many artists and novelists, one passes the well-frequented café-theater **Théâtre Le Grand Edgar** along the Boulevard Edgar-Quinet. In the **Rue de la Gaîté,** which was once famous for its artists' studios and concert halls, sex shops and theaters promoting related themes tend to be more predominant today.

In the **Rue Campagne-Première**, not far from the cemetery, artists such as Picasso, Miró, Kandinsky and Friesz resided between the World Wars. While sightseeing, take notice of the façade of house nr. 6 with its pine cones. House nr. 31 conceals the unusual, tiled **Maison Céramique**.

In the **Rue Vavin** (Métro Vavin) at the intersection of the Boulevards Raspail and Montparnasse, look for the house nr. 26. Its façade, dating back to the year 1912, is completely covered with white ceramics. Sauvage and Sarazin were its architects.

Above: Montparnasse Tower. Above right: On a bistro terrace with a cup of café crème.

Next door in the **Rue de la Grande-Chaumière**, the *Maison Fourniture pour Artistes Sennelier* carries all of the necessary artists' supplies. Here you will also find the **Académie de la Grande Chaumière**, founded in 1904 for painters and sculptors.

The cafés, bars, movie theaters and bookstores on the Boulevard Montparnasse and in the surrounding streets are open until deep into the night. Some of the artists' bars and clubs have preserved their old flair.

If you saunter down the **Boulevard Montparnasse**, you will soon reach the Boulevard de Vaugirard close to the Place du 18 Juin 1940. The 15 rooms in the back building of house nr. 34 contain the **Musée de la Poste**.

If you are not particularly interested in the history of the French post office, you can immerse yourself in the former studio of the sculptor **Antoine Bourdelle** where there are 1000 sculptures, 6000 sketches of frescos, drawings, aquarelles and oil paintings. If you want to look beyond the

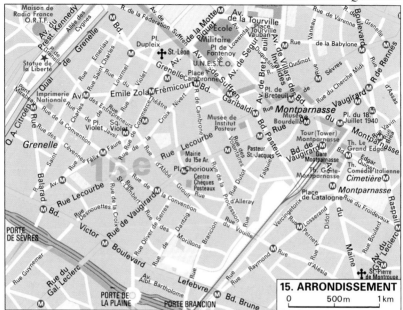

15. ARRONDISSEMENT
0   500m   1km

columns of your local newspaper, you will find the large building of the French daily *Le Monde* at the corner of Rue Antoine-Bourdelle and Rue Falguière.

THE PARKS QUARTER
15th Arrondissement

The *Quinzième* provides neither historical buildings nor grandiose perspectives. It is more suitable for relaxed walking along shady avenues and small business streets away from the hectic pace of the big city.

In the 19th century, the city of Paris spread out towards the south. Here in the 15th Arr., you will find a characteristic of the urbanization that took place during the Second Empire, the so-called *square parisien*, a small spot of repose in the middle of the turbulence of the city.

Most of the parks were created during that period, and they bear the typical hallmarks of the French park: straight paths with park benches, lawns with trees and playgrounds for the children, and kiosks

with refreshments. And they always seem to have creaking entrance gates.

The local city hall, the **Mairie du XVIème Arrondissement** (Métro Vaugirard) hands out city maps, which show all of the squares. The city hall is an excellent starting point for a lovely walking tour of this arrondissement. Adolphe Chérioux gave his name to the square in front of the city hall.

There are two curious sights worth visiting in close proximity to the **Square Chérioux**. The first one will particularly interest fans of architecture: Across from the métro exit is a large grating which you have to pass through to reach the **Square Vergennes**. Here you will find yourself in a private street, but no one will stop you from admiring the façade of the old house of the glazier Barillet with its wonderful glass windows at the end of the cul-de-sac. It is by Robert Mallet-Stevens.

The second curiosity awaits in the Rue de Vaugirard nr. 226. A sun made of gold-plated wood shines above the entrance

115

door. The old inn, the **Auberge du Soleil d'Or**, once stood here, site of a conspiracy during the French Revolution. In 1796, a group of conspirators who wanted to topple the government of the Directoire held their meetings there. However, their plans were betrayed: 130 people were arrested and 53 beheaded.

From the square in front of the city hall, you can also see the Square Saint-Lambert. Cross it and enter the Rue des Entrepreneurs. Continue straight ahead to the **Square Violet**, whose garden is among the most pleasant in this arrondissement. It is the remnant of a park that once belonged to the house of Léonard Violet, a co-founder of the village Beaugrenelle. (His house now accommodates a fire station).

Beaugrenelle, which lies directly on the Seine, is today a typical business district of the 1970's with terraces, high-

rises, and shopping centers. On Place Charles-Michels is a newspaper stand with one of the best assortments of international newspapers in the city.

It takes no more than five minutes to reach the **Imprimerie Nationale** in the Rue de la Convention. All official government documents and publications are printed here. A Gutenberg monument stands in the park of the house and seems to keep an eye on tradition. Guided tours are only possible once a week in groups, and you must apply for one in writing to the director of the Imprimerie Nationale (75732 Paris Cedex). On the other hand, the building's library is open all week long. Here you can admire some of the most beautiful examples of the book-printing art. A reverent atmosphere dominates in the library, as if it were almost a sacred place. It is easy to forget all sense of business there.

A pleasant walk along the river connects the Pont Mirabeau with the **Pont de Grenelle**. In the middle of the bridge towers the French version of the **Statue**

Above: The Statue of Liberty greets her far-off American sister. Right: A center of attraction for children.

of Liberty *(Statue de la Liberté)*, created by the Alsacian sculptor Auguste Bartholdi. Its gold-plated torch stretches towards its American sister. The **Allée des Cygnes** (avenue of the swans) starts behind it. It forms a dyke that runs down the middle of the Seine and connects the Pont de Grenelle with the **Pont de Bir-Hakeim**. This long, narrow, man-made island was built up in 1825. It extends for over 850 meters and is planted with trees.

The Allée des Cygnes has an observation point at one end, upon which an equestrian statue with an extended sword is displayed. Its title is *La France Renaissante,* ("France Reborn").

On the Pont de Bir-Hakeim you can enter the métro station, which is located above the ground and ride one stop further. Get out at Dupleix. The **Square Dupleix** is just another 100 meters. Here the **Saint-Léon** church attracts attention. With its Eastern flair, polished tiles and gentle colors, it appears to have originated in the Orient. This impression is further accentuated by the interior. A soft yellowish light floats around the diagonal ribs, which are decorated with mosaics. The church was constructed in the years 1925 to 1934 and was dedicated to the Cardinal Léon Amette.

From the Square Dupleix, it takes five minutes to reach the **Village Suisse**, the "Swiss village," a residential area for the very rich. Its name harks back to the World Exhibition of 1900. Today there is an art and antique market here known unfortunately for having exorbitant prices. But you should still wander through the ensemble of alleys and small squares and take a look at the marine antiques and Art-Déco objects.

Afterwards, take a rest in one of the terrace cafés on the Avenue de la Motte-Piquet or in the Kinopanorama, one of the last large movie theater halls. Nearby, there is a relatively unknown place which is worth a visit: the **Musée de l'Institut Pasteur**. It is located at in the Rue du Docteur-Roux nr. 25 (Métro Pasteur) in the onetime dwelling of the scientist, which was converted after his death in

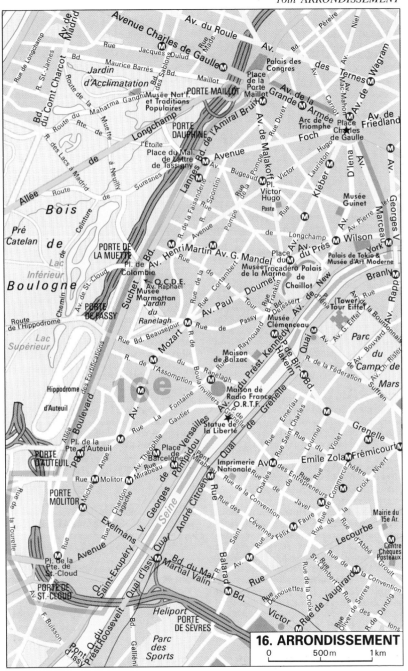

16. ARRONDISSEMENT

0   500m   1 km

1895. In the interior of the residence of this 19th-century humanist, a world of medical and scientific accomplishments opens up for the visitor.

In the Shadow of the Sword
7th Arrondissement

Every visitor to Paris is probably driven by an irresistible urge to pay a visit to the 7th arrondissement. There are, of course, quite a number of legitimate reasons for this: It does contain such major attractions as the Eiffel Tower and the Hôtel des Invalides.

In addition, the 7th arrondissement has up to this day maintained a certain independent character, which is rooted in its comparatively short history. From the 6th to the 16th century, only the Saint-Germain-des-Prés and Saint-Geneviève abbeys, with their extensive estates were located here on what is called the Grenelle Plain. The uncultivated pastureland belonged to the kings of France and was used only when they felt the desire to go hunting for small game. The area is also said to have had a certain popularity as a place to carry out forbidden duels with swords or pistols.

A great rock on the plain indicated where the boundary between the two monasteries was located. This boulder, the *Gros Caillou*, was destroyed in 1738. The name naturally lived on in the surrounding village, which had already come into existence 100 years earlier. Up to 500 washerwomen and their families lived here at times. Later, when the growing metropolis had incorporated the village, the sign of a well-known brothel by the name of Gros Caillou lured customers to the historic spot.

Obstinate Swans

One of the most obvious characteristics of the 7th arrondissement is its homogeneity. The district has preserved the appearance of a one- to two-hundred year-old part of the city. It has remained spared of the architectural sins of modern times – except for the headquarters of **UNESCO**, which were constructed in 1958. The concrete and glass palace of the World Organization for Education, Science and Culture, which stands directly behind the École Militaire, certainly compares favorably with other buildings of that era. However, it couldn't be more inappropriate considering its surroundings in this particular spot.

Many Parisians feel that their Eiffel Tower is even more annoying since it cannot be overlooked despite one's best efforts. Yet detractors and supporters alike are seldom aware of the incidental fact that two of its imposing support pillars stand on what was once a river island. In the 16th century, the Seine was broader than today. Because of mud and earth deposition, a number of tiny islands grew together to form what was called at the time the Ile Maquerelle. Why the island was given this rather unrefined name (*maquerelle* means procuress) of all things can no longer be determined. There can be no doubt, though, that it was not considered to be a pleasant location. In 1544, the victims of the plague were buried there, as were those Huguenots who fell victim to the Catholic rage during the Massacre of St Bartholomew.

Louis XIV selected the island to be the home of his royal swans, which he had purchased in England. Parisians were forbidden access to the island, and fishermen were not allowed to navigate the narrow channel between the island, now referred to as **Île des Cygnes**, Swan Island, and the Grenelle Plain. Despite all the care they were given, the swans proved to be obstinate, freedom-loving beasts. Time and again they escaped. In 1678, Colbert even had a party searching for them as far away as in the area of Rouen. In 1773 the Île des Cygnes was attached to the left bank of the Seine.

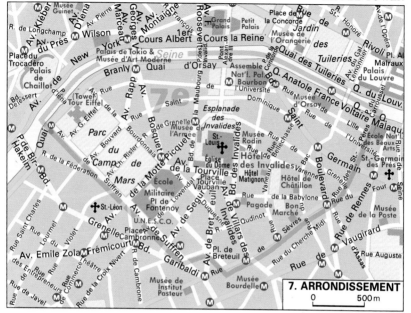

7. ARRONDISSEMENT

0   500 m

EIFFEL TOWER

It was on March 31, 1889, that the **Eiffel Tower** was quietly dedicated on the occasion of the Paris World Exhibition. This was important to its constructor, Gustave Eiffel, an engineer of German descent. He hated big performances. A handful of guests of honor climbed up the tower on foot since the elevators had not yet been completed. They covered the 1789 steps in just less than an hour.

In the meantime, the landmark of Paris – for a long time the highest building in the world – is now more than 100 years old, and controversy between its opponents and its admirers has been simmering for exactly the same period of time. If there is any truth to the off-paraded notion, that taste is something one does not argue about, then it does not apply to Parisians whenever the topic is the Eiffel Tower.

Around five million visitors a year come to see the ingenious construction of iron. However, only five percent of them are inhabitants of Paris itself. A good portion of these has never been able to get used to the "terrible skeleton," as Guy de Maupassant called the Tower. Because of his initial shock about the "monster," the writer left the city. Later he made a daily pilgrimage to the very good, but also very expensive restaurant in the first storey of the Eiffel Tower: "It is the only place in Paris from which one cannot see the damned thing..."

With an eye on their pocketbooks, most French people do not want to follow his example. They are satisfied with giving the Eiffel Tower vicious nicknames: "giraffe's cage" is one example; other epithets include "tragic floor lamp" and the "rusty suppository."

This was at least the case until 1986. At that time, the old structure experienced a far-reaching change, which robbed its opponents of half of their arguments. A 44-year-old Breton, an electrical engineer by profession, Pierre Bideau, went to work on the lighting system of the Eiffel Tower. The result of his efforts was as-

119

tounding: The 320-meter-high tower is no longer illuminated from the outside, but glows from within. Each one of its massive girders shines like gold. Fragile, yet simultaneously majestic, it appears to float above the city of lights at night.

For his part, thanks to the Tower, Gustave Eiffel not only became famous throughout the entire world, but also immensely rich. From the 700 proposals for the construction of "a new world wonder" for the World Exhibition, it was his plan that had been chosen. Although its critics maintained that the tower would collapse when a height of 220 meters had been attained, the city of Paris gave him a credit of 1.5 million gold francs for its construction. Nevertheless, trust in the calculations of the experienced engineer was by no means unequivocal. It was only after Eiffel declared himself prepared to endorse liability for the stability

Above: Gustave Eiffel's daring iron construction. Right: A view towards the east of Paris from the Eiffel Tower.

of the Tower with his complete assets that he was allowed to begin work on the controversial structure

The Eiffel Tower was erected in just 26 months. Eiffel, who had done the work under the condition that he was to be granted the entire revenue from the operation of the Tower during its first 20 years, had struck the deal of his life.

In 1889, the Eiffel Tower was exactly 300.65 m high. Today it boasts a height of 320.755 m. The forest of antennas at its tip accounts for the growth. From this point, television stations provide 15 million viewers with pictures, the military inspects the air space with its radar, and meteorologists observe the weather. The Tower weighs 9000 tons and was assembled from 15,000 iron pieces which are held together by 2,500,000 rivets. The most intense fluctuation of its tip was measured at 18 cm during a severe storm in 1894.

The Eiffel Tower, which could properly be construed as the grandiose Sunday afternoon fantasy of a frustrated en-

gineer, rules over a sober, symmetrical urban complex. "Behind it," if you will, linked to the left bank of the Seine by the Pont d'Iéna, are the **Jardins du Trocadéro**, embraced by the two halves of the **Palais de Chaillot**.

In front of it lies the **Champs de Mars**, a well-groomed, geometrically laid-out park, whose shaded avenues provide some breathing space for lethargic boules players, apartment dogs and rows of babbling school children.

The peaceful atmosphere of the Champs de Mars belies its name, Mars being, after all, the ancient Romans' god of war. An old Chinese saying which states that "repose can be found in the shadow of the sword" would apply perfectly to this area, as war is indeed a major theme here. The most stately blocks of buildings owe their existence to the assistance the military received from the crown. Under Louis XIV, the Hôtel Royal des Invalides, which encompasses a large church, was built in the 17th century. A century later, Louis XV gave the

order to have the imposing École Militaire (a royal military academy) constructed. Together with the gardens spread out in front of them – the **Esplanade des Invalides** between Pont Alexandre III and the Dôme des Invalides conveys spatial generosity and urban harmony just like the Champs de Mars between the military school and the Eiffel Tower. These two impressive complexes comprise almost one quarter of the total surface area of the 7th arrondissement.

A Mummy in a Hero's Grave

The **École Militaire**, founded once upon a time to educate up to 500 destitute noblemen to be upright officers, today also serves as an educational and administrative center for the French army. (Placing the UNESCO right behind it was either a coincidental irony or the cynicism of some Parisian ministry). On the other hand, the **Hôtel des Invalides**, where until the beginning of this century 4000 soldiers who had been injured in the

fields of honor could find care, room and board for the rest of their lives, today houses the French army museum. It possesses an unusually comprehensive collection of uniforms and weapons. Another quite remarkable exhibit is the collection of models depicting all the major fortified places of France.

The military **Church of Saint-Louis**, a structure with three naves, is impressive in its soldier-like austerity. The only ornamentation decorating this house of God is a selection of enemy banners captured after bloody fighting on the battlefields. In the year 1800, the great military leader Turenne was buried for the second time in the crypt of the church. (During the turmoil of the Revolution, it was only the richness of the botanist Defontaine's imagination that saved the corpse of Turenne from the raging mob by having it declared a mummy and temporarily

Above: The majestic Dôme des Invalides.
Right: Boule players in the autumn sun on the Esplanade des Invalides.

placing it in the Musée du Jardin des Plantes.) The church has since become the final resting place for a multitude of marshals and war heroes, who had done their service for the *Grande Nation*.

The generously gold-plated cupola of the **Dôme des Invalides** covers one of the loveliest monuments erected in Paris since the Renaissance and a masterpiece of the French Classical style. The cathedral and Saint-Louis church were originally joined by a common sanctuary and together formed a large church similar to the cathedral in Aachen. The members of the royal family were accustomed to attending the same Sunday services as the soldiers and the disabled veterans, but they kept themselves spatially separated in the nave of Saint Louis. In 1840, on the occasion of the return home of Napoléon I's remains, renovations transformed the Cathedral of the Invalides into a gigantic mausoleum. And apparently the symbolic value of the emperor's grave, a monumental coffin tower in the middle of the church, which was excavated for this purpose, surpasses all esthetic standards of values. It should be noted that the remains of the great Corsican are surrounded by the panels of no less than six coffins that could come apart like a Russian doll. The innermost consists of polished iron, the second of mahogany, numbers three and four of lead, the fifth of ebony, and the one visible to the eye of the beholder is made of oak.

Idylls Behind High Walls

How idyllic life can be behind the high walls of the approximately 200 old private villas in the 7th arrondissement is conveyed perhaps by a visit to the **Rodin Museum** in the Rue de Varenne. Most of the famous works of the great French sculptor (from *The Kiss* to *The Burghers of Calais* to *The Thinker* and *Balzac*) are displayed in the rooms of a well-proportioned building from the 18th century and

in its inviting and extensive garden. Even if you are not one of Rodin's fans, you will still be enchanted by the charm and relaxing atmosphere of the premises.

A further treasure of the district is **La Pagode**. This oriental villa, built in 1896 according to Japanese models, may make a strange, even mysterious impression in the middle-class Rue de Babylone. However, it is in no way unsightly. Constructed at the wish of the capricious spouse of a Parisian department store owner, it was the showplace for fashionable receptions and balls to which *tout Paris* thronged at the turn of the century. Louis Malle, the famous film director, later saved the pagoda from being torn down. The Asiatic palace with its exotic decor has now become the home of a unique movie theater, which incidentally is the only one in this district, and a tea salon that is just as distinctive.

The 7th Arrondissement could hardly be described as a shopping paradise. It does, however, boast the first department store built in the Seine metropolis. The

Bon Marché first opened its doors in the Rue de Sèvres in 1863. Incidentally, it was Gustave Eiffel who designed the metal skeleton that supports the spacious building. It allowed the interior of the construction to have large rooms not separated by intrusive, supporting walls, a design unheard of in those times.

Initially, though, the Bon Marché attracted attention for other reasons altogether. Its builder and director Aristide Boucicaut was the pioneer of free admission without an obligation to buy, clearly visible price tags and the possibility of later exchanging articles purchased in his store. At that time the height of modernness, the Bon Marché today tends to reflect the life style of the quarter's residents: In comparison to other department stores, it appears to be a bit conservative, sedate and aristocratically distinguished.

CITY PALACES

The true urban development of the 7th Arrondissement began (and peaked) in

123

the 17th century. Representatives of the French nobility who no longer were happy with the loud and overpopulated Marais district discovered the left Seine bank across from the Tuileries. In the subsequent time period, a multitude of town houses, so-called *hôtels*, rose up on the grounds acquired from the Saint-Germain abbey. These flamboyant villas, which usually concealed their beauty, their inner courtyards, and their gardens behind high walls, determined the appearance of the quarter back then just as they do today.

The lordly ambience has in no way been lost since then. The places where the former aristocracy used to hold court are still the scene of a considerable portion of the political and diplomatic life of Paris today, and indeed of all of France as well. The district has no less than 19 ministries situated in it. The **Palais Bourbon** (Rue de l'Université nr. 126), which Louis XIV had built in 1728 for one of his daughters, is now where the parliament meets, and the **Hôtel Matignon** (Rue de Varenne nr. 57), constructed in 1722, today serves as the official residence of France's prime minister.

The wish to be as close as possible to the Ministry of Foreign Affairs, quartered on the Quai d'Orsay, resulted in 23 countries situating their embassies in the 7th arrondissement. Few can, however, compete with the German embassy residing within the magnificent framework of the **Palais Beauharnais** (Rue de Lille nr. 78). It was built in 1713 and provides the pleasure of an exclusive view of the Seine.

The Marquis de Torcy, the last foreign minister under Louis XIV, had the house built. In 1803, Eugène Beauharnais purchased it. He had this villa redecorated in the purest Empire style for an outrageous amount of money and then presented the

Right: In the train station's former hall in today's Musée d'Orsay.

bill to his stepfather Napoléon I. The emperor paid – after he had suffered one of his notorious fits of rage.

Prussia, however, obtained the property for a ridiculously low price in 1817. One of the most beautiful private town houses in Paris, the residence is today classified as a historical monument. It is only possible to take a tour of it in exceptional cases and after arrangements have been made by telephone.

On the other hand, a true pilgrimage site for devout Catholics has always been the **Hôtel de Chatillon** (Rue du Bac No. 136). It was originally built in 1760 and has housed the order of the nuns of Saint-Vincent-de-Paul since 1813. Louise de Marillac, a saint no less, was buried in the chapel of the building in 1824. Furthermore, it is said that the Virgin Mary appeared five times in this chapel to the novice and former servant Cathérine Labouré in the year 1830. On these occasions, the Mother of God is reported to have instructed the young girl to have a coin minted in her honor.

It took two years until the Parisian archbishop recognized the miracle of the appearances of the Virgin Mary and consented to having coins minted according to the specifications of the nun. Four years later, there were already 20 million examples of this Virgin Mary medallion in circulation, which was considered to have miraculous healing powers. The armchair in which the Holy Virgin took a seat across from the praying Cathérine Labouré is still honored today as a cult object in the chapel.

The aristocracy did not only relinquish the 7th arrondissement to the politicians and diplomats in the course of time, but also, and primarily, to the well-to-do upper middle class. The "seventh," with its unrivaled, high real-estate prices and rental fees and its buildings that radiate *la bonne situation*, is an arrondissement of and for the rich. This is also a reason why – despite its central location – it has still

been able to preserve the reputation and rhythm of life inherent to a comparatively quiet, residential sector.

MUSÉE D'ORSAY

The **Musée d'Orsay** is the youngest temple of art in Paris and has proven to be a favorite with the public from the start. Since it opened in December of 1986, the mandatory program for all art aficionados in Paris has had three incomparable highlights: After a tour of the Louvre, with its treasures from four milleniums, and before an excursion to the futuristic Centre Georges Pompidou, which is dedicated to the 20th century, a visit to the transformed Gare d'Orsay is definitely considered to be *de rigueur.*

Where the trains once departed for Orléans, Tours and Bordeaux, the loveliest objects created by artists of the *Grande Nation* during the fruitful epoch between the years 1848 and 1905 are exhibited in extravagant surroundings. The Gare d' Orsay was erected in a brief 22 months

according to the plans of the architect Victor Laloux. The construction work was finished just in time for the Paris World Exhibition in the year 1900. Located directly on the left bank of the Seine, the new station allowed travelers from the southwestern section of the country to arrive right in the heart of the capital city. Many of the most affluent also chose to stay overnight in the elegant hotel integrated into the building. The splendor of the *Belle Epoque,* with its playful stucco and gold ornamentation, celebrated one of its last great triumphs here.

As early as 1935, with the electrification of the railroad complete, the Gare d'Orsay had sunk into insignificance. Its platforms of just 135 m were simply too short for the new trains. Together with the steam locomotives, it had to give up operations. The hotel survived on its own, losing, however, one star after the other until 1970.

The giant, 32-m-high and 140-m-long hall of the station, its artfully surrounded, light iron construction enabling the abun-

125

dant use of glass, was deserted by all, except for the rats. By the 1960s, the dilapidation had progressed to the point that this scenery inspired Orson Welles to film Kafka's *The Trial*. In 1971 it was finally decided to tear the building down.

Fortunately, this did not occur. During Georges Pompidou's term of office as president, the idea of transforming the train station into a museum first emerged. His successor, Giscard d'Estaing, eventually gave the go-ahead for the time-consuming and expensive renovations. The work began in 1980. Some 270 million U.S. dollars flowed out of the taxpayers' pockets before President Mitterand could proceed to ceremoniously dedicate it.

When you enter the vast old train station hall, it will remind you of the choir of a cathedral. In the central area on this floor, sculpture sets the tone. Two rows of smaller halls are laid out on either side of

main one. Within them, almost all of the currents that influenced the great schools of painting of the epoch, from Realism to the beginnings of Impressionism, from the students of Romanticism (Delacroix) to those of Neoclassicism (Ingres) are well represented.

In the second storey, the actual attraction awaits you in the form of the Impressionists' exhibits. On a considerably larger surface than that of the Jeu de Paume, which many people still mourn for, there are numerous pictures that had previously slumbered in the archives because of a lack of space. Even if the illumination appears to be just as successful as that of the Jeu de Paume – the ventilation is undoubtedly much better – the playful decor of the museum is not always compatible with the works of Renoir, Manet, Cezanne or Monet.

In conclusion, you should allow yourself a breather in the terrace café of the uppermost story. Enjoy the view across the Seine to the Tuileries, one of the loveliest panoramas that Paris has to offer.

Above: The monumental station clock in the Musée d'Orsay gives recollection to its early beginnings as a train station.

126

7th ARRONDISSEMENT
Accommodation

LUXURY: **Hôtel Montalembert**, 3, rue Montalembert, Métro Rue de Bac, Tel: 45 48 68 11. *MODERATE:* **Hôtel Derby-Eiffel**, 5, av. Duquesne, Métro St.-François-Xavier, Tel: 47 05 12 05. *BUDGET:* **Grand Hôtel Leveque**, 29, rue Cler, Métro École Militaire, Tel: 47 05 49 15.

Restaurants

La Fontaine de Mars, 129, rue St. Dominique, Métro École Militaire, Tel: 47 05 46 44, typical Parisian bistro, good, hearty fare. **La Ferme Saint Simon**, 6, rue St. Simon, Métro Rue de Bac, Tel: 45 48 35 74, excellent food, good value for money. **Le Télégraphe**, 41, rue de Lille, Métro Rue de Bac, Tel: 40 15 06 65, popular restaurant, although the prices are more impressive than the food. **L'Arpège**, 84, rue de Varenne, Métro Varenne, Tel: 45 51 20 02, absolutely stunning Nouvelle Cuisine.

Museums / Sightseeing

Musée d'Orsay, 1, rue de Bellechasse, Tel: 40 49 48 14, Métro Solférino, in summer 9.00 a.m.-6.00 p.m., in winter 10.00 a.m.-6.00 p.m., Thur until 9.45 p.m. **Invalides**, Tel: 45 55 37 70, Métro Invalides, a stunning architectural threesome: **Hôtel des Invalides** (military museum), **Église du Dôme des Invalides** (containing the sarcophagus of the emperor Napoléon I) and the **Église Saint-Louis des Invalides**, (the soldiers' church). **Musée Auguste Rodin**, 77, rue de Varenne, Tel: 47 05 01 34, in summer 10.00 a.m.-5.45 p.m., in winter 10.00 a.m.-5.00 p.m.

Tourist Information

Tourist Information in the Town Hall (in the Hôtel de Villars, built in 1645), 116, rue de Grenelle, Tel: 45 51 07 07.

15th ARRONDISSEMENT
Accommodation

LUXURY: **Holiday Inn**, Porte de Versailles, Tel: 45 33 74 63. **Sofitel Porte de Sèvres**, 8, av Louis-Armand, Tel: 40 60 30 30. **Nikko**, 61, quai de Grenelle, Tel: 40 58 20 00. **Hilton**, 18, av. de Suffren, Tel: 42 73 92 00. *MODERATE:* **Fondary**, 30, rue Fondary, Tel: 45 75 14 75. **Pasteur**, 33, rue du Docteur-Roux, Tel: 47 83 53 17 (closed in August). **Terminus Vaugirard**, 403, rue de Vaugirard, Tel: 48 28 18 72. **Tourisme**, 66, av. de la Motte-Picquet, Tel: 47 34 28 01. **Beaugrenelle Saint-Charles**, 82, rue Saint-Charles, Tel: 45 78 61 63. **Résidence Saint-Lambert**, 5, rue Eugène-Gibez, Tel: 48 28 63 14.

Restaurants

Chez Quinson, 5, pl. Etienne-Pernet, Tel: 45 32 48 54, Mediterranean cuisine, Bouillabaisse,

credit cards not accepted, closed Sun and Mon. **Lal Quila**, 88, av. Émile-Zola, Tel: 45 75 68 40, Indian specialities to the sound of a sitar, relaxed atmosphere, Hollywood-style interior, closed lunchtime Sun and Mon. **Bistrot 121**, 121, rue de la Convention, Tel: 45 57 52 90, a classic restaurant of this quarter, French food, closed Sun and Mon. **Café du Commerce**, 51, rue du Commerce, Tel: 45 75 03 27, an institution since 1925, plain but good food for a shoestring budget, daily until 11.00 p.m. **Le Vasco da Gama**, 39, rue Vasco da Gama, Tel: 45 58 21 28, pleasant Portuguese restaurant, closed Sun and Mon. **Le Passé Retrouvé**, 13, rue Mademoiselle, Tel: 42 50 35 29, restaurant in memory of Edith Piaf, dishes from the southwest of France, closed lunchtime Sat and Mon, closed all day Sundays. **Morot Gaudry**, 6, rue Cavalerie, Tel: 45 67 06 85, elegant, reasonable prices, closed Sat and Sun. **Les Célébrités**, 61, quai de Grenelle, Tel: 40 58 20 00, restaurant on the 8th floor of the Nikko Hotel, elegant, expensive, open daily.

Museum

Musée de l'Institut Pasteur, 25, rue du Docteur-Roux, 2nd floor, Métro Pasteur, open Mon-Fri 2.00-5.00 p.m.

Tourist Information / Post

Town Hall: 31, rue Péclet, Métro Vaugirard, Tel: 48 28 40 12. **Post Office:** 19, rue d'Alleray.

MONTPARNASSE
Theaters

Théâtre Le Grand Edgar, 58, bd. Edgar-Quinet, Tel: 42 79 97 97. **Théâtre Montparnasse**, 31, rue de la Gaîté, Tel: 43 22 77 74. **Théâtre de la Comédie Italienne**, 17, rue de la Gaîté, Tel: 43 21 22 22. **Théâtre Gaîté-Montparnasse**, 26, rue de la Gaîté, Tel: 43 22 16 18. **Théâtre Le Guichet**, 15, rue du Maine, Tel: 43 27 88 61.

Brasseries

Le Dôme, 108, bd. du Montparnasse, Tel: 43 35 25 81, seafood. **La Coupole**, 102, bd. du Montparnasse, Tel: 43 20 14 20, original interior of the 1920s. **La Closerie des Lilas**, 171, bd. du Montparnasse, Tel: 43 26 70 50.

Bars

Rosebud, 11 bis, rue Delambre, popular, crowded jazz bar. **Le Ciel de Paris**, Tour Montparnasse, bar and restaurant on the 56th floor, breathtaking panorama of Paris. **Méridien Montparnasse**, 19, rue du Commandant-Mouchotte, quiet hotel bar with piano music. **Café Pacifico**, 50, bd. du Montparnasse, very popular, though not an authentic Mexican – in spite of cocktails with Tequila, Mezcal and Pisco.

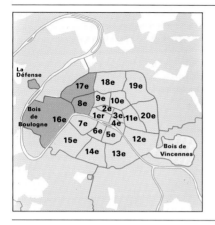

POMP AND PARKS

PLACE DE LA MADELEINE
PLACE DE LA CONCORDE
CHAMPS-ÉLYSÉES
PLACE DE L'ÉTOILE
PLACE DU TROCADÉRO
BOIS DE BOULOGNE
LA DÉFENSE
17th ARRONDISSEMENT

Today the west side of Paris is among the city's finest residential areas. It didn't become a city district until 1860. Before then, the quiet villages of Neuilly, Monceau, Batignolles and Clichy still slumbered in the midst of green pastureland. There were farms, dairies and lowland gardens, scattered here and there with quite isolated, middle-class homes. Financial entrepreneurs caught a whiff of the opportunity here, buying up land and making up contracts with the stipulation that the land be developed within the ensuing six months. As a result, within a few years, entire residential districts had shot up out of the ground, all in the Haussmann style. Nowadays these are among the preferred addresses for the seats of French and international corporations, concentrated particularly in the 8th, 16th and 17th arrondissements. Besides touring the better-known sites of interest, one should not pass up the opportunity to leave the well-trodden tourist paths, where, for example, you can discover the 17th-century Place de Clichy. This Paris of old was not that of traffic jams on the main thoroughfares rather it was a pleasant city, full of provincial dialects.

Previous pages: Pont Alexandre III with Place de la Concorde in the background. Left: Along Champs-Élysées.

PLACE DE LA MADELEINE
8th Arrondissement

Start out from the **Gare Saint-Lazare**, the major rail terminal from which trains depart towards the northern and western regions of the country. From here you can take a both interesting and pleasant stroll.

The Gare Saint-Lazare and around which is always a bustle of activity, struck fear and dismay into the enemies of progress among the old guard, to whom locomotives appeared to be some sort of monsters – as in Baudelaire's *The Trains Gone Wild*. However, it also fascinated people with a more modern viewpoint, including Monet, who immortalized it on canvas, and Offenbach, in whose operetta *La Vie Parisienne* a throng of travellers invades the Gare Saint-Lazare. Since quite a number of bus lines and taxi rides also end at the station, the scene is constantly turbulent and noisy.

In order to get to the **Chapelle Expiatoire**, Louis XVI's chapel of atonement, make your way along the Rue de Rome to the Boulevard Haussmann. A detour down the Rue de Madrid to the **Conservatoire Nationale de Musique**, in which all varieties of instruments and musical scores can be viewed, is worthwhile. The church will enthuse those with an interest

– albeit a macabre one – in the events of the French Revolution.

1343 victims of the guillotine, along with the royal couple, were buried in the cemetery, over which a small Gothic chapel now rises. In 1815, under Louis XVIII, the corpses of Marie Antoinette and Louis XVI were transported to the royal cemetery in Saint-Denis. The staircase leading to the chapel is flanked by the graves of other famous deceased: Danton, Desmoulins, Charlotte Corday and Philippe Égalité.

A walk along the Boulevard Haussmann offers an opportunity for some inexpensive shopping in expensive stores, namely by window-shopping. Here you will find the major department stores that at one time robbed many small businesses of their livelihoods. Turning into the Rue Tronchet with its luxury boutiques, one soon arrives at the **Place de la**

Above: This sculpture in front of Saint-Lazare train station symbolizes the trauma of missing a train.

Madeleine, on which stands the neoclassical **Church of the Madeleine**, which lacks a cross. It is a replica of the Parthenon in Athens. Its onerous style is not exactly everyone's cup of tea. The foundations of the church date back to the 8th century. At that time a chapel dedicated to Mary Magdalena stood at what is today nr. 8 Boulevard Malherbes. It has disappeared, but hasn't been forgotten, having lent its name to the new church (on which construction began in 1764). Constant d'Ivry, its architect, followed the plans for Saint-Louis-des-Invalides.

Couture, his successor, wanted to erect a building modelled on the Pantheon here instead and began with the demolition work. He was interrupted by the Revolution. In 1806, Napoléon I ordered the construction of a Greek temple on the site for the glorification of his *Grande Armée*. This temple was dedicated by Louis XVIII to that repentant sinner healed by Jesus in the Gospel according to St Luke. It narrowly escaped destruction when the Belgian anarchist Pauwels threw a bomb its way in 1852. As it turned out, the only thing blown sky-high was the perpetrator himself.

A pleasing silence usually dominates inside La Madeleine, which also features admirable sculptures by Rude and Pradier, masters of Classicism. If you descend the 28 steps at the front of the church, a splendid view opens up down through the Rue Royale, past the Obelisk of Luxor to the Palais Bourbon and the domed Cathedral of the Invalides.

For gourmets and gourmands alike, the Place de la Madeleine is a true never-never land. Chocolate, strawberries in winter, rare wines, caviar...go ahead and let your mouth water, as it inevitably will. The delicatessen shop **Fauchon**, only a little store in the 19th century, is now a flourishing enterprise exporting worldwide, with customers of long standing in the USA, Japan and various other spots on the globe.

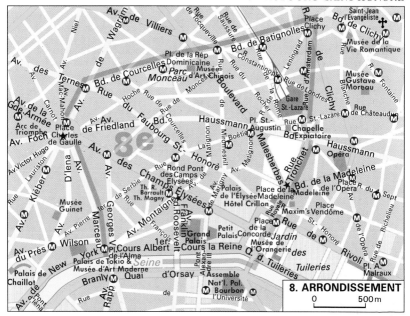

8. ARRONDISSEMENT

0   500m

Now's a good time to wander down the **Rue Royale**, which was able to boast some rather prominent residents over the centuries. Cardinal Richelieu, interior minister under Louis XIII, lived in nr. 3, which now houses **Maxim's**. If your budget permits, taste the duck with strawberries. This famous restaurant also offers a delightful *belle époque* ambience, featuring splendid original wainscotings of mahogany and lemon wood. Jacques-Ange Gabriel, the architect of the Place de la Concorde, lived in house nr. 8, not far from Madame de Staël, who, at the beginning of the 19th century, achieved international renown with her book *On Germany*, which was one of the first to make a real contribution to the two countries' understanding of each other.

Before arriving at the Place de la Concorde, take a look to the right down the **Rue du Faubourg Saint-Honoré**. From here the luxurious Paris (in rivalry with the Faubourg Saint-Germain) can be seen. Since the reign of Louis XIV, the aristocrats have been ensconcing themselves in splendiferous mansions here. This quarter is now the realm of money and power, displaying every imaginable luxury on the Rue du Faubourg Saint-Honoré. Just beyond it stands the **Élysée Palace**, the impressive residence of the French president.

Since as early as the 19th century, boutiques the likes of Henri, Les Montagnes Russes, Hermès and Jeanne Lanvin have held beautiful, wealthy women from around the world under their spell. Virtually all the world's ranking fashion designers are represented here, including Yves Saint Laurent, Ungaro, Tarlazzi, Stéphane Kélian, Mugler, Sonia Ryckiel, Kenzo and many others. Contemptuous of all this vile, worldly pomp, in this very neighborhood the Darbyist sect has erected its church in a quiet cul-de-sac (the little Impasse Villa-Wagram-Saint-Honoré). This community of faith, related to the Anglican-Puritan branch of Christianity, lives on costly turf but in ascetic isolation from what it views as an evil and defiled world.

133

Having left the Faubourg behind, you proceed to the Champs-Élysées via the **Rue Marigny**, having by a theater of the same name. The pleasant alleys here, shaded by chestnut trees, serve as a traditional marketplace.

PLACE DE LA CONCORDE

Having arrived at the **Place de la Concorde** by way of the Rue Royale or the Rue Boissy d'Anglais, pedestrians tend to feel rather lost and bewildered on the gigantic plaza, with the automotive traffic roaring and careening about seemingly in all directions. Two commanding edifices, whose colonnades are copies of the Perrault wings of the Louvre, rise up over the north side of the plaza. Currently situated in the right-hand building is the **Naval Ministry**; the Army Ministry was previously housed here. During the 18th

Above: Resting at the large fountain at the center of Place de la Concorde. Right: Marly's horse at the Place de la Concorde.

century Queen Marie Antoinette used it as a meeting place for her amorous escapades. The **Hôtel Crillon** is among the citadels of Parisian snobbism. Today it houses the French automobile club. Formerly, its elegant salons served as the winter quarters of the famous Chateaubriand family.

The Place de la Concorde, once known as the Place Royale, was constructed for the glorification of Louis XIV, the Sun King. The assessors of Paris, officials of the magistrate, had the plaza laid out around the equestrian statue of the king. The sculptures were provided by Bouchardon, and the plaza was designed by Gabriel, who had won the commission in a call for entries. The grounds consisted of eight hectares of swampland, at that time located outside of the city limits. From 1755 to 1775 an octagonal plaza was planned, though only the north side was actually constructed.

Many historical scenes were played out here. For example, in 1770, 133 spectators were trampled to death at a huge

pedestals serve as broom closets for the municipal sweepers. Eight female figures have now taken up residence on the pedestals. They symbolize the cities of Brest and Rouen (in the northwest), Lille and Strasbourg (to the northeast) Lyon and Marseille (on the Quai des Tuileries) and Bordeaux and Nantes (in the southwest).

CHAMPS-ÉLYSÉES

The *Marly Horses* at the entrance to the **Champs-Élysées** were sculpted by Couston. Actually, they were originally intended to grace the garden of the Château Marly, but the painter David liked them so much that he wanted to bring them to Paris. Today, the originals stand in the Louvre, but the reproductions in shining white marble compare surprisingly well.

Setting foot onto the Champs-Élysées, one may well have a difficult time imagining that this magnificent boulevard consisted of nothing more than fields and swamplands in the 17th century. In 1616 Maria de Medici had the Cour de la Reine (literally: the queen's courtyard) laid out here, a shady avenue, which was later extended to the Tuileries gardens by André Le Nôtre and yet further to the Butte Chaillot (today the Place de l'Étoile) by the Duc d'Antin. In 1709 this promenade was given the name it still bears today.

This is where the kings of France once made appearances before the people. When they were in a benevolent mood they distributed bread and wine to their subjects. This tradition was preserved until the advent of the Revolution, a period during which the general irritability often lead to brawls and riots flared up over every trifle. Furthermore, the monarchy had been abolished.

Into the 18th century, the Champs-Élysées had a thoroughly vile reputation. At night it was better not to go for a walk along it. Nonetheless, ever-increasing

Right: The entrance to Petit Palais.

numbers of well-to-do citizens were constructing houses in the fields on both sides of the street. Gradually it became fashionable to reside here and to drive along the avenue in an elegant carriage. But the night hours continued to be dangerous. Philippe Lebon himself, who contributed to the city's safety with the invention of the gas street-lamp, was murdered on the Champs-Élysées by Napoléon's soldiers in the night of December 2, 1804.

When Napoléon abdicated in 1814, the Allies marched into the city via the Champs-Élysées and bivouaked their army on the city's dignified parks. The Prussians and English deployed in the Tuileries and on the Place de la Concorde, while the Russians camped on the Champs-Élysées. In late March of that year, winter delivered one more icy blow to the city, and the Czarist troops were compelled to fell many trees for firewood. The street took some time to recover and once more pass as the "most beautiful in the world."

The Champs-Élysées has been within the limits of Paris proper since 1828. The sidewalks were subsequently widened, the night illuminated with gaslamps. The on-going modernization attracted the city's wealthy and they brought their favorite pastimes with them: balls, restaurants and fashionable cafés.

Today the Champs-Élysées is flanked by a row of fast-food joints and discount department stores the likes of *Prisunic*, while young people stream into the *Virgin Megastore*. Nowadays along the historic avenue one finds – besides "normal" Parisians – an eclectic mixture of business people, high-class prostitutes and gypsies with their children.

Facing the Seine on the Place de la Concorde, toward the right you will glimpse two structures covered by domes of iron and glass. The **Petit Palais** and the **Grand Palais** are turn-of-the-century architectural masterpieces erected for the

1900 World's Fair, which steered Paris into the 20th century.

Since 1902 the Petit Palais has housed the **Musée des Beaux-Arts de la Ville de Paris** with works of Etruscan, Egyptian, Greek and Roman origin. Paintings from the Middle Ages and Renaissance are to be found here alongside Dutch and Flemish works from the 16th and 17th centuries, as well as French painting from the 18th and 19th centuries, and exhibits of 18th-century furniture, tapestries and handicrafts. The Grand Palais puts on art exhibitions of world renown. When one of these is on, visitors from around the globe must patiently wait for admission in long lines.

A degree more interesting, perhaps, for children and those with a scientific mind is the **Palais de la Découverte**. Installed in the Grand Palais' west wing, this museum provides vivid and generally comprehensible explanations of discoveries from all branches of the natural sciences, including astronomy, mathematics, physics, medicine, chemistry, biology and geophysics. Don't forget to visit the **planetarium**. At fixed intervals, a mechanism sets the huge dome (15 m diameter) in motion. Then you will witness a truly "heavenly" performance.

On leaving the Grand Palais from the exit of the Palais de la Découverte, it is best to go up the Avenue Franklin D. Roosevelt to the **Rond Point des Champs-Élysées**. This neat circular plaza was designed by Le Nôtre. Sitting on one of the benches in the shade with the sounds from Paris' most important traffic arteries in the background, it is difficult to imagine how idyllic this place once was.

Under Napoléon III, the English governesses of the city's upper class came here with strollers to bring their little charges into the fresh air. In the shade of these chestnut trees, Marcel Proust also drew inspiration from watching these dainty little scenes. To this day, elegant ladies still stoop to dig about in the sandboxes with their toddlers, and sandwich peddlers hawk their wares to the hungry passers-by. Saunter along to the **Théâtre Renaud-Barrault**. The restaurant in this

old glass palace is unexcelled in popularity as a place for meeting up with friends.

Branching off from the Rond Point is **Avenue Montaigne**, along which the big names of the *haute couture* are established, among them Dior, Givenchy and Nina Ricci, places which, in the words of Baudelaire exude *luxe, calme et volupté*, luxury, calm and voluptuousness.

Before leaving the Avenue Montaigne, you might want to indulge in a costly coffee at the bar of the **Hotel Plaza Athénée** to enjoy the sumptuous surroundings. In this place it's quite probable that you will meet a journalist from Antenne 2, or perhaps Radio-Télévision Luxembourg will be shooting a film.

PLACE DE L'ÉTOILE

As can be seen from Place de la Concorde on clear days, the Champs-Élysées lead all the way to the **Place de l'Étoile**,

Above: Champs-Élysees flanked in Christmas lights, and the Arc de Triomphe.

known today as Place Charles de Gaulle, but only officially.

In 1730, five streets radiated out from this *Étoile de Chaillot* (Star of Chaillot) forming a star. Haussmann, who was responsible for re-designing Paris during the 19th century, added another seven boulevards to the existing five. Hittdorf assured that the façades of the newer buildings were harmonized with the older ones. In 1758, there were thoughts of erecting a bizarre monument in the midst of the square – a gigantic elephant housing ballrooms and a theater. However, the plans appeared a bit too ambitious. Napoléon I had in mind a monument for the glorification of his *Grande Armée*, a triumphal arch in classical style – the **Arc de Triomphe**. When Marie Louise of Austria, Napoléon's I second spouse, made her festive entry into the city, the arch had not yet been completed. Huge backdrops of painted cloth and makeshift plaster sculptures disguised its gaping nakedness.

The monument wasn't dedicated until 1836, during the reign of Louis Philippe.

Its purpose was to extol the glories of the military, but its founder, Napoleon, one of France's great commanders, only "saw" his creation in 1840, when his remains were brought to Paris from St Helena, and the procession passed through the arch on the way to the Cathedral of the Invalides. Every year on the 14th of July, France's national holiday, is commemorated with festivities here.

An underpass (on the Champs-Élysées or Avenue de la Grande Armée) leads to the center of the plaza where one can get a closer look at the Arc de Triomphe. Only then will you fully appreciate its tremendous scale of a height of 50 meters and width of 45. The massive piers of the arch are decorated with reliefs depicting scenes from the revolutionary era (including the First Empire). To the right on the side facing the Champs-Élysées is the *Marseillaise* by Rude (the departure of the volunteers to the front in 1792); to the left is *Napoléon's Triumph* of 1810 by Cortot. The resistance of 1814 and the Peace of 1815 are on the other side of the arch, modestly facing away from the city. With the elevator one can ride up to the observation platform, which offers the beholder one of the most beautiful views to be had of the city. There is also a little museum documenting the arch's history.

PLACE DU TROCADÉRO
16th Arrondissement

If you want to enjoy a view over the Seine, walk down the Avenue Marceau to the **Place de l'Alma**.

Since 1970 an iron structure has stood in place of the old stone bridge, of which only the renowned *Zouave* has been preserved, a symbol of the 1854 victory over the Russians in the Crimean War. This sculpture by Georges Diebolt adorned what was then Paris' most modern bridge, and it thoroughly pleased the Parisians. It also served as a high-water marker, and almost "drowned" in 1910.

Once you have crossed the bridge, take a side-trip into the **Musée des Égouts**. It explains how the Parisians have dealt with their sewage problem from 1370 to the present. The museum was established by Belgrand, the engineer who also renovated the entire sewage network during the period of Baron Haussmann's reshaping of the city. It is still functioning to this day. It is possible to view the *égouts* and even walk a piece into one. Surprisingly, the place does not stink as much as one might imagine.

By way of the Avenue du Président Wilson you arrive at the **Place du Trocadéro**. Fans of modern and abstract art should visit the **Musée d'Art Moderne de la Ville de Paris**. The equestrian statue of Maréchal Foch stands in the center of the square, from which major streets lead towards l'Alma, l'Étoile, the Bois de Boulogne and Passy.

The **Palais de Chaillot** is majestically enthroned on this large, mostly vacant plaza. Its terrace affords the visitor a wonderful view. The interior provides cultural diversity, with theaters and several museums. Its history extends back to Catherine de Medici (16th century). The spouse of Henry II had a country manor erected here on a hill so that she could enjoy the view over the city. Maréchal de Bassompière purchased it and turned it into the stage for his numerous, amorous affairs. The building burned down, but fortunately his collection of some 6000 love letters could be saved. In a new building, Henriette of England, a sister-in-law of Louis XIV, established a convent for ladies of the nobility, the *Convent de la Visitation*. Its occupants were soon nicknamed "Bassompières' daughters" in common parlance. Napoléon I had the edifice demolished; however, he was no longer able to execute his plans for the construction of a palace for his son, the King of Rome, on this site so close to the end of the imperial period (1814). An Oriental-style palace

Passy

Passy, essentially still a little village of sorts, begins at the cemetery (**Cimetière de Passy**) tucked in a angle where Avenue Georges Mandel and Avenue Paul Doumer enter Place du Trocadéro. It does offer a glimpse into French culture, in a way. Playwright Jean Giraudoux, artist Édouard Manet, and the composers Gabriel Fauré, Claude Debussy and other personalities who passed away after 1850 are buried here.

By way of the Rue Franklin, one arrives at the **Musée Georges Clémenceau**, the unaltered residence of this versatile statesman known as "the tiger," who was a mayor of Montmartre during 1870 und 1871 and still going strong (as prime minister) in 1920. Here, where he passed away in 1929, are exhibits documenting his life and work.

On taking a walk through this upper-class residential district, it should be kept in mind that in 1900 there were still huge vineyards here. Passy was a simple village with vintners, many cows and a rural atmosphere – still reminiscent in the little **Rue Vineuse** (meaning "winy"). The village became wealthy when a spring with ferruginous water was discovered in the 18th century.

Over time, the spring eclipsed the vineyards in significance, though in the **Rue des Eaux** a small wine museum recalls days gone by. As time went on, increasing numbers of townsfolk – including many artists – moved into the village. By the turn of the century, it had become *chic* to live here.

Right next door in the **Hôtel de Lamballe**, at Rue d'Ankara nr. 17, you will find the renowned Institute of Docteur Blanche. Gerard de Nerval resided in it during the three months before his suicide, and Guy de Maupassant, who out of his syphilitic nightmares created the demon *Le Horla* in the book by the same name, passed away here in 1893.

was put up here in 1878 for the World's Fair. It was torn down before the next World's Fair, to make room for the cubical pavilions seen here today. Between the two buildings lies a 60-meter-wide terrace with a splendid vista. The left-hand building houses the **Théâtre de Chaillot**, which has had a capacity of 1800 guests since its renovation in 1975. Its director is Jean Vilar, one of the most important reformers of the French theater.

The four museums of the Trocadéro consist of the **Musée de l'Homme** (essentially a museum of ethnography and anthropology); the **Musée des Monuments Français**, documenting French architecture; the **Musée du Cinema**, and the **Musée de la Marine**, a fascinating exploration of maritime history. In the evening, especially when the weather is warm and dry, people often stroll from the terrace in front of the museums down to the Seine. Watch out for the motorcyclists who ride up and down the stairs!

Above: On the steps of the Trocadéro.

du Steinkerque, you will be climbing directly up the *butte*. The way uphill is steep and fatiguing, but even so one should definitely not miss covering this stretch on foot. Anyway, driving through the narrow lanes and finding a parking place are not simple matters!

The road leads directly to the church Sacré-Coeur. Before arriving at it, one must still climb the many, tree-shaded steps. An alternative is to take the rack-railroad (*funiculaire*) to the top; it runs from 6 am to midnight, departing from Rue Tardieu (the fare is one métro ticket). Having made it to the top of the hill, the **Halle Saint-Pierre** (Rue Pierre Ronsard nr. 2) appears to your right.

This beautiful, 19th-century iron structure was constructed by a student of Baltard, the architect of Paris's old market halls. Today the Halle Saint-Pierre shelters the **Musée en Herbe** (a children's museum), and a modern art museum called the **Musée d'Art Naïf** (open daily from 10 am to 6 pm).

Located directly opposite it, extends the **Marché Saint-Pierre**, which has a great diversity of fabrics for sale on its three levels. After this, make your way back to the **Rue Tardieu**.

In nr. 7 there is a shop filled with the pleasant aromas emanating from its numerous phials of perfume. Now you have the option of heading left down the Rue des Trois Frères to the tranquil **Place Charles Dullin**. Here you can behold the neo-classical façade of the **Théâtre de l'Atelier** (illuminated at night), which dates back to the Restoration. Then take a left into the **Rue Yvonne Le Tac**. At nr. 11 on the **Place de Martyrium** is a chapel erected in memory of the death of Saint-Denis (Dionysus). In the crypt of the church, the Spaniard Ignatius of Loyola founded the Jesuit order in 1534 (open to the public from 10 to noon daily except on Thursdays and from 3-5 pm).

On the **Place des Abbesses** (named as a memorial of the cloister destroyed here

in 1794) there is one of the two remaining original signed glass panes from the métro stations. Their ornate Art Nouveau style, fashioned of glass and iron, was personally created by Hector Guimard. To the left is the imposing **Église Saint-Jean l'Évangéliste**. The Mairie de Montmartre, the old city hall, stands on the **Square Jehan Rictus**. Now cut across the plaza and turn right into the **Rue Ravignan**. On the right-hand side of the street, you might take a breather in the bar *Chez Camille* and have a drink at the *zinc* (counter). This is the favorite pub of Montmartre rockers.

The **Place Émile Goudeau** is a rather romantic sight with its aged trees, old-fashioned pavements and the Wallace Fountain. The most famous of all artists' studios was once located at nr. 13 – the **Bateau-Lavoir**, a wooden shack which once gave shelter to some 20 artists around the turn of the century. Max Jacob, Van Dongen, Modigliani, Juan Gris and Georges Braque were among them. Picasso painted his *Demoiselles*

The great writer Honoré de Balzac, after going through his wild years of love and passion, moved to Passy to spend his last years in peace. His home on the **Rue Raynouard** brings the days of *Cousine Bette* and *Le Père Goriot* to life. The desk where he wrote is still here; his paintings and drawings still hang on the walls. The house also has a rear exit to the Rue de Berton, through which the novelist often fled from the throng of devotees that virtually knocked down his front door.

When strolling down the Rue de Passy, you should pay a visit to the **Jardins du Ranelagh**. During the 18th century, this was where the *jeunesse dorée* and Marie Antoinette danced in a great pavilion.

The Avenue Raphaël brings one to the **Musée de la Radio**, where Radio France maintains its FIP departments, France-Inter, France-Culture, France-Musique, France-Info, RFI and Radio-Bleue. These

Above: On the way to Bois de Boulogne. Right: Les Cascades, a man-made lake in Bois de Boulogne.

stations pump out information, music of all kinds and entertainment programs around the clock. A hectic atmosphere permanently surrounds the building, with journalists, musicians and famous people coming and going. The small museum on the ground floor can also give the visitor the feeling of being a part of it all.

The Rue Fontaine guides you to **Auteuil**, where the fabulist La Fontaine as well as the critic Boileau and Molière, France's greatest 17th-century playwright, resided. The village was annexed by Paris during the Second Empire, as was Passy.

Chic, provincial and discreet at the same time, Auteuil has attracted many artists over the years. The renowned Arletty lived in the Rue Rémusat. The architect Héctor Guimard, creator of the ornate Art Nouveau entrances to the métro, lived in the Rue La Fontaine and the Rue Agar. Reposing between the two is the 17th-century **Lycée Jean Baptiste Say**, reminiscent of an enchanted castle.

On the Square du Docteur Blanche, the **Fondation Le Corbusier** is housed in the Villa La Roche. In the museum and private residence of this modern architect, one can obtain some revealing insight into his trail-blazing projects in interior decoration and landscaping.

BOIS DE BOULOGNE

On speaking of landscapes: The good people of Auteuil and Passy who feel a need to get away from the rough and tumble of their busy social and professional lives have Paris' most important area of vegetation at their doorstep. For exhausted tourists, for joggers in need of fresh air, for track gamblers and horseback riders, for children and parents looking for entertainment, for the sorely-tested toilers of the giant city and, some are sorry to say, for those in search of purchasable sex, the Bois de Boulogne is a horn of plenty.

Originally, in the Middle Ages, this area was covered with holm oaks, lending the forest the name Forêt du Rouvray (*rouvre*= holm oak). Unfortunately, these magnificent trees were cut down in 1814. They served that year as firewood for the camps of the allied troops. The park now has stands of sycamore, acacia and chestnut. During the Middle Ages, this forest also extended out to Chaville, Meudon, Montmorency and Germain-en-Lay.

The woodcutters' guild, on return from a pilgrimage to Boulogne-sur-Mer, in 1308, constructed a church with the financial support of King Philip the Fair in the middle of the forest, which they named **Notre-Dame-de-Boulogne**. The church became the namesake of the neighboring village as well as the entire forest region, which served as a hunting ground for the nobility. It was dangerous to get off your horse – even for the moment it takes to hike up your leggings – since the woodlands were full of prowling wild bears and wolves in addition to stags and wild boars. Travelers in

the postal coaches were plagued with fears of robberies and bandits.

Francis had a castle built here, the Château de Madrid, the name of which was to remind him of his captivity in Spain. Don't be too surprised when you no longer find the castle at the **Porte de Madrid**, since this symbol of the monarchy was completely destroyed in 1793.

Henry III was a fan of deer-breeding. He had a corral constructed here, surrounded by a high wall with eight gateways. Colbert had the forest transformed into a park and improved its roads. Louis XIV opened the Royal Hunt (formerly the exclusive province of the king) to the general population, which had become increasingly attached to the forest. Following the Regency (1715-1723), members of the nobility built summer residences here, whom they sometimes gave rather peculiar names, among them La Muette (the mute woman), Bagatelle (the only one still standing), Saint-James and Le Château de Neuilly. Finally, Napoléon III had additional small, convoluted *allées* and two small lakes put in, the **Lac Inférieur** and the **Lac Supérieur**, which are quite appealing for romantic boat rides.

The **Musée des Arts et Traditions Populaires** is situated at the Porte de Maillot in the north of the Bois de Boulogne. It has exhibits on the handicrafts and customs of the French peasantry from every century up to the time of the Revolution.

If your children are still too small to have much interest in ethnology, it's better to take them to the nearby **Jardin d'Acclimatation**, a recreation and amusement park for small children. The dolphin pool, the animals in the Normandy farmyard, the plant museum, the Lilleputian railroad and many other diversions really make time fly.

Another way of spending some pleasurable hours is to go rowing in the **Lac Supérieur** and the **Lac Inférieur** some way to the south of the Jardin d'Acclimatation. Close by, beyond the grounds of the **Racing Club de France**, is a small park-within-a-park called the **Pré Catelan** (admission is free). The name of the park has a poetic ring. An old legend tells of a troubadour who, after having returned from Spain, was murdered here. At the site of the purported event is a cross with his name.

Today many botanists are necessary to maintain the splendid extravagance of the **Bagatelle's** well-known flowerbeds. A gleaming white pavilion appears west of the forest. It owes its existence to a wager between the Count of Artois and Marie Antoinette and was constructed in three months. The Rococo period lives on here. A host of flowers provides the backdrop both visual and aromatic. They include tulips, hyacinths, narcissus, crocuses, rhododendrons, vetches and especially roses in all shapes and color. The garden displays its most seductive traits from mid-June to the middle of July and from September until October.

The horticultural adventure here continues in the **Jardin de Shakespeare**, an unusual translation of Shakespeare into the language of the trees. One explores the way the great playwright described nature in his plays. A small theater puts on productions of Shakespeare. Those traveling with children can safely leave them at a well-supervised playground called **Relais du Bois** during the show.

Last but not least, the Pré Catelan has a place of worship, if you will, for the gourmet sect, a restaurant considered to be the best in all of Paris, which is no small feat.

Towards the south, on the edge of the Bois, there are still two active horse-racing tracks – the **Hippodromes d'Auteuil** and **Longchamps** – where turf-races are held on a regular basis. This sport was once considered the province of the suburbanite; nowadays, the jockeys are predominantly *pied noirs* – which means French people born and raised in France's erstwhile North African colonies. The gripping atmosphere during the races has remained the same since the early days. Another sporting grounds is situated not far from the **Fleuriste Municipale** – the "Municipal Flower-breeding Research Garden."

In the **Stade Roland Garros**, an international tennis championship, the *Internationaux de France*, is played each year in late May/early June. Don't go to the tennis courts without a water-bottle and some sunglasses – even the audience sweat at these matches. Tickets should be reserved well ahead of time, since they are so coveted that they are even traded on the black market.

LA DÉFENSE

Immediately to the north of the Bois de Boulogne lies the peaceful area of **Neuilly**, divided in two by the Avenue Charles de Gaulle. This comfortable residential section used to be a final oasis

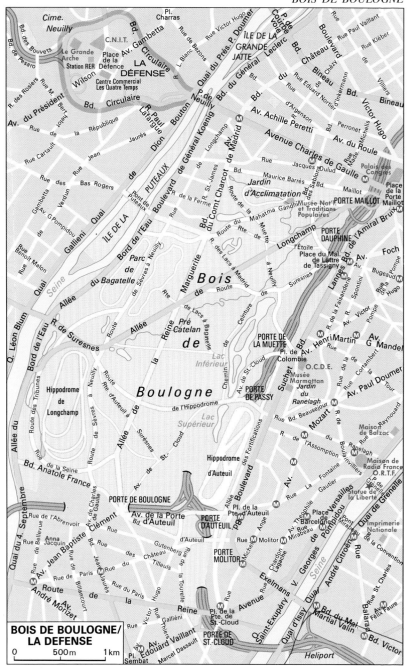

**BOIS DE BOULOGNE/
LA DEFENSE**

0   500m   1 km

before a desert known as **La Défense** and lying beyond the city limits, was built on the other side of an arm of the Seine.

At the beginning of the fifties, the government decided to erect a business and office center five kilometers outside of Paris in this dilapidated district. In those days, nobody had the least bit of interest in the ugly suburb with its junkyards, small factories and run-down buildings.

The district is named after a statue by Barrias, *La Défense de Paris,* that once stood in the middle of a traffic roundabout on the Butte de Chantecoq (now completely built up) and was relocated to the Rond Point de la Défense in 1983.

The first complex of buildings, the **CNIT (Centre National des Industries et des Techniques)** was dedicated in 1958. It resembles an immense upside-down seashell supported from only three points on the earth.

Above: A light and sound show in La Défense. Right: La Défense with Arc de Triomphe in the background.

Since that time, 21,000 private residences, some 2,000,000 sqm of office space and 200,000 sqm of business premises (retail space, etc.) have come into being, offering a total of approximately 120,000 jobs.

The first plan for this gigantic project, referred to as the *Charte d'Athènes,* was drawn up by Le Corbusier in 1963. One of the basic notions behind the design was a systematic separation of humanity from the motorized vehicle. The automobile is confined to arterial routes and subterranean parking ramps, while up above only pedestrian zones course about the highrises.

The first generation of office towers rose to heights of about 100 m. Since 1969, the construction of skyscrapers with cantilevered (self-supporting) skeletons has also been permitted. All of these structures are fully climate-controlled and equipped with artificial lighting – not necessarily to the pleasure of the employees within.

Since 1970 a new track of the RER, the suburban train line, has brought passengers right into the center of La Défense. The stretch from the Arc de Triomphe to this stop can be covered in a mere five minutes. But perhaps you will already have noticed that the people who work there don't have any desire to reside there as well – and the other way around.

The third generation of skyscrapers arose following the great energy crisis in the seventies. In the meantime, it had occured to the powers that be, that energy doesn't simply flow from some endless reservoir, but is fed by a limited and precious supply of raw materials. From then on, the office spaces were no longer continuously illuminated by artificial means, so the employees once again went about their work by daylight.

In 1981, the **Les Quatre Temps** shopping center opened its doors. It relieved the quarter of its oppressive silence and brought life into the streets.

In the same year, the architect Von Spreckelsen won a competition for which the President of the Republic had invited entries. His project was entitled **La Grande Arche**. It closes off the Champs-Élysée's lines of perspective. Twelve columns, each 30 m in height, bear a weight of some 300,000 tons. It boasts a large exhibition hall. Various ministries have their offices in these supporting pillars, major corporations and the human rights commission *Fondation des Droits de l'Homme* also have space here.

Seated up above on the terrace one can admire the impeccable success of its perspective, whose lines can be followed to the Arc de Triomphe, along the Champs-Élysées to the obelisk on the Place de la Concorde, over the Tuileries gardens to the Louvre's Cour Carrée.

At the kiosk on the ground floor there are pamphlets with information about each of these ultra-modern architectural gems. It is obvious to the naked eye, too, that the designers have paid attention to the surface decoration, and have not ignored modern artists either. Sculptures, mosaics, frescoes and fountains keep the eyes busy, when gazing at otherwise quite pedestrian ventilation shafts.

When taking a stroll through the district, it is like wandering through some sort of futuristic universe where form and content meet in beauty. Active and lively during the day, deathly silent at night, this stronghold of international business attracts men and women from the world over – even when there doesn't happen to be any major international trade fair or exhibition in the CNIT or on the roof of the Arche.

The CNIT serves as the location of quite a number of cultural events, including exhibitions, concerts and theater performances, which in combination with its numerous restaurants and hotels have contributed to the development of a pleasant atmosphere in the district. Each year on the 21st of June an impressive

musical festival is put on. With its architecture, concerts and play of light and water, the organizers attempt to present an aesthetic whole – a *Gesamtkunstwerk* reflecting both the conceptions of Stravinsky and Wagner.

17th ARRONDISSEMENT

The Avenue Charles de Gaulle leads back to the city, whose proportions, after the concentration of modern architecture at La Défense, appear pleasantly human. **Porte Maillot** has become a traffic hub. For one, it is the gateway to the Bois de Boulogne. In fact, a little train takes people directly to the Jardin d'Acclimatation. Porte Maillot is also the south-western tip of the 17th arrondissement, which stretches from the prosperous shores of Passy all the way to the foothills of Montmartre.

This area, where many streets' names recall French military history, has become a rather busy residential and commercial strip. In the 19th century, there

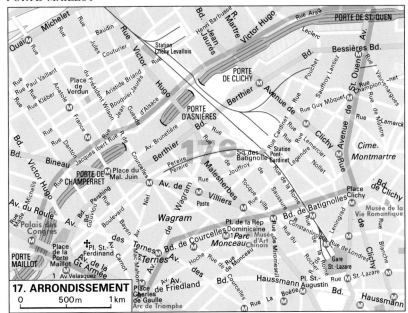

was nothing more than a few farms here, attracting Parisians suffering from urban fatigue. Today this area is completely developed. Throughout the year, the **Palais des Congrès** attracts business people from around the world as well as a great many tourists. Shops and restaurants have a steady clientele on the Avenues des Ternes and the Avenue Gouvion Saint-Cyr. Jazz fans also make pilgrimages to the latter in order to visit the **Club de Méridien** that awaits them with the finest of the genre.

These bits of current news should not, however, obscure the old history, bloody anecdotes, and other peculiar events that are somehow related to this street.

A shrieking child in a police station brought about a popular rebellion in 1750 at the Porte Maillot. The Parisians thought they had seen the king lift him up and attempt – vampire-style – to suck its blood. According to another version,

Right: An 18th century woman in the traditional dress of the Sansculottes.

small children were shipped to Louisiana and sold as slave laborers. The people banded together, marched to Versailles and called King Louis XV to account. Since that time, both of the streets have born the nickname "Street of the Revolt."

Children were also Saint Just' s main focus of attention. This young, brillant, ruthless philosopher of the Revolution co-founded the École Militaire, also named École de Mars. Spartan drills dominated the routine in this institution for child rearing. It was constructed on a parcel of land in the poverty-stricken district between the Porte Maillot and the Place du Marché, and was surrounded by a blue, white and red fence. Its presence irritated the residents of Neuilly, who were thus forced to make a lengthy detour through the Avenue des Ternes in order to get to Paris.

The stern discipline of the institute exacted many privations of its 16 and 17-year-old inmates. The painter David captured some of them on canvas: The children wore uniforms – in a style resembling a cross between Roman, Scottish and Polish stage costumes – which were so thin that they nearly froze in them. Their board was limited to thin soup and vinegar water. They received neither bed nor bedding, but were forced instead to sleep on the bare floor. Altogether, these conditions lead to countless symptoms of deficiency, and illnesses including tonsillitis and dysentery. If the childrens' health couldn't further endure the conditions in the school, they were sent back home.

On another sorry note, the **Chapelle Notre-Dame-de-la-Compassion** on the Boulevard Aurelle-de-Paladines calls to mind the tragic death of the Duc d'Orléans in 1842. He was making for his castle in Neuilly in his coach when it overturned here. The seriously wounded duke was carried into a grocery store on the Boulevard Gouvion Saint-Cyr, where he succumbed to his injuries soon afterwards. The small, Byzantine-style church that commemorates the accident was originally built on what is today the Avenue Pershing. But when the Palais des Congrès was built, it was relocated (scrupulously, stone by stone) to its current location.

The tracks of the Gare Saint-Lazare separate this district into a north and south side, both of which can look back on their own, differing histories. The north developed into an industrial area with the construction of the railroad ringroute surrounding Paris, while for a long time the south remained farmland.

At the close of the last century you would have been trudging through meadows, fields and swamps as well. To the north lay the old villages of Clichy and Batignolles, to the south Neuilly and Monceau, which was conquered by two brothers.

Before 1800, Louis XVIII had military grounds established in the commune of **Batignolles**. Speculators publicized the fresh air, attracting more and more Parisians, who built country residences for

La Femme du Sans Culotte

themselves, wishing to enjoy simple country life. The idyll quickly became overpopulated, as ever more houses were constructed. To this day the streets bear the names of the old land speculators.

In the center of Batignolles a chapel was built in 1828 which proved to be too small just six years later. Since Grecian columns were quite "modern" at the time, the chapel was expanded in this style.

At this time the community of Batignolles, which belonged to Clichy, wanted to become independent again. Together with the village of Monceau, it strived towards the founding of a new community. This was indeed established in 1830, but existed only until 1860, at which time all of the villages in the vicinity of Paris were incorporated into the city.

In this region, too, outside of the city, in 1850 Pereire acquired ten hectares of the park at a low price in order to engage in land speculation. Not much later, he had earned a fortune through its sale. Between 1878 and 1884, a new district was quickly established, since the brothers

Pereire attached to the sale of each parcel the condition that it be developed within six months. The exterior design of the houses had to correspond to the Haussmann style. In this manner, a harmoniously coordinated residential district came into being.

Soon, the townsfolk no longer had the district to themselves. Businesses popped up, especially along the Rue Bayen, on which the **Château des Ternes** is also located. Constructed in the 16th century on the foundations of an old farmstead, it belonged to the Bishop of Paris; from the beginning of the 18th century, a wealthy state official. Since it was split into two parts by the Rue Bayen, it looks even more original. Its peculiar mutation is due to the remodelling efforts of architect Nicholas Renoir in 1778. The castle was previously surrounded by a hamlet that went down in history when the rebellious elements of the Neuilly Commune assembled there.

Above: Music from the accordéon – the typical accompaniment for chansons.

In the village of **Monceau**, the feif of the Duc d'Orléans, a small hamlet existed in the 9th century. It was populated by the farm hands, farmers and gardeners who had settled around Monceau Castle. If it were still standing its entrance would be located in the Rue Legendre.

Several streets away from the Gare Saint-Lazare, at the borderline between the 8th and 17th arrondissement, is the **Parc Monceau**, a real paradise for children. The Duc d'Orléans had his hunting grounds here, later transformed by Hubert Robert into a landscaped park in the English style fashionable at that time. Robert also had "modern," romantic ruins installed – newly renovated, they still lend the gardens a rococo character.

In May 1871, during the suppression of the Paris Commune by the troups loyal to the French government in Versailles, the dead from the violent street battles with the *Fédérés* (the rebellious National Guard of the city) were hastily buried in the Parc Monceau and the Square des Batignolles.

8th, 16th AND 17th ARRONDISSEMENT
Accommodation

LUXURY: **Hôtel Georges V**, 36, av. Georges V., Tel: 47 23 54 00. **La Villa Maillot**, 143, av. de Malakoff, Tel: 45 01 25 22. **Le Méridien Paris Etoile**, 81, bd.Gouvion St.-Cyr, Tel: 40 68 34 34. **Sofitel Paris**, CNIT 2, pl. de la Défense, BP 210, 92053 Paris la Défense, Tel: 46 92 10 10. *MODERATE:* **Hôtel La Boétie**, 81, rue La Boétie, Tel: 42 25 56 54. **Résidence Trocadéro**, 3, av. Raymond Poincaré, Tel: 47 27 33 30. **Etoile Péreire**, 146, bd. Péreire, Tel: 42 67 60 00. **Hôtel Madeleine Opéra**, 12, rue Greffuhle, Tel: 47 42 26 26. **Le Hameau de Passy**, 48, rue de Passy, Tel: 42 88 47 55. **Élysée Étoile**, 5, rue de l'Étoile, Tel: 43 80 22 19. **Hôtel Wilson**, 10, rue de Stockholm, Tel: 45 22 10 85. **Résidence Orion**, 8, bd. de Neuilly, La Défense 1, 92400 Courbevoie, Tel: 47 78 15 01. *CAMPING:* **Camping du Bois de Boulogne**: Allée du Bord de l'Eau, Tel: 45 24 30 00 (open all year).

Restaurants / Nightlife

Le Bacchus Gourmand, 21, rue François 1er, Tel: 47 20 15 83, Nouvelle Cuisine. **Le Bonaventure**, 35, rue Jean-Goujon, Tel: 42 25 02 58, Nouvelle Cuisine. **Le Pré Catelan**, Route de Suresne, Bois de Boulogne, Tel: 45 24 55 58, excellent French cuisine, interior in the style of Napoléon III, very expensive. **La Péniche**, Allée du Bord de l'Eau, Tel: 42 88 01 88, traditional food. **La Cloche à Fromages**, 71, bd. Gouvion Saint-Cyr, Tel: 45 72 50 06, cheese specialities, wine. **Chez Fred**, 190, bd. Péreire, Tel: 45 74 20 48, pub with sausage specialities from Lyon. **Café de France**, Parvis de la Défense, Tel: 47 76 15 28, traditional food. **The Blue Fox Bar,** 25, rue Royale, Métro Madeleine, wine bar for connoisseurs, Mon-Fri 12.00 noon-10.00 p.m. **L'Écluse**, 64, rue François 1er, Tel: 47 20 77 09, wine bar. **Lido**, 116, av. des Champs-Élysées, Tel: 45 63 11 61, spectacular variety shows from 10.00 p.m.

Museums / Sightseeing

Arc de Triomphe, place de l'Étoile, April 1–Sept 30 open 10.00 a.m.-5.30 p.m., Oct 1–March 31 open 10.00 a.m.-5.00 p.m. **Tour Eiffel**, Champ de Mars, Tel: 45 55 91 11, Métro Trocadéro, in summer 9.30 a.m.-midnight, in winter 10.00 a.m.-11.00 p.m., observation platform on the 3rd story, restaurant. **Musée d'Art Moderne de la Ville de Paris,** 11, av. du Pt. Wilson, Métro Iéna, open 10.00 a.m.-5.30 p.m., closed Mon. **Musée Guimet**, Asian art, 6, pl. d'Iéna, Métro Iéna, 9.45 a.m.-5.15 p.m., closed Tue. **Musée des Arts et Traditions Populaires**, 6, av. du Mahatma Gandhi, Métro Porte Maillot,open 9.45 a.m.-5.15 p.m., closed Tue. **Maison de Balzac**, 47, rue Raynouard, Métro Passy, 10.00 a.m.-5.40 p.m., closed Mon. **Musée d'Arts Chinoises,** 7, av. Velasquez, Métro Monceau, open 10.00 a.m.-5.40 p.m., closed Mon and public holidays. **Musée en Herbe Jardin d'Acclimatation Bois de Boulogne**, open 10.00 a.m.-6.00 p.m., closed Saturday mornings.
The **Palais de Chaillot**, 17, pl. du Trocadéro, contains the **Musée du Cinéma,** (Tel: 45 53 74 39, open 10.00 a.m.-12.00 noon and 2.00-5.00 p.m., closed Tue), the **Musée de la Marine** (Tel: 45 53 31 70, open daily 10.00 a.m.-6.00 p.m., closed Tue), the **Théâtre Chaillot** (State Theater) and the **Musée National des Monuments Français** (Tel: 47 27 35 74, open daily 9.00 a.m.-6.00 p.m., closed Tue).
Musée Marmottan (Institut de France), 2, rue Louis Boilly, Métro Muette, 10.00 a.m.-5.30 p.m., closed Mon. **Palais de la Découverte**, av. Franklin Roosevelt, Métro Champs-Élysées Clémenceau, open 10.00 a.m.-6.00 p.m., closed Mon. **Musée du Petit Palais**, av. Winston Churchill, 10.00 a.m.-5.40 p.m., closed Mon. **Musée de Radio France**, 116, av. du Pt. Kennedy, Métro Passy, open 10.30 a.m.-4.30 p.m., except Sun and public holidays. **La Grande Arche de la Défense**, open Mon–Fri 9.00 a.m.-5.00 p.m., Sun and public holidays 10.00 a.m.-7.00 p.m.

Shopping

Boutiques: Elegant shops along the Champs-Élysées and the rues du Faubourg Saint-Honoré and Royale tempt the more affluent visitors. **FNAC:** bookstore selling international literature, records, hifi etc., 26, av. Wagram.
Stamp Exchange: Carré Marigny, Métro Champs-Élysées Clémenceau, Thur, Sat, Sun.

Boat Trips

Departure from the Pont de l'Alma bridge, Métro Alma Marceau, daily at 11.00 a.m., 2.30, 4.00 and 9.00 p.m.

Post / Police / Pharmacy

Post Offices: 8th Arr.: 71, av. des Champs-Élysées. 14, rue du Colisée. **16th Arr.:** 3, pl. Victor Hugo. **17th Arr.:** 110, av. de Wagram. **Police: 8th Arr.:** 1, av. du Général Eisenhower. **16th Arr.:** 58, av. Mozart. **17th Arr.:** 19, rue Truffaut. **Pharmacy:** Dhéry, 84, av. des Champs-Élysées (open 24 hours daily).

Exchange

13, rue Royale, Mon–Sat 9.00 a.m.-6.30 p.m., Sun and public holidays 10.00 a.m.-6.00 p.m. **CFC**, 25, av. des Champs-Élysées, daily 9.00 a.m.-8.00 p.m. **Thomas Cook,** Gare St.-Lazare (rail terminal), daily from 7.00 a.m.-9.00 p.m.

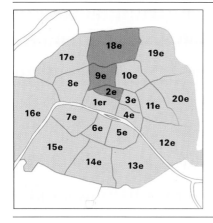

THE PULSE OF PARIS

**SENTIER DISTRICT
GRANDS BOULEVARDS
L'OPÉRA
MONTMARTRE
PIGALLE
FLEA MARKETS**

The Sentier district is known for its chic boutiques selling high-class *prêt-à-porter* fashions; Saint Ouen, on the other hand, has a world-famous flea market, complemented by a host of run-down junk stores. The throng strolling along the Grands Boulevards can choose from a number of luxurious department stores that date back to the wild capitalist days of the late 19th century. These areas may strike one as being utterly different in style – and they are –, but they are linked by a solid mercantile tradition going back over 100 years.

From the center of Paris to the northern *Périphérique*, the scene is dominated by a constant bustle of activity. In the shadow of the flurry, though, one can still visit the city's last remaining glass arcades with their little luxury boutiques (preserved in original style). These structures formed the center of retail life until the turn of the century. In the meanwhile, the old owners have given up their shops and several of the smaller arcades now look quite dilapidated. Others have become occupied by expensive galleries, spruced up in post modern fashion, but still inviting you to press your nose on

Previous pages: Toulouse Lautrecs – affordable for all pocketbooks. Left: Steep steps leading up to Sacré-Cœur.

their windows. These include the Galerie Vivienne, Passage de Choiseul and Passage des Panoramas.

La Butte (hill) Montmartre, towers over the entire area, which has managed to preserve its original village charm, although it has also developed into a significant tourist center.

Day and night, the curious public moves around Montmartre and along the boulevards of Pigalle, climbing up the stairs to the Sacré-Cœur and back down again. The narrow side-streets, which often suddenly turn into steep stairways, are among the "must sees" – and a valuable "must do" for physical fitness – for visitors to Paris.

Several steps removed from *La Butte* is the district Barbès-La Goutte d'Or, an inviting place for an exotic window-shopping tour: African baskets, a complete tea service for mint tea, spices and jewelry from the Antilles, among many other items can be admired (and purchased!) here. Unknown treasures from faraway lands and islands await discovery.

SENTIER DISTRICT
2nd and 9th Arrondissement

The loading hoists in the narrow, crowded streets of the **Sentier district** have disappeared. This area is now in-

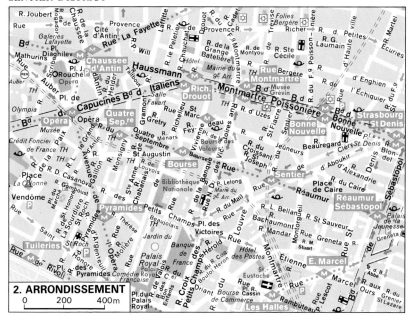

2. ARRONDISSEMENT

0   200   400m

habited by fashion moguls, whose stylish shops sell ostentatious creations at astronomical prices. Still, sprinkled here and there among them are the odd old butcher shops, fishmongers and greengrocers. Consuming quite literally kilometers of fabric in the process, the designers' collections originate in their often rather well-hidden studios above and behind the shops.

The roofed-in, occasionally rather sleepy-looking shopping arcades between the Sentier district and the Grands Boulevards provide some insight into the world of 19th century luxury items, as they were frequently described by Balzac. In those days, Paris had more than 130 such arcades. With their abundantly decorated display windows, filled with the accoutrements of affluence of the emerging industrial society as well as artisans' handicrafts, they attracted the ladies of the upper class like some kind of magic charm. People shopped here, went out to eat, strolled about and met their friends for a tête-à-tête. The arcades were

rendered "superfluous," by and large, by the development of the automobile and the construction of the major department stores. About 20 in all have been preserved, and additional ones are now being restored.

If you are standing before the Saint-Eustache Church behind the Forum des Halles, you should take a walk through the weekly markets in the **Rue de Montorgueil** and the **Rue des Petits-Carreaux**, the old halls of which have been preserved as the last relics of the so-called "belly of Paris." Then you will come upon the **Place du Caire** with its heavily ornamented, hieroglyphic façades. (The street names Caire, Aboukir and Alexandria are in memory of Napoléon's 1798 Egyptian campaign).

In the 17th century the *Cours des Miracles* was located here – literally, the Courtyard of Miracles – complete with tightrope walkers, storytellers, prostitutes and petty criminals.

In his novel *The Hunchback of Notre-Dame*, Victor Hugo brought this world back to life: Its inhabitants subsisted from begging and theft, straying through the streets and choosing their own king and queen (who didn't necessarily conduct themselves in a particularly noble manner). Today it is the pulsating center of the Sentier district.

Across the Place du Caire is the **Passage du Caire,** a lively market street. Keep in mind that the majority of the arcades lock their gates at 7 pm.

One of the passages leads to the notorious **Rue Saint-Denis,** which was already a prime turf for Parisian ladies of the night during the reign of Charlemagne. Their services are still available around the clock.

Continue from here straight down to the **Rue Réaumur.** Since the days of the Revolution this section of the Sentier has been a center of the press, roughly corresponding to London's Fleet Street, with many printers and newspaper publishers. During the seventies and eighties, however, a number of newspapers either moved away or had to close their doors. Their former offices in these buildings, which feature a characteristic steelwork construction, have been filled by a growing number of clothing wholesalers. In 1989, *France Soir* also moved out, leaving only *Le Figaro* to carry the torch (on the Rue de Louvre).

Right next door to the stock exchange, in the large building of the **NMPP** (*Nouvelles Messageries de la Presse Parisienne),* all the major French as well as the most important European and American newspapers and magazines are available. Not far from here, opposite the exchange, is the headquarters of the **AFP** (*Agence France Presse),* the third-largest press agency behind AP and UPI.

The **stock exchange** (*La Bourse* in French) is now situated in the former Palais Brongniard. In this 19th-century temple of capitalism, through which a teeming throng of speculators streams between 11:00 am and 1:00 pm, one can find out about the latest market quotations (for information call 42-33-99-83).

Standing on the **Place de la Bourse** you find yourself in the midst of the city's glass arcade "center." The Rue Vivienne alone has two outstandingly well-restored and revivified examples of these glazed structures, which were formerly threatened by utter decay.

The **Galerie Vivienne**, which begins opposite the stock exchange, is particularly impressive. United under its roofs (resembling a huge, idyllic conservatory), are a tea room and some extraordinary boutiques, interior decoration shops and booksellers.

This is also where the renowned young French fashion designer Jean-Paul Gaultier has his post-modern boutique, spartanly appointed in iron, steel and neon, and worth a detour to get a look at. If you're interested in fashion, the most daring of Parisian whimsy can be viewed here. Among other notable works, Gaultier designed Madonna's costume for her most recent film.

The freshly restored **Galerie Colbert**, opposite the Bibliothèque Nationale, has frequent exhibitions of old fashions, books and antiques in a very pleasant atmosphere amid its columns of amber. Between 12:00 noon and 6:00 pm one should pay – without fail – a visit to the **Bibliothèque Nationale**, the national "book sanctuary" (entrance on the Rue Richelieu). For centuries, thousands of books, magazines and unpublished works of French authors have been collected here – to date some eight to ten million volumes. Frequent special exhibitions are displayed in its beautiful Mazarine and Mansart galleries.

Rightwards down the Rue des Petits-Champs takes you to nr. 42, where the **Passage Choiseul** begins. It was made famous by the poetry of Paul Verlaine and re-dubbed the *Passage des Bérésinas* by the novelist Louis-Ferdinand Céline. In the latter's *Mort à Credit* novel *(Death on the Installment Plan)* he drew an apo-

calyptic vision of life in this passage, a view one can hardly connect with its present-day quiet charm. In the beginning of this century, Céline lived here for several years; his mother ran a small shop where she sold antiques and old-fashioned lace underwear.

The publishing firm of Alphonse Lemerre, which printed the works of many poets of the Parnasse, had also its offices here. Today, there's only the sizeable *Lavrut* stationery store, selling a wide variety of paper, writing utensils and erasers – a very modest reminder of this passage's literary tradition. At nightfall, this street frequently has a rather peculiar look to it; in fact, sometimes it's downright creepy.

The Rue Saint-Augustin connects back to the Place de la Bourse. The Rue

Above: The glass dome in Galeries Lafayette department store. Above right: In the Galerie Vivienne near the stock exchange. Right: The opera house Garnier is a magnificent building of its time.

Vivienne continues alongside the stock exchange to the Rue Saint-Marc, where some of the livelier arcades leading to the famed Grands Boulevards are situated.

The **Passage des Panoramas** begins at nr. 10, Rue Saint-Marc, where the city's first gas lanterns were installed in 1817. The little shops here survive from their regular customers. The copper engraving firm *Stern* has been housed here for over 150 years. The residents of the second stories maintain the pleasant tradition of decorating their windows with flowers.

At the other end of the passage, on the Boulevard Montmartre, is the **Théâtre des Variétés**, which has been a traditional showplace for vaudeville theater and operettas such as Offenbach's *La Vie Parisienne* since 1807.

If one crosses the Boulevard Montmartre after leaving the Passage des Panoramas, one can proceed into the **Passage Jouffroy** at nr. 12. A brisk whirlwind of commercial activity predominates within its confines. Neon advertisements in three languages bid the tourist welcome.

On the other side of the Rue de la Grange Batelière, this passage empties into the **Passage Verdeau**. The shopkeepers here are sometimes heard to complain of too few customers, even though here are real gold mines for such rarities as old photographic equipment, art postcards and travel souvenirs behind some of their doors.

On the boulevard opposite the entrance to the Passage de Jouffroy is the **Musée Grévin**, where one can admire wax figures of personalities from French history, famed television stars, actors, singers, other entertainers and soccer players. It first opened its doors in 1882. Among its special exhibits is an ancient *laterna magica,* a precurser of the movie camera, and indeed a popular form of entertainment in the days of yore.

Paris' most recent passage, relatively speaking at least, is the 1860 **Passage des Princes,** starting at nr. 5, Boulevard des Italiens. It was a favorite meeting place for the Surrealists during the period between the two World Wars.

GRANDS BOULEVARDS

The traditional promenades of the **Grands Boulevards** extend some three kilometers from the Opéra to the Place de la Bastille. Unfortunately, today they look somewhat abandoned in spite of their busy night life. Their erstwhile charm, so praised by Yves Montand in the song *J'aime flâner sur les Grand Boulevards* (I like to stroll along the Grands Boulevards) has vanished. With their numerous cinemas, theaters and brasseries, sidewalk cafés, the boulevards – from **Saint-Martin** to **Bonne Nouvelle**, **Montmartre**, **Italiens** and **Capucines** – continue to be the heart of Parisian nightlife. They lead directly to the Place de l'Opéra and the incomparable *grands magasins* (the department stores) on the Boulevard Haussmann.

During the 17th century, the first boulevard along the old northern city wall was still located outside of the municipal limits. Shortly before the Revolution, it was a popular route for

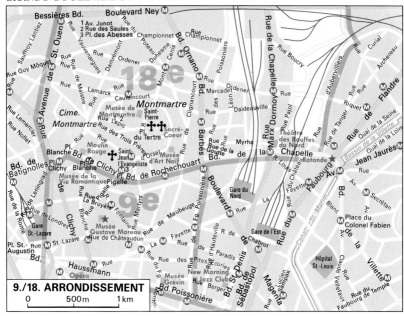

9./18. ARRONDISSEMENT

0   500m   1km

pedestrian and coach excursions. Peddlers and shopkeepers came, then restaurants and cafés were built, followed later by dance halls and theaters. The latter primarily featured melodramatic pieces dealing with love, murder and perfidy. Maybe because of them, the street eventually acquired the nickname *Boulevard du Crime*, the Boulevard of Crime. The stretch between the Boulevard des Italiens and the Boulevard Montmartre developed into its most renowned section. Both history and fashion were, quite literally, made here.

When Baron Haussmann re-designed the streets between the Place de la République and the Place de l'Opéra, he obliterated the greater part of the *Boulevard du Crime* by laying out the main axes dead straight through the urban landscape. Nonetheless, the brasseries and theaters stayed where they were, and the boulevard continued to be a popular place for amusements of every sort.

In the evening one can attend a witty comedy in the Théâtre du Boulevard, or perhaps see a performance in the Caveau de la République, the Théâtre de la Porte Saint-Martin, in the Opéra Comique or in the Bouffes Parisienne, followed up by dinner in a brasserie.

L'OPÉRA

In 1860, the young architect Charles Garnier prevailed with his vision of a new Parisian opera. He designed and built it in the gingerbread style of the Second Empire, but completed it during the Third Republic, in 1875. Tickets for admission to the Opéra are hard to come by. Even if you are unable to obtain some, you should try to experience the gold and velvet ambience of the building itself (the main entrance hall is open from 11 am to 4:30 pm). The *grand escalier,* the ostentatious staircase at the entrance, leads to the *grand foyer*, through which one proceeds to the pompously ornamented loges of the auditorium.

Despite its 11,000 sqm, this gigantic structure can only admit an audience of

2200. Only quite recently, the non-operatic theater company moved out. It relocated to the Opéra de la Bastille, which was opened with great pomp and ceremony in 1989, on the occasion of the French Revolution's 200th anniversary.

The ceiling frescoes of the Opéra were conceived and painted in lively colors by Marc Chagall in 1964. Hanging in the center, is an immense crystal chandelier weighing six tons.

It is of interest to note that the massive opera house was constructed above a subterranean river that still feeds an underground artificial lake to this day. The *Phantom of the Opera*, created by Gaston Leroux, is said to continue his sinister doings down below.

The Department Stores

On a visit to Paris one should by all means take time to explore the department stores **Printemps** and **Galeries Lafayette** on the Boulevard Haussmann. The tradition of these institutions extends back to the year 1850. Since that time these famous *grands magasins* have been attracting their predominantly female clientele as though there were a magical spell over them.

The Printemps (1869) and the Galeries Lafayette (1894) still have their heavily ornamented original façades. The stores' selections range from elegant *prêt-a-porter* (ready-to-wear) fashions, exquisite fabrics and linens, to lingerie, lovely porcelain, valuable rugs, perfumes, cosmetics and select gifts.

These huge department stores are themselves distributed among several buildings, divided into mens', womens' and childrens' sections with additional services, including an underground parking garage, interpreters, currency exchange booths and banks, as well as an outstanding retaurant (naturally).

The Printemps' top-floor restaurant, for example, is underneath an Art Nouveau glass dome that has deservedly been placed under historical preservation.

The New Athens

About half way between the *grands magasins* and Pigalle one should take advantage of the opportunity to explore – on foot – the little-known **Nouvelle Athènes**. In the middle of the last century, a multitude of newly-erected townhouses in neo-classical style gave this neighborhood its name. George Sand, Chopin, Berliosz and Delacroix were among the area's residents.

Place Saint-George with its somewhat portly architecture of sandstone ashlars with monumental entrance portals is characteristic of this quarter. There are also a number of antique shops here with display windows full of 19th-century paintings from the French Academy.

Continue along the Rue de la Bruyère to get to the Rue de la Rochefoucauld and the **Musée Gustave Moreau** at nr. 14. Already in 1895, the Symbolist painter had remodeled his private residence into a public museum to provide a lasting setting for his 6000 oil paintings, drawings and watercolors. The visitor is allowed free movement throughout the house to admire his luscious and audacious treatments of mythological and biblical images. The house's rather peculiar atmosphere attracted André Breton and the Surrealists in the period between the two World Wars.

The **Musée de la Vie Romantique** also constitutes a part of Nouvelle Athènes. It is located at 16, Rue Chaptal, an address frequented by such figures as Ingres, Delacroix, Liszt and Chopin in the days when George Sand held court in its salons on a regular basis some 150 years ago. The museum is dedicated primarily to her. It displays books, portraits, furniture and personal collector's items gathered with romantic sensibility by George Sand herself.

At the Foot of Montmartre

Before climbing *la butte,* one should become familiar with the boulevards extending along its base. This is a good place for a concentrated experience of the proverbial "Paris by night," since a peculiar blend of people wanders through these streets. Only in the wee hours, when the proper tourist is snoozing soundly in his or her hotel room, do the shady characters of the city once again have their bars to themselves.

Up into the fifties, **Place Clichy** was the heart of this entertainment district. The renowned Gaumont Palace, then the largest cinema in Paris, stood on the corner of Rue Caulaincourt and Calais. Despite angry protests, it was demolished in the seventies to make room for a shopping street and two new hotels. The *Wepler,* which still stands, is one of the last grand old cinemas here.

Above: Some like it hot! Right: The Moulin Rouge is said to be the birthplace of the famous cancan.

Walking along the **Boulevard Clichy** one passes a multitude of cinemas, restaurants and brasseries on the way to **Place Blanche,** which owes its name to its formerly white pavement stones. The world-famous **Moulin Rouge** is located on this square. During the *belle époque* the notorious *chahut,* later called the *cancan* – the dance with the kick made famous by Jacques Offenbach and immortalized on the posters of artist Henri Toulouse-Lautrec – had its première here. A big scandal brewed up over the Moulin Rouge in 1896 when a women undressed right down to her birthday suit in a striptease competition at a *bal des quat'z'arts* (the ball of the four arts) arranged by students of the art academy. The event's organizers were sentenced to three months in prison, which lead to protest marches in the Quartier Latin, the student district.

Further along the Boulevard Clichy, one eventually reaches **Place Pigalle** by weaving between innumerable tourist buses. Here, in the midst of the *milieu,* many *films noirs* were shot during the fifties and sixties. Even if an occasional street criminal snatches an occasional handbag or two and some pretty shady-looking characters are hanging around, the big-time gangsters disappeared from this neighborhood quite some time ago.

Nowadays, all the brightly-lit streets around here are filled with sex-shops, porno shows and some more-or-less tasteful cabarets, enticing their customers with rather graphic photos. If you allow yourself to be lured in by a doorkeeper, be aware that the entrance price bears no relationship to bill that must be paid at the conclusion of the performance. Since the 18th century this area has been a frequented stronghold of the most time-honored profession.

Now head onto the **Boulevard de Rochechouart**, on which a major street festival is held in December. The renowned **Cabaret Chat Noir** ("The Black Cat") was once located in nr. 84, a night-

spot frequented by humorist Alphonse Allais, Toulouse-Lautrec and *chanson* singer Aristide Bruand. This noisy little smoke-filled salon was also a popular meeting place for groups of avant-garde artists and people in revolt against the academic traditions – the *Hydropathes* and the *Hirsutes*, the predecessors of Dadaism.

To this day, the **Élysée-Montmartre** is located in nr. 72. This ballroom was opened in 1807 and continued to serve as the most popular meeting place for those afflicted with dance mania until it was supplanted by the Moulin Rouge. La Goulue, Nini Pattes en l'Air and Jane Avril once performed there. Presently, a rock club lurks behind its splendidly preserved façade.

MONTMARTRE

Artists have been living in this most picturesque of all Parisian districts, **Montmartre**, for generations. Utrillo and Toulouse-Lautrec have immortalized it in their works. Whether summer or winter, it is one of the most popular destinations for tourists from around the world, lending the bistros and souvenir shops at the Place du Tertre a cosmopolitan accent. Nonetheless, beyond the main paths of the tourist stampede there are still quiet side streets on the *butte* which have retained their old village charm.

In the days when the Gallic city was still named *Lutetia,* a temple to the god Mercury during the period of Roman occupation crowned the hill. Around AD. 250, according to the local legend, Saint-Denis, the first Bishop of Paris, and several of his compatriots were tortured and then decapitated here.

Since that time, the place has been called *Mons Martyrium*, Hill of the Martyrs, from which the present-day name Montmartre was derived.

From 1134 until the Revolution, a famous cloister, directly subordinate to the king, stood on Montmartre. A religious community had settled here and lived quite well from the production and

sale of its wine. In 1794, the last abbess was beheaded, the cloister was leveled, and the hill renamed Mont Marat. All that remains of the wealthy old convent is the **Église Saint-Pierre** next to the church of Sacré-Cœur.

In 1860, when Baron Haussmann incorporated Montmartre into the city, the small village was still situated amidst pastures and fields. No less than 30 windmills ground wheat into flour. However, the millers' guild could no longer keep up the competition with industrial mills. At the same time deposits of gypsum were discovered under the hill, which was gradually hollowed out in Swiss-cheese fashion. Parisian workers, who could no longer afford to live in their old city districts after the re-designing job of Haussmann, settled in increasing numbers in Montmartre. In 1871, following the capitulation before the Prussian army,

Above: A typical narrow street in "Butte Montmartre". Right: An emulator of Pissarro tries to make a living with the paint brush.

they participated quite actively in the Paris Commune, which ended in a bloodbath and renewed oppression. The mayor of Montmartre at the time was Georges Clemenceau.

From 1880 to the turn of the century, Montmartre experienced its heyday as the great anti-establishment quarter, the haven of the famous *Bohème*. In its cabarets, "immoral" performances were put on, which sent shivers of fear and horror up the spines of residents in the city's fancier neighborhoods. To this day, one can still detect this tradition of anarchism and struggle for free expression in Montmartre.

Poets and painters come to the hill for inspiration. Located near the center of Paris, cabarets, bistros and ballrooms have also been constructed. A motley crowd of workers, prostitutes, criminals, philosophers, artists of every sort and and experts in the "art of life" mingle together in public.

When from the corner of Élysée-Montmartre you head to your left on the **Rue**

d'Avignon here, a work heralding the beginning of Cubism.

The **Place Jean-Baptiste Clément** was created in memory of the mayor of Paris during the period of the Commune. Clément also wrote the revolutionary song *Le Temps des Cerises (*The Time of the Cherries). In his honor, cherry trees have been planted on the plaza.

The neighborhood's smaller side-streets, which often make one forget the proximity of hypermodern Paris **La Bonne Franquette**, on the corner of the Rue Saint-Rustique and Rue des Saules, was a renowned cabaret around the turn of the century. This street corner also appears in some of Utrillo's paintings. The narrow **Rue Saint-Rustique** is the oldest of the village's streets (from the 9th century!) and features aged cobblestone pavements and gutters running down the center. In addition, it is the highest point in Paris at 129.37 m above sea level.

Above: Many, Parisians and tourists, yearn for the idyllic past of Montmartre.

The **Rue Poulbot** looks like a little country road. It is named after the creator of the *Gamins* (little rascals) *de Montmartre*, reproductions of whose works are sold by the dozen on the Place du Tertre.

There are depictions of the most important episodes in Montmartre history, from the 12th-century abbey to the *Cabaret Chat Noir* during the period of the Commune, in the **Historial Wax Museum** (nr. 11, Rue Poulbot; open daily from 10 am–6 pm).

The **Place du Tertre**, Montmartre's old market square, is now the hill's primary tourist attraction. Early in the morning before it has come to life, it offers a delightfully calm atmosphere in which one can enjoy breakfast at a streetside café. During the day, however, it is inundated with a flood of tourists. Dozens of canvas-daubers put their masterpieces on sale here. The surrounding restaurants are also besieged by the sightseers. With their red-and-white checkered table-cloths, "authentic" bar counters and cabaret spectacles, these tourist traps are still trying to convey a feeling of being original. One is better off avoiding them.

The **Église St Pierre**, which can be seen to the right behind the Place du Tertre, is Paris' oldest church and the only remaining portion of the abbey founded there in 1133 by Louis VI the Fat. Standing in its interior are four Gallo-Roman marble columns. They may well have originated in the ancient Temple of Mercury.

The **Sacré-Cœur Basilica** is located only a few meters from the Place du Tertre. Even now, some 80 years after its completion, the church's architectural style is still the subject of heated controversy. The Parisians themselves scoffingly refer to their city's dominant landmark as "Neo-Byzantine gingerbread." In 1873, the Catholic church decided to erect a basilica in "atonement" for the "crimes" of the Communards at the germinal point of the Commune that erupted after the Franco-Prussian War. Financed with subscriptions to a "national people's vow," the church on this venerated location was intended to morally re-arm the "true France." When the contract for its design was awarded to then-fashionable architect Paul Abadie, a multitude of artists and intellectuals protested against this "abberration of taste."

A tour of its profusely ornamented interior might well be disappointing. Mosaics depict the pilgrimage haltingplaces of the *Eternal Adoration*. In the main dome one can view the ceiling fresco *France's Adoration of the Sacred Heart of Jesus*. A total of 237 steps lead up to the dome, from which there is a commanding view of Paris and, when the weather is right, of the surroundings to a distance of more than 30 km. The Sacré-Cœur possesses one of the largest bells in the world, the **Savoyarde**, named after Savoy where it was cast in 1895. It weighs a total of 19 tons. Behind the Sacré-Cœur take a left into the Rue du

Chevalier de la Barre and then go right into the **Rue du Mont Cenis**. There you will see a century-old water tower.

The **Musée de Montmartre** (nr. 12, Rue Cortot) was installed in a 17th-century country manor by Rose de Rosimond, a member of Molière's theater troupe. Renoir, Raoul Dufy, Suzanne Valadon and her son Utrillo have resided within its walls. The salons are filled with memorabilia from the good old *bohème* days in Montmartre. Works by Van Dongen, Dufy, Utrillo and many unknowns hang here, as well as a number of posters, caricatures and old photographs. An old bistro has also been reconstituted within its walls, and many of its souvenirs hark back to the days of the Commune.

A bit further downhill, in the **Rue des Saules**, you will discover a vineyard. Tiny though it may be, the **Vigne du Clos Montmartre** is a source of pride for the local residents. A renowned wine was once cultivated all over the *butte*. The now largely symbolic grape harvest takes place on the first Saturday of October, accompanied by a great festival, the *Fête des Vendanges.* About 500 bottles of the *Vin du Clos* are produced; they can be purchased (very pricey) in the **Mairie du 18e** (the city hall of the 18th Arrondissement). The proceeds from its sale are still devoted to the preservation of Montmartre.

Directly opposite the vineyard at nr. 22 is the **Lapin Agile**. This rose-hued building with its green window-shutters is one of Montmartre's biggest attractions. In 1860, the *Cabaret des Assassins* (the cabaret of the "hashish-eaters") was founded within it. It continued until 1880, when André Gill established a restaurant here. This is the place famed for rabbits jumping out of its casseroles, hence the building's name *Le Lapin à Gill* (Gill's Rabbit, whereby *agile* also means agile). Verlaine, Renoir, Utrillo, Toulouse-Lautrec, Apollinaire and Clemenceau used to stop in here to drink and

listen to *chansons*. Picasso, who was usually broke in those days, paid for a meal with one of his harlequin paintings. The chansonnier Aristide Bruand purchased the building in 1903 and thus protected it from demolition.

Nowadays, the *Lapin Agile* has the best cabaret in Montmartre; its decor has scarcely changed through the years. The walls are filled with paintings by Fernand Léger, Gill and drawings by Bruand. Every evening the performance in this small hall is sold out.

The younger generation of *chanson* singers has also studied here: Annie Girardot, Georges Brassens and Claude Nougaro all made their first appearances here. The evening production, *La Veillée*, begins at 9 pm daily except Mondays.

Now ascend the Rue des Saules again and turn right into the **Rue de l'Abreuvoir,** named for a spring once used for watering livestock. Turn into the **Allée**

Above: Palette upon palette – "true" artists and hobby painters in Montmartre.

des Brouillards, which is surrounded by charming houses with little front gardens. Renoir lived in nr. 8. The large white building to the left is the **Château des Brouillards**, an 18th-century folly. A climb down a flight of stairs brings one to the old castle garden, which has now been transformed into the **Square Suzanne Buisson**.

From this point you should head into the **Avenue Junot**, which in 1910 was struck through the "Montmartre ungle," a peculiar turf filled with brothels and dubious meeting places of crooks and swindlers – not especially recommended for a night-time stroll. Nowadays the apartments in its numerous Art-Deco era buildings are among the most coveted in Montmartre.

Head back uphill to your left. Turning off beside nr. 23 is the **Villa Léandre**, most probably the quietest street in Paris. Lined up along this cul-de-sac are low, diminutive cottages with attractive little gardens, quite reminiscent of London's Kensington district. The actors Jean Marais and Anouk Aimée reside here.

The **Place Marcel Aymé**, at the top of the Avenue Junot, is named after the author of *Passe mureille* (The Man Who Could Walk through Walls), who once lived here. His monument is a figure that appears to be jumping out of a wall, a bronze sculpture created by Jean Marais. Across the way, Louis-Ferdinand Céline resided from 1940 to 1944 in the Rue Girardon.

By following it, you arrive back at the **Rue Lepic**. Here on the corner, the **Moulin Radet** is still located above the restaurant *Da Graziano*. At the lower end of the Rue Lepic, across from the Rue Tholozé, you can admire the famed **Moulin de la Galette**, whose ball goings-on have been rendered unforgettable by Renoir. (The painting in question hangs in the Musée d'Orsay.)

The **Cimetière de Montmartre** (entrance located on the Avenue Rachel at the Place Clichy; open from 8 am to 5:30 pm) is surrounded by a high wall. Crowded tightly together here are the graves of Stendhal, Degas, Offenbach, Sacha Guitry, François Truffaut, Dalida and Heinrich Heine, among many others.

La Goutte d'Or
– The Orient in Paris –

Beyond the pretty houses and the fashionable unconventionality of old Montmartre, to the east of the hill, lies a quarter with quite a different character: Maghrebine Paris. Having been a workers' district since the 19th century (it was the setting for Zola's *L'Assommoir*), the **Goutte d'Or** ("drop of gold") quarter absorbed a wave of Arabic immigrants during the fifties and sixties of the 20th century. Since the seventies it has also been home to a large number of African immigrants.

A new world opens up to you on leaving the Barbès métro station. **Barbès** is the center of the Islamic community and a bustling business district. Clustered along its narrow lanes are Muslim bakeries, butcher shops and textile merchants. This is also their most important cultural center. Many Arabic musicians have installed their studios in the rear courtyards. Millions of cassettes are produced here and distributed in North Africa.

In the meantime this quarter has also come under threat from some real-estate sharks. Many run-down buildings have been demolished, giving way to sterile concrete bunkers.

The neighborhood does not exactly enjoy the best of reputations, particularly because of its drug scene. Even today, many of the bars serve coffee with a spoon with a hole in the middle, so that it can't be used by the junkies for preparing their next fix. Nonetheless, one can still move about in the majority of its streets without danger to one's body.

Begin your walk on the **Rue de la Goutte d'Or**, which runs between the Barbès-Rochechouart and the Château Rouge Métro stations.

Many cafés are located here, illuminated with fluorescent lights and full of men playing dominoes or *trictrac*; there are swelled-to-bursting textile shops and plenty of little bazaars featuring cheap knick-knacks.

Every sort of African headgear as well as other exotic souvenirs can be found in nr. 42. Press the doorbell to enter the **Villa Poissonière**, which stands across a paved courtyard. Enveloped in its extraordinary quietude are wild gardens and country houses from the 19th century, many of which are decorated with ceramic tilework.

Now turn back to the lively street full of Muslim butcher shops unabashedly displaying their lambs' heads and legs. By following the **Rue Myrha** uphill, one lands right in the middle of "Africa", since all sorts of that continent's specialties are here to be discovered, ranging from sweet potatoes to undreamed-of spices and vegetables.

Restaurants, Nighttime Bars and Rock Clubs

An astounding density of entertainment spots are crowded together on the north side of Paris. In contrast to the "refined" districts on the west side of town, here one can find establishments open for eating and drinking at any hour of the day or night, especially in the streets around the Grands Boulevards, in Pigalle and Montmartre. This is where you will encounter the night-owls on their flight from one cabaret to the next.

In recent years this district has become increasingly popular amongst the 18-30 set. *Musette* (traditional) and rock-and-roll enliven the old theaters, many of which have recently been transformed into concert halls.

Above: Village atmosphere and quaint restaurants are among the typical features of the backstreets of Montmartre. Right: Romantic Montmartre, apparently far from the maddening crowd.

On the Grands Boulevards

The restaurants here squeeze their way right out onto the edge of the street. If you're looking for a special place, though, duck into the unobtrusive entrance of **Chez Chartier** (nr. 7, Rue du Faubourg-Montmartre, open daily until 9:30 pm). Thanks to its renowned speedy service there's never much of a wait. Chez Chartier has existed for over 150 years. In the rear courtyard you push on the heavy doorknob and suddenly find yourself in a dream world – a swarm of waiters buzz around with overflowing trays, and, miracle of miracles, though the place is overflowing and loud, they will be immediately at your service!

This spot is always full, but nobody has to make reservations. One can partake of their hearty traditional cuisine quickly and without much ado. Everything on the menu is quite tasty and rarely costs more than 50 francs. The waiters even permit the guests to add up the check themselves.

Those with an appetite for something exotic should head for **Chez Bébert** (Boulevard de Montmartre nr. 18). This immense restaurant, appointed in Oriental style, doesn't do its thing half-way: Even Gargantua (the giant created by the French Renaissance author Rabelais) could scarcely master one of their *couscous* platters. The service is very attentive. The first American restaurant, opened in 1947, is quite another thing. **Chez Haynes** is located at nr. 3, Rue Clauzel (open evenings except Sundays and Mondays until 12:30 am). The decor seems a bit florid; the music is an unending drone of country-and-western tunes and blues. But they serve outstanding, "classic" American cooking.

One has to have seen it to believe it. Even the *Guinness Book of World Records* takes note of it: The cheapest restaurant in the world is located in the 9th arrondissement! You have to figure on at

least an hour's wait on the street to get a seat in **La Casa Miguel** (nr. 48, Rue Saint-Georges). But the wait will definitely pay off. For many years Madame Maria, an octogenarian at the last count, has been cooking up a complete 3-course meal (appetizer, entrée and dessert with a glass of wine) for only 5 francs!

PIGALLE

When at the Place Clichy, you should seek out the **Brasserie Wepler**. Despite the somewhat gauche decor (in fake *belle époque* style), the brasserie has managed to retain its old, pre-war charm, harking back to the days when its public consisted of artists and the people coming in after a show in one of the grand old cinemas. Traditional French cuisine and seafood are its primary offerings.

Just a couple of strides further on, at Place Clichy nr. 12, you will find the **Charlot, Roi des Coquillages** ("king of the shellfish"), which remains open until 2 in the morning. It is an outstanding spot

to have dinner after attending the theater or cinema. Granted, in the last few years the inundation of tourists has driven the prices into the heights – its roster of customers has changed as well – but no matter what, their seafood continues to boast truly outstanding preparation.

In the night or early morning you can also sip a glass of champagne or a *kir framboise* in the **Pigalle** (on Place Pigalle). In the process, you might admire its pastel, fifties ambience. This spot is a hangout for night-owls and some rather dubious characters. The menu includes seafood and traditional cuisine.

In the Heart of Old Montmartre

Don't hesitate to stop into the minute restaurants along the narrow lanes of Montmartre. Look particularly for the *grands classiques*, such as **La Pomponnette** at nr. 42, Rue Lepic. The time-honored appointments of many of these places are still intact. Old posters are still glued up on the walls; drawings and pho-

171

tographs have stayed where they are since the turn of the century, thoroughly yellowed from decades of cigarette smoke. There is also some outstanding, classic French cuisine. Stroll up the Rue Lepic, to the renowned **Virage Lepic** (nr. 61). In its densely-packed atmosphere one can experience the real Montmartre. Whether intellectual or laborer, its customers are primarily French people who value good prices. A large selection of country wines and simple, good food awaits you here. **Négociants** is situated at the foot of the *butte* in nr. 27, Rue Lambert. This restaurant serves excellent traditional cuisine in a family atmosphere (large selection of wines).

Another insider's tip (and a gourmet rendezvous) is **La Casserole** at nr. 17, Rue Boinod. Although located a bit off the beaten track, this place is certainly

Above: Who will order the next "café express"? Above right: Even the organ-grinder "melts" at the sound of her music. Right: Nightlife in Pigalle.

worth the detour. From its walls and ceilings hang a variety of bizarre articles, stuffed animals and the like. An extraordinarily substantial cuisine is offered here, in autumn including wild game (wild boar, venison and rabbit) and even beaver and shark.

Restaurant chains are also trying to win a foothold in old Montmartre. In the **Tortilla Flat** (corner of Rue Lepic and Rue Tourlaque), rock music has assumed the place of the traditional *musette*. "Mexican" food accompanied by *tapas* and *tequila* is served there at tolerable prices amid a kitschy decor of ceiling fans and contemporary art.

Rock on the Pigalle

It's been a few years ago now since the rock clubs left the Halles district, and re-established themselves in Pigalle, where they brought new life to dilapidated theaters and converted former striptease joints to fit their needs. Meanwhile, the area has also become the location of most

of the city's music and instrument shops. The amateur looking for an electric guitar will discover a real gold mine along the Rue de Douai.

La Locomotive, located at Boulevard de Clichy nr. 90, is directly opposite the Moulin Rouge (Tel. 42573737). It was a legendary place in the sixties; *The Who* have also given some concerts there. The "Loc" was re-opened in 1986.

La Nouvelle Eve at nr. 25, Rue Fontaine is a striptease joint which opens its stage to rock musicians once a week.

In **Le New Moon**, nr. 66, Rue Pigalle, a steep staircase leads up to a tiny hall with coquettish decor from the seventies. This is the exclusive domain of rockers wearing skin-tight leather. At midnight it presents many rock concerts featuring Parisian groups. The club opens its doors nightly at 10:30 pm.

La Cigale on the Boulevard Rochechouart is a cabaret founded in 1887, in which Mistinguette once appeared. It then declined to the level of a porno cinema, later turning into a karate school.

Re-opened in 1987 after a remodelling effort by designer Philippe Stark, who had even the gilded balcony – along with everything else – painted black, it is now the most "chic" of all Parisian rock clubs. Concerts begin nightly at 8:00 pm.

After the passing of its heyday, the **Élysée-Montmartre** at nr. 72, Boulevard Rochechouart featured boxing and wrestling matches, then ran porno films for a time. After that nadir it rebounded to become a venue for such acts as *Mick Cave, Mano Negra, Suicide* and others.

FLEA MARKETS

The biggest flea market in the known universe is held on Saturdays, Sundays and Mondays only (Métro Porte de Clignancourt). Pandora's box gapes wide open here: For only a very few francs one can acquire various articles of wrought iron, while (hopefully) genuine, signed furniture pieces often go for a small fortune. Burned-out wretches sell their record albums, a couple of books and their

last tatters of clothing right on the side-walk. Even though the flea market is primarily manned by professional second-hand merchants and antique dealers, a carnival atmosphere still prevails, especially in the morning hours.

The market has existed since the middle of the last century. Rag dealers and ironmongers, *clochards* (bums) and ropemakers settled outside of the old city walls and sold their wares as well as discarded old furniture and household utensils scrounged from the wealthier districts. One could also purchase old, often flea-ridden mattresses at the market, which is how it ultimately got its name. At first, the market was held every Sunday, expanding gradually but persistently from there. In the surrounding booths, you can buy a glass of wine and dance to the strains of accordeon music. The market achieved fame around the turn of

Above: African handicrafts on Marché aux Puces. Right: Goods found at the flea market – clothes and old furniture.

the century when several art lovers accidentally discovered several genuine masterpieces there. Nowadays one can acquire all manner of worthless trash at the flea market, but only in a very limited section does it have truly valuable antiques for sale.

With a bit of luck you can still find clocks from the fifties and sixties, but here, as well, all the really good pieces have their price, and they are frequently more expensive than in the city.

If you leave the métro at the **Porte de Clignancourt**, you will find yourself in the middle of the sidewalk, again surrounded by a jumble of street stands selling leather goods, carpets, T-shirts and jeans in every hue. The prices are a lot better than those found elsewhere in Paris. From this point, the above-mentioned flea market is located behind the **Boulevard Périphérique** – just go under the bridge and follow the throng.

Officially, the flea market starts at 7:30 am. However, the real business is done earlier, between 5 and 7 am – the pro-

fessionals refer to it as the "prelude" – when the **Rue Paul-Bert** and **Rue Jules-Vallès** are jam-packed with delivery vehicles unloading wares from all the provinces of France.

Mighty crates are unpacked in the glare of electric lights; the *came* (wares) is then displayed on the sidewalk. Disassembled cabinets of various types, furniture of all sizes and prices, old editions of the Bible and so on.... Then the dealing starts, and cash begins changing hands rapidly. The whole process takes place in a rather suspenseful atmosphere – one can never be sure how "genuine" the items are.

If you pay with cash, it's often possible to push down the asking price by another 25%. Beware of deals that seem *too* good, though; it could be a case of *bidouille* (stolen goods). The *came chaude* (hot goods) often "disappeared" in the provinces.

In the mass of humanity on the **Rue Jean-Henri Fabre**, which runs parallel to the Périphérique, you will find the en-

trance to the **Marché Malik**, one of Paris' most popular markets. Up into the eighties it was a paradise for the chance purchase. One could acquire precious objects from all periods: top hats and derbys from the 19th century, clothing from the forties, jackets from the fifties. Today, however, only newly produced goods are offered.

The majority of stalls have specialized in American cowboy fashions, jeans and T-shirts or paramilitary fatigues. At *Lyonnel's*, a specialist in sixties' and seventies articles, the observant shopper can still come across exciting finds from the psychedelic era as well as associated jewelry and bell-bottom pants. Several of the record shops sell cheap bootleg pressings.

The **Marché Vernaison**, founded in the twenties, is the oldest and most "typical" flea market (entrance at nr. 99 Rue des Rosiers or Nr. 136, Avenue Michelet). In its numerous side streets you will find more-or-less antique furniture, old clothing and other articles from around the turn of the century, as well as old toys.

175

The cheapest of the flea markets is probably the **Marché Jules-Vallès** at the end of the Rue Jules-Vallès. Neither the period furniture nor the paintings are overpriced; old books, lamps and porcelain also find new and truly delighted owners.

The **Marché Serpette** on the Rue Paul-Bert is more of an antique market than a real flea market. Beautiful Art-Deco pieces and paintings from the 18th and 19th centuries can be found here, as well as old bathroom articles and turn-of-the-century bar stools. Here, however, your wallet may wind up looking as though it's been on a crash diet.

The remaining markets, **Cambo**, **Rosiers**, **Paul-Bert** and **Biron** are located in the immediate neighborhood. They also deal in antiques, furniture, copper engravings, crystal chandeliers, paintings and so forth, although they bear a greater semblance to the traditional second-hand market (especially the engaging Marché Paul-Bert).

Restaurants at the Flea Market

The flea market may not have any stars in the restaurant guide to show for itself, but there's good food to be found.

In **À la Bonne Franquette** you can dine amid very pleasing surroundings. **Chez Louisette**, at the rear of the Marché Vernaison, could be considered the most typical of the flea market restaurants. One can enjoy a simple meal (mostly *andouillette* and *faux-filet*) to strains of accordeon and the *chansons* of Edith Piaf, Jacques Brel and Aristide Bruand. What really counts here is the "French" atmosphere. Other restaurants even engage live orchestras, for example the **Au Baryton** on the Rue Vallès. It serves fried clams and grilled blood sausage to the strains of electric guitar music.

If you take a stroll through the streets of this area you will discover plenty of similar establishments.

Above: After a stroll through the flea market – food and music at a flea market pub.

2nd, 9th AND 18th ARRONDISSEMENT
Accommodation

MODERATE: **Hôtel André Gill**, 4, rue André Gill, at the foot of the hill, near Pigalle, Tel: 42 62 48 48. Quiet, excellent value for money. Métro: Abbesses or Pigalle. **Hôtel Bouquet de Montmartre**, 1, rue Durantin, Tel: 46 06 87 54. Small hotel with pleasant atmosphere. **Tim Hôtel**, 11, place Émile Goudeau, next to the Bâteau-Lavoir, Tel: 42 55 74 79. With a view over the most romantic square of Vieux Montmartre. Extremely popular with nostalgic Americans. Métro: Abbesses. *BUDGET:* **Hôtel Tholozé**, 24, rue Tholozé, Tel: 46 06 74 83. A favorite of those wanting to spend one night at the steps of this legendary hill. Double rooms with wash basin. Métro: Blanche or Abbesses.

Restaurants / Nightlife

Au Crus de Bourgogne, 3, rue Bachaumont, Métro Les Halles, Tel: 42 33 48 24, closed Sat and Sun. **Au Petit Riche**, 25, rue le Peletier, Tel: 47 70 68 68, French food at moderate prices, closed Sun. **Beauvilliers**, 52, rue Lamarck, Tel: 42 55 82 76, closed Sun and Mon. **Chez Chartier**, 7, rue du Faubourg Montmartre, good, hearty fare at 9.30 p.m. **Le Zen**, 40, rue du Faubourg Montmartre, Tel: 47 70 06 88, vegetarian dishes. For further restaurants see pages 170–172, and page 176.

Bar-Tabac Le Diplomate, 19, bd. de Rochechouart, open until 1.00 a.m. Métro: Anvers. **Le Pigalle**, 22, bd. de Clichy, daily until 3.00 a.m., popular bar for night owls. Métro: Pigalle. **Harry's New York Bar**, 5, rue Danou, Métro Opéra, 11.00 p.m.-3.00 a.m.

Folies Bergère, 32, rue Richter, Métro Cadet, Tel: 42 46 77 11, variety shows from 9.00 p.m., closed Mon. **Au Lapin Agile**, 22, rue des Saules, Métro Lamarck, Tel: 46 06 85 87, cabaret from 9.30 p.m., closed Mon. **Moulin Rouge**, 82, Boulevard de Clichy, Métro Blanche, Tel: 46 06 00 19, variety shows from 11.00 p.m. **Olympia**, 28, bv. des Capucines, Métro Opéra, Tel: 47 42 25 49, the most famous "Temple of Chansons" in Paris, closed Sun and Mon. For further night bars and rock clubs see page 172 onwards.

Museums / Sightseeing

Musée Grévin, 10, bd. Montmartre, Tel: 47 70 85 05, daily 1.00-7.00 p.m., during school holidays 10.00 a.m.-7.00 p.m., museum of waxworks. **Musée de la Parfumerie**, 9, rue Scribe, Tel: 42 42 04 56, Mon-Sat 9.00 a.m.-5.30 p.m., Tue 10.00 a.m.-4.00 p.m., history of perfume production. **Musée de la Vie Romantique**, 16, rue Chaptal, 10.00 a.m.-5.30 p.m. closed Tue.

Musée Gustave Moreau, 14, rue de la Rochefoucauld, Tel: 48 74 38 50, daily 10.00 a.m.-12.45 p.m. and 2.00-5.15 p.m., closed Tue. **Musée Vieux Montmartre**, 12, rue Cortot, Tel: 46 06 61 11, Tue–Sat 2.30-5.30 p.m., Sun 11.00 a.m.-5.30 p.m. **La Villette**, Parc de la Villette, Museum of Technology and Industry, Métro Porte de Pantin, Tel: 42 78 70 00, Tue, Thur, Fri 10.00 a.m.-6.00 p.m., Wed 12.00 noon-9.00 p.m., Sat and Sun 12.00 noon-8.00 p.m. **Bibliothèque Nationale**, rue Richelieu. **Cimetière de Montmartre**, av. Rachel, pl. Clichy, 8.00 a.m.-5.30 p.m., last resting place of celebrities such as Degas, Stendhal, Heine and Truffaut. **Opéra de Paris**, pl. de l'Opéra, Tel: 40 17 33 33, with ceiling paintings by Marc Chagall, open to the public 11.00 a.m.-4.30 p.m., closed in August. **Sacré Coeur**, Métro Anvers, or with the cog railway from the Marché Saint-Pierre. Basilica: 6.45 a.m.-11.00 p.m., Crypt: in summer 9.00 a.m.-7.00 p.m., in winter 9.00 a.m.-6.00 p.m.

Entertainment for Children

Atelier du „Musée en Herbe" de la Halle Saint-Pierre, 2, rue Pierre Ronsard, Tel: 42 58 74 12. Activities for children from 4 years onwards, Métro: Barbès or Anvers. **Atelier pour Petits**: 26, rue Durantin, Tel: 42 27 68 81. Painting and games for children. Métro: Abbesses. **Babysitting**: Alpha Baby, Tel: 43 65 16 16.

Post / Pharmacy

Main Post Office, 2nd Arr.: 5, place des Petits-Pères, Métro: Bourse or Sentier. **Post Office, 9th Arr.:** 21, rue Joubert, Métro: Chaussée d'Antin. **Main Post Office, 18th Arr.:** 77, rue du Mont-Cenis, Métro: Jules-Joffrin. **Main Post Office** (24 hours): 52, rue du Louvre, Tel: 48 28 20 00, Métro: Louvre or Sentier. **Pharmacy Machelon**, 5, pl. Pigalle, until 1.00 a.m.

Exchange

Exchange Bureau C.C.F. in the Galeries Lafayette, 40, bd. Haussmann, Tel: 45 26 20 63, Mon–Sat 9.30 a.m.-5.45 p.m. **American Express:** 11, rue Scribe, Paris 75009, Tel: 47 77 77 07. Sale and exchange of traveler's checks, foreign exchange, handling of loss or theft of checks. Métro: Opéra. Exchange counter in the **Tourist Information Vieux Montmartre**, pl. du Tertre, 10.00 a.m.-midnight. Métro: Abbesses.

Tourist Information

Town Hall, 2nd Arr.: 8, rue de la Banque, Tel: 42 61 55 02, Métro: Bourse. **Town Hall, 9th Arr.:** 6, rue Drouot, Tel: 42 46 72 09, Métro: Richelieu-Drouot. **Town Hall, 18th Arr.:** 1, pl. Jules-Joffrin, Tel: 42 52 42 00, Métro: Jules-Joffrin. **Tourist Information Vieux Montmartre**, pl. du Tertre, Tel: 42 62 21 21, Métro: Abbesses.

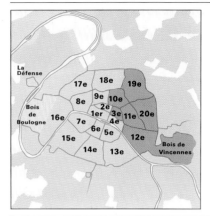

THE EAST OF PARIS

MARAIS AND TEMPLE
10th ARRONDISSEMENT
LA VILLETTE
BELLEVILLE
PLACE DE LA BASTILLE
BERCY
BOIS DE VINCENNES

3rd, 10th, 11th, 12th, 19th and 20th Arrondissement

Paris is divided in two by a rigid axis cutting through the city from north to south. On its western side is the Promised Land, where those in possession of power and wealth have their homes. Dwelling in the East are the people who have neither money nor influence – the so-called common folk.

As is the case with most clichés, this one is long-lived – and certainly not entirely devoid of truth. After all, the situation just described still hasn't been fully abolished. Historically, Paris' western districts have been a residential area with stately houses, quiet streets and clean air. On the other hand, in the east the first industrial facilities were established quite early on, environmental pollution was considerable, the infrastructure lacking and houses tended to go to seed. The daily struggle for existence was the prime molding force of these proletarian quarter, and demands for social reforms and justice repeatedly culminated in popular rebellions. The French Revolution began here on the Place de la Bastille in the 11th

Previous pages: A fountain sculpture on Place de la Nation. Left: Inside the courtyard of the city palace Sévigné.

Arrondissement, and the Paris Commune breathed its last in the 20th.

In the meantime, in a certain sense, capitalism has conquered the eastern arrondissements as well. The supply of land suitable for construction is tight: Lots are accordingly expensive, and a wave of speculation has continued uninterrupted for decades. As a result, the city's administration has (for once) selected the east side for a program of improvements. This is no whim: Even today a quarter of the dwellings in this capital are equipped with neither bath nor toilet. This situation is particularly characteristic of the former workers' districts.

The costly rehabilitation measures being undertaken are destroying the original social fabric by driving people of lesser means out of the renovated dwellings, which are then taken over by others a couple of rungs higher on the social ladder. Furthermore, besides the architectural upgrading, there are also aspirations towards a change in the area's overall image. Some symptoms of this include locating of the Ministry of Finance in Bercy, the construction beginning on the American Center, as well as the planned Center for Crafts and Trades, all to be situated in the city's eastern districts.

The common man's Paris is being sold out. Everywhere you look is the sign:

181

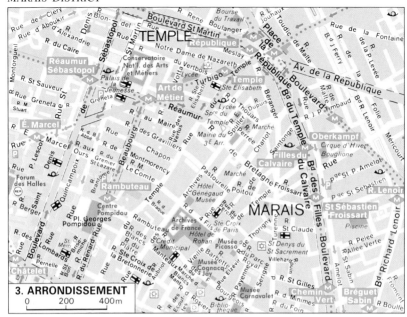

3. ARRONDISSEMENT

0   200   400m

Caution – Construction Zone. What is being left behind in this renovation mania, however, is the historical face of this people's Paris, with all of its tortuous passages and arcades, the little workshops, the wild gardens – in short, everything which, to our eyes, made up the charm of days past.

MARAIS AND TEMPLE DISTRICTS
3rd Arrondissement

One thing is quite certain – the 3rd Arrondissement, one of the most beautiful in Paris, is architecturally homogeneous by and large. Here one has the opportunity to stroll through the streets, hemmed on either side by buildings of historical significance, or to saunter through passages and medieval lanes.

One way to discover the district's true charm is to unabashedly open doors and

Right: Picasso's famous goat looks not exactly well-fed.

explore the paved courtyards and green spaces behind them. One can scarcely help but fall for the charm of this part of the Marais tucked away behind the Marais of Beaubourg. At night the curtain rises on an entirely different play. Floodlights illuminate the building façades bathing the streets in an enchanting, nearly unreal glow.

The real heart of Paris throbs in this district, with the current upswing manifesting itself in some pleasant ways. This area has always been a patchwork of very different populations. Today, its primarily Asian residents live from the production and marketing of leather goods and fashionable jewelry. There are also many Yugoslavs; they have settled primarily around the **Carreau du Temple**.

The Carnavalet, Cognacq-Jay and Picasso Museums

The Saint-Paul Métro station is the place to reach to begin the tour of this area. In the Rue Sévigné stands the

Musée Carnavalet (nr. 23). The Marquise de Sévigné (1629-1696), a rather distinguished member of the aristocracy famous for the letters she wrote to her daughter, resided in this house for some 20 years. The museum is dedicated to the history of Paris. It houses the most complete and vivid collection of documents on a rather decisive period of French history – the French Revolution. The red cap of the *sans-culottes*, notes on the constitution and on the question of human rights, a sketch of the Bastille carved into a stone of the demolished prison and a number of other legacies tell of the confusion of that period.

The Rue Sévigné leads into the **Rue du Parc Royal**. The extravagant residences from the 17th and 18th centuries along this street will spark any visitor's attention. Awaiting the fashion-conscious woman in nr. 17 is shop of designer Alaia's. It's worth crossing the threshold even if you have no intention of buying anything. After the Rue Payenne and the Rue des Francs-Bourgeois, you should

turn towards the **Rue Elzévir**. Nr. 8, the 16th-century Hôtel Donon has become the home of the **Musée Cognacq-Jay**. The exhibits were collected by the businessman Ernest Cognacq, who opened the city's first major department store, the Samaritaine (Rue Rivoli), in 1869. Here one can admire works by Chardin, Fragonard, Boucher, Watteau and Daumier, among many others. The museum has a charming, intimate atmosphere.

The Rue Elzévir leads to the **Place de Thorigny**. Since this section's renovation it looks like some sort of jumbled conglomeration and, sadly, scarcely brings to mind that this was once the heart of Molière's quarter. Since 1985 the **Musée Picasso** has been housed in the Hôtel Salé, Rue de Thorigny nr. 5. The building itself was constructed in the 17th century for a member of the *nouveau riche* who had made his fortune in the collection of salt taxes. The Picasso collection extends through a series of bright exhibition rooms, a successful unification of older architecture and modern

183

painting. Significant works from each of the artist's periods bear witness to his extraordinary creative powers.

Fans of contemporary art will find a number of galleries in the vicinity of the Musée Picasso. The most renowned of these is the Galerie Yvon Lambert at nr. 105, Rue Vielle-du-Temple. A pamphlet is available there listing the addresses of galleries in the Marais.

In the "Archive Quarter"

Besides art from a very wide range of epochs, this quarter is also noted for its inviting tea houses. Proceed from the Rue Elzévir into the Rue Barbette, which opens into the **Rue Vielle-du-Temple**. One of the oldest streets in Paris, it was already known by the same name in the 12th century. Follow along it towards the Place de la République. On the way there you cross the **Rue de la Perle**, which was named Rue Crucifix-Maquereau in the

Above: The entrance to Place des Vosges.

16th century because the cross that once stood on it was the preferred hangout of the local prostitutes *maquereau* being a slang word for a procurer.

By turning onto the Rue des Quatre Fils, one arrives eventually to the **Rue des Archives**. This district offers a real overdose of residences once belonging to the nobility and the wealthy middle class.

Observant pedestrians will discover small portals ornamented with stone rosettes or fine wrought-iron work. At the intersection of the Rue Braque and the Rue des Archives is a Gothic portal with two small watchtowers, a rare remnant from the Middle Ages. By way of the portal, one enters the **Hôtel de Clisson**, which once belonged to the Dukes of Guise, offshoot of the family descended from Claude of Lorraine, who fought together with the French king Francis I against the Habsburg emperor Charles V at the beginning of the 16th century. The Italian painter Le Primatice had a chapel erected here, the decor of which was done by his student Nicolo dell' Abbate.

Now turn off the Rue des Archives onto the Rue des Francs-Bourgeois. At nr. 60, the semi-circular entrance gate of the **Hôtel de Soubise** opens onto an oval courtyard, which conveys something of the past greatness of this residence. During the 18th century, this magnificent residence held all of Paris under its spell. The Prince of Soubise, a music lover, put on concerts for connoisseurs – which even Mozart attended on the occasion of his journey to Paris.

Presently, the **National Archive** is housed here and connected by gardens to several neighboring, aristocratic houses as well. The **Museum of French History** is located in a wing of the Hôtel de Soubise. The private apartments, decorated by major French painters of the 18th century, are open to public view. At nr. 55-57, one can refill one's slimmed-down pocketbook – if need be – in the pawnshop **Mont-de-Piété**. This institution was established in 1777 to compete with other pawnbrokers and set some moral standards in the branch.

Writers and Readers

Continue along the Rue des Archives towards the Hôtel de Ville, eventually crossing the **Rue des Blancs-Manteaux**. Here in the 13th century, parchment factories once produced the material on which monks wrote their Biblical texts. For this reason it was formerly named the "Street of Parchment Making." Its present name springs from a mendicant order that wore white frocks. The order's library, one of the richest of its kind, is said to have comprised some 12,000 manuscripts and documents at the time of the Revolution, all of which were destroyed. The theater-café at 15 Rue des Blancs-Manteaux features a variety of performances, with humorists and chansonniers appearing on its stage.

Upon crossing the **Rue Sainte-Croix-de-la-Bretonnérie**, one should bear in mind that as early as the 14th century the administration of the funeral parlors was established here. Historians claim that the town criers went through the street with portentous voices wailing: "Pray for the dead!" In contrast, today the street is a vibrant and high-spirited place. The theater-café *Point Virgule* is (Semi-colon) located here, and quality bistros like **Le** *Petit Gavroche* or *Au Rendezvous des Amis,* as is the restaurant *l'Aviatic-Club* and the bookstore *La Nef des Fous and Au-dessus du Volcan.*

Back on the Rue Vielle-du-Temple heading towards Place de la Republique, you will come upon the shop *Mélo* with its abundant selection of gift items, clothing, perfumes and textiles from every part of the globe (nr. 46). And in nr. 47, the **Hôtel Amelot-de-Bisseuil**, Beaumarchais penned *The Marriage of Figaro.*

From the "Provincial Streets" to the Museum of Technology

The walk from the Rue Vieille-du-Temple to the Quartier du Temple leads through a number of streets which are named after France's provinces. The itinerary is a little off the beaten track: With the exception of a few interior courtyards one could hardly describe it as being studded with major tourist attractions, but it *does* lead one through some picturesque old streets.

So, take a turn into the Rue du Perche, then into the Rue du Saintonge, and after that into the Rue du Poitou. Cross the **Rue Charlot**, whose name originates from a 17th-century banker. Now follow the Rue Pastourelle. Take a glimpse at the alleyway **Sourdis** to your left, which has retained its medieval charm. Now you'll arrive at the intersection of the Rue du Temple and the **Rue des Gravilliers**, a street typifying this quarter of Paris. Shops with costume jewelry and fairground-type, baubles and gewgaws make for quite a flurry of customers. At nr. 44

the first international workers' union, supported by Karl Marx once met.

Now turn into the **Rue des Vertus** ("street of the virtues"), whose name was ironically derived from the métier that was once practiced here.... Then, at the Rue Réaumur, turn to the left towards the suburb of Sébastopol.

The **Technical Museum** (270, Rue Saint-Martin), is open daily except Mondays. All sorts of inventions and technological developments are exhibited in a precise and didactic manner, even though the descriptions seem a bit outdated now and then. Here, one can learn a lot about the development of standard units for weights and measures as well as gain an understanding of various everyday technologies. Among other things, it features the first pressure cooker (1686), the laboratory of the chemist Lavoisier, the

Above: The first sunrays entice the Parisians outdoors and onto the streets. Right: A cosy, secluded bridge over the St Martin canal.

aircraft in which Blériot crossed the English Channel, and the first automobile – Cugnot's steam-powered towing truck.

Square du Temple

Not far away from the Museum of Technology is the **Square du Temple**. It's worth taking a stroll in this park which was laid out on the location of a former prison of the Knights Templar.

There is a monument dedicated to the singer and polemicist Pierre Jean de Béranger (1780-1857). He is little known, although his songs during the revolutions of 1830 and 1848 had considerable political impact.

Here, in the northern section of the Marais, the streets are lively and the area has its own special atmosphere. Arabic coffeehouses, Chinese restaurants and dance performances in the Rue au Maire and Rue Volta indicate that you are approaching the Place de la République and the 10th and 11th Arrondissements, which are quite distinct from the Marais.

Street, boulevard, square and area may bear the names of the Templars, but nothing else remains of the order. Even the tower that was remodeled into a prison for Louis XVI and his family (and from which the king went to the guillotine) no longer stands.

Between Rue Perrée and Rue Dupetit Thouars, the renowned **Carreau du Temple** is an enjoyable place to rummage around a bit. This reasonably-priced clothing market, located under a great glass-and-metal skylight, was established at the end of the 18th century. During the 19th century, Parisians of modest means clothed themselves here. In the seventies there was a move afoot to demolish the Carreau as part of a district renovation effort. The local residents succeeded in defending their market. At 7:30 am, when the market bell chimes, things start hopping in the renovated hall. You can clothe yourself from head to toe here at prices undercutting any competition. Nowadays, the clothing is new for the most part, but the old custom of haggling remains and helps create an informal atmosphere. Small businesses and artisans' shops have settled in alongside the Carreau. On weekdays, you should take a stroll through the old town of **Dupetit-Thouars** where, in addtion to old workshops, you can still discover Hénin senior's former billiards factory.

Nocturnal Scenes

When night settles in, it plunges the quarter into a whirl of color and lends it an atmosphere of tragic, metropolitan poetry. The young people crowd around shooting galleries or gather together in huts in front of pinball and gambling machines. Gloomy old passageways send shivers up your spine. Meanwhile, the "New Wave" generation has discovered this part of town as well. Two discothèques illuminate this attractive nocturnal scene: *Les Bains* (in a former bathing facility at nr. 7, Rue du Bourg-l'Abbé) and the best African dancing club, Le Tango (nr. 13 Rue Au-Maire).

187

10th ARRONDISSEMENT

The 10th Arrondissement is composed of the suburbs of Saint-Denis and Saint-Martin. It is one of the districts of Paris that was most decisively altered by the sweeping re-designing of Haussmann during the mid-19th century. Expansive boulevards between the northern and eastern railroad stations, located quite close to each-other, lend the area an urban flair. Walking the area is the best way of discovering its sights, which so well reflect the history of the city.

Canal Saint-Martin

By way of the Rue du Faubourg du Temple, walk from the Place de la République to the **Quai des Jemmapes**. Then follow the **Canal Saint-Martin** towards the Bassin de la Villette, bring-

Above: The entrance hall of Gare de l'Est is impressive to anyone who is interested in architecture.

ing you to Place Stalingrad. The canal was installed during the Restoration, connecting the Canal de l'Ourcq with the Seine. During the 19th century, tanneries and paper factories were established along its banks. Except for a very few, such as 130-132 Quai de Jemmapes, these structures have either disappeared or been remodeled into lofts.

The banks of the Canal Saint-Martin allow for some leisurely sauntering. Between the **Square Frédéric Lemaître** and the **Rue Récollets**, the landscape is particularly romantic with its tree-lined banks, green spaces, a swing bridge and some metal foot bridges.

From the swing bridge on the Rue de la Grange-aux-Belles, the tile façade of **Saint-Louis Hospital** can be seen at the end of the street. It was constructed in 1608 when the plague broke out. The facility is composed of an odd grouping of individual buildings, a layout supposed to cut down the danger of infection. This often overlooked 17th-century edifice is well worth a visit.

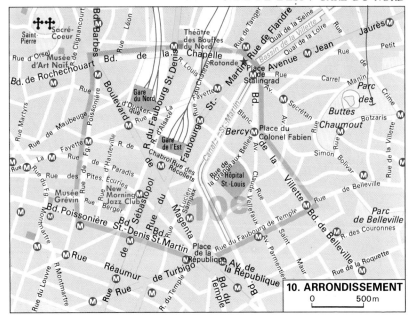

10. ARRONDISSEMENT

0   500 m

Hidden in the angle between the Rue de la Grange-aux-Belles and the Rue des Vinaigriers is the **Hôtel du Nord,** which lent the film by Marcel Carné its name. On the building opposite is the catwalk where the scene was played in which the lead actress Arletty spoke the famous words: "Atmosphère, atmosphère".

Actually, though, the scene was played before a reconstructed backdrop in the studio. It, the backdrop, can be viewed in the Cinema Museum (Palais de Chaillot on the Place du Trocadéro).

Through the Streets of Saint-Martin and Saint-Denis

Follow along the Rue des Récollets in the direction of the suburb Saint-Martin. On the right-hand side, the **Gare de l'Est** can be distinguished by its façade of glass and steel.

After the Rue d'Alsace and the Rue Dunkerque you will come upon the **Gare du Nord**. Even if your stomach isn't growling, at least take a look at the menu of the restaurant *Le Terminus*. It is considered one of the finest dining establishments in Paris. After that, you should continue your journey via the Boulevard Magenta until you reach nr. 85, where the **Saint-Quentin market** is housed in a 19th-century hall.

Afterwards, take a turn into the ancient **Rue du Faubourg Saint-Denis**. It is connected with the Rue du Faubourg Saint-Martin by a number of passages. During the day, the Passages du Prado, Brady and de l'Industrie teem with humanity. On top of that, the Rue du Faubourg Saint-Denis is enlivened by a considerable number of truly distinctive shops, a reflection of this district's cosmopolitan side.

The gourmet restaurant *Le Julien* (nr. 16) has held onto its glass and metal Art-Nouveau decor. Also highly recommended is the restaurant *Flo* at nr. 7, Cour des Petites Écuries. It pampers its guests with turn-of-the-century interior decoration and menu selections of excellent quality.

189

Back on the Rue du Faubourg Saint-Denis, duck into the **Passage Reilharc**, which is connected to the Boulevard de Strasbourg by a series of little, interior courtyards. The boulevard was laid out by Haussmann to connect the Northern and Eastern stations.

Entertainment after Dark

Theater fans should reserve at least one night to attend a performance at the **Théâtre des Bouffes du Nord** (nr. 37, Boulevard de la Chapelle). Though its auditorium is unadorned and its walls are equally naked, the cordial atmosphere of the works themselves is quite infectious. One of the best jazz clubs in Paris, the *New Morning,* opens its door to enthusiasts of the genre at nr. 7, Rue des Petites Écuries. The discothèque *Le Parisien Libéré*, installed in a former newspaper publishing house, offers a diversified musical program with something for almost any taste, ranging from traditional to the newest of experimental jazz and on to blues, salsa and African rhythms.

LA VILLETTE
19th Arrondissement

Located within in the city's north-eastern reaches, the 19th Arrondissement looks Janus-faced, with two different sets of characteristics. An avant-garde, new territory is breaking ground all around **La Villette**. Among other things, it is the location of the world's largest museum of science and technology. In contrast, the scene around the **Parc des Buttes-Chaumont** tends toward the bucolic, with the park grounds serving as a close-at-hand recreation area for the local inhabitants – besides being steeped in memories of the "good old days."

The Villette quarter had its origins in a Roman road which connected Paris with Flanders. In 1806, during construction of the Canal de l'Ourcq, discoveries were made of objects from the Gallo-Roman period. In all probability, the historical settlement on the Roman route was the foundation for the later village of La Villette-Saint-Ladre.

At the beginning of the 19th century, the newly-created Villette Basin and the Canals de l'Ourcq, St.-Denis and St. Martin attracted industrial development. In 1860, during the Second Empire, the village of La Villette was incorporated into the French capital. Not long after that, the city fathers decided to consolidate La Villette's livestock market and slaughterhouse within the district's confines. For over a century, it supplied the entire metropolis with meat.

The **Avenue Jean-Jaurès** was one of the most important transportation routes to and from Germany. At the time it was even called la Route d'Allemagne. Today it separates La Villette from the Parc des Buttes-Chaumont, one of Paris's most beautiful green spaces.

The earliest known mention of it dates from the ninth century. Up until the later Middle Ages, the grounds were used as a "back-to-nature" garbage dump. The Cossacks and the French waged a gruesome battle at the foot of the hill in 1814. Finally, during the 19th century, gypsum, sand and clay were mined here in huge quarries. The park itself was laid out 130 years ago.

Champs-Élysées of the East

The Métro lines 5 and 7 transport one to the Stalingrad station and the square of the same name, which resembles a huge amphitheater extending over an area of three hectares. To the left the automobile traffic winds around the facility in adventurous curves, while to the right one can cast one's gaze into the blue yonder over the **Bassin de la Villette**.

The "Champs-Élysées of the East", as the basin has been dubbed in common parlance, was officially dedicated by

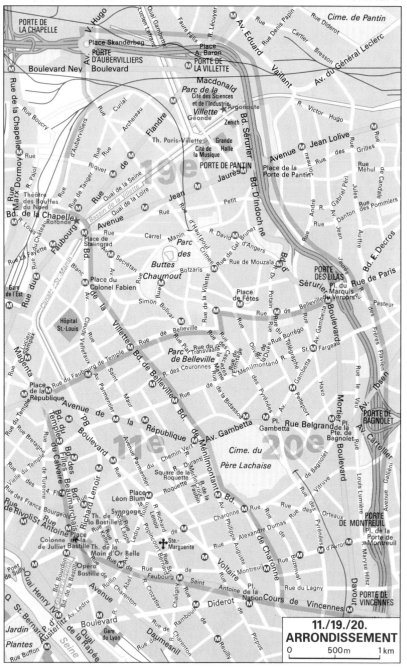

11./19./20.
ARRONDISSEMENT

0   500m   1 km

Napoléon in 1808. Just a few years later, enthused city dwellers were doing their laps on ice skates, while some seasoned entrepreneurs even organized rides in Russian-style sleighs for the ladies.

The "little Venice of Paris" continues to attract people seeking recreation. The water is sprinkled with canoeists, and a boating school offers a two-day crash-course for the sailing license examination; one can also rent a houseboat for a journey through the canals.

The **Rotonde** dominates Place Stalingrad. Nowadays, this domed edifice of light sandstone gleams once again, having undergone a complete renovation. The elegant structure was erected in 1784 as one of four customs pavilions along the municipal taxation belt. It now houses the headquarters of the city's archaeological department. Visitors will find exhibits on the city's history.

Above: Today's Cité des Sciences was a slaughter-house at one time. Right: The Géode houses a monumental movie theater.

Now follow the left side of the Bassin de la Villette. After about 800 m, you will come upon the last remaining Parisian drawbridge. With its ingenious hydraulic system, a weight of only four kilos is used to set the bridge in motion. This miracle of engineering dates from 1885, and was designed by the firm responsible for the east and west elevators in the Eiffel Tower. The bridge is still in service. One of the area's old brick warehouses stands opposite.

Those who have set out on their walking tour of the area on a Thursday or Sunday ought to fit in time for a brief excursion to the **Marché de Crimée** (behind the none-too-significant Church of Saint-Jacques-Saint-Christophe). Squeezed onto a small square, this market exudes a village-like atmosphere.

Via the right bank of the Canal de l'Ourcq you arrive at the Parc de la Villette and finally the **Cité des Sciences et de l'Industrie**. This is the former location of the livestock market's central slaughterhouse. Today the 55-hectare grounds are a center for the sciences, culture and recreation, luring countless visitors each year.

Several buildings can be recognized at a considerable distance: the gigantic, angular glass-and-steel edifice of the Cité des Sciences and, right next to it, the **Géode**, an immense sphere with a diameter of 36 meters, covered by 6533 triangular, aluminum plates. Sky and earth are reflected in its gleamingly polished exterior walls. In the structure's interior, audiences can view films projected onto a gigantic (measuring 1000 sqm) hemispherical screen. Don't pass up the opportunity to partake of this three-dimensional sensory experience.

Not far away from the Géode, the submarine *Argonaute* has cast anchor and opened its air-lock portal for curious visitors. Inside you can experience the feeling a landlubber gets when he finds himself 20,000 leagues under the sea.

A City of the Future

In the sixties, the municipal administration wanted to completely renovate the century-old slaughterhouse and expand it into the largest meat-processing facility in the world. Shortly before its completion, though, things went badly awry – the high-powered project turned out to be an economic dud.

However, then-Prime Minister Valéry Giscard d'Estaing came up with the surprising idea of transforming the distribution center into a Science City. The **Cité des Sciences et de l'Industrie** opened its gates punctually on the 13th of March 1986, just in time for the passage of Halley's Comet.

The permanent exhibit **Explora** is divided into four sections: *From the Earth to the Universe, The Adventure of Life, The Tool and Human Labor,* and *Language and Communication.*

Children will be especially thrilled with the **Inventorium**, which includes a planetarium and a "mediathèque" as well

as three gigantic greenhouses. In addition, major exhibitions dealing with science, engineering and industry are held at regular intervals. "Please touch" is the surprising notice posted on many of the articles on display – after all, the institution is an exponent of "critical knowledge conveyance."

This concept is obviously being well received. During its first five years of existence, the center recorded a proud 21 million visitors, with the number continuing to climb. Of course, foreign guests are in the minority, but they are not neglected. The personnel can communicate in several languages, and for special exhibitions tour cassettes are available in English, German and Spanish.

Nonetheless, the visitor should be warned ahead of time – in order to make an exhaustive exploration of the Cité des Sciences, one should plan on about 30 hours – even a "quick, superficial" tour takes two to three hours.

Beyond the foot bridge you can see the **Grande Halle,** one of the most beautiful

remaining examples of a 19th-century steel construction. The building once served as a livestock auction hall. Today it is used for exhibitions, concerts, lectures and avant-garde theater performances. Three movable stages enable the hall to be transformed according to need.

An adjacent building, the former leather exchange, has become home base for the **Théâtre de la Villette** and the **Arletty Cinema**, which presents scientific films (admission free).

The **Cité de la Musique** was opened in Winter 1990 directly behind the Grande Halle's main hall. It is France's largest conservatory, equipped with an appropriately large concert hall and state-of-the-art technology necessary for performances of modern music.

The **Zénith** is a temple of popular music; its tent-shaped auditorium creates a circus-like atmosphere.

Above: Is he looking back at May 1968 in Paris? Right: A short stop in the park of Buttes-Chaumont.

A Park for the People

The **Parc des Buttes-Chaumont** lies about 20 minutes by foot to the south of the Cité de la Musique (by Métro the journey lasts almost as long). Today, there is nothing more to be seen of the barren hill for which the area was named, ever since Napoléon III commissioned his chief designer Haussmann to establish a park for the neighboring working class population.

A full-blown network of roads crisscrosses the park, which is spread over 25 hectares. All routes lead to the artificial lake, in the center of which boulders were piled up to an imposing height of 50 m. The "hill" is crowned by the **Sibylline Temple**, from which one can take in a splendid panorama of the Montmartre. The island can be reached by way of two bridges, and through the picturesque **Chemin des Aiguilles**, a staircase of 200 steps carved right into the stone, it is also possible to climb through the interior of the rock right up to the top.

Take time to explore the grotto on the lake's eastern shore as well. It has been carved 15 meters into the hill's flank, and is enlivened by an artificial waterfall. Gypsum was mined at this location until the mid-19th century. On the other hand, the largest and best-known quarry, the Carrière de l'Amérique (so named because most of its output was exported to the New World) was filled in when the park was established.

Across from the lake's western shore, next to the main entrance gate, is a chart providing an overview of the exotic plantings. (The 19th Arrondissement city hall also offers a map of the quarter which shows the park's nature trail).

The puppet theater's open-air performances, held diagonally opposite the entrance gate, are great fun for children. The season runs from spring to autumn – also depending, naturally, on the weather. When it's sunny and warm, every spot on the 18 wooden benches is occupied.

Summer concerts can be heard in the little music pavillion. And, after a strenu-

ous rowboat tour, there is appetizing food at the Restaurant *La Puebla* (an interesting sight as well). When leaving the park at the corner of Rue Crimée/ Rue Botzaris, the extension of which is named **Rue de Général Brunet**, there are countless passages lined by single family houses to the right and left.

At the end of the Rue Miguel Hilbage, turn left and head uphill along the Rue d'Hautpoul, then turn left once again onto th**e Rue Crimée**. At nr. 50, switch over to the other side of the street in order to better contemplate its façade. Elaborate cast-iron balustrades grace the windows and balcony parapets and provide a pleasing contrast to its successful terracotta work.

The adjacent house provides a futuristic contrast to this thirties' gem: Constructed in 1970, it quite obviously bears the imprint of the *Starship Enterprise* era. The mailboxes resemble flying saucers, while the entrance hall divulges that day's notions of 21st-century habitation. The Rue de Crimée comes to an end at

the **Place des Fêtes,** once a fairground for the community of Belleville and backdrop for some rather turbulent Mardi Gras parades.

After an urban redevelopment effort, which resulted in the plaza's being surrounded by towering skyscrapers, people appear to have lost interest in holding festivities here – the Métro can rapidly transport you to greener pastures.

BELLEVILLE / MÉNILMONTANT
20th Arrondissement

With the battle cry "wine, women and song" on their lips, the Parisians used to head eastward in the 18th and 19th centuries, full of enthusiasm, to **Ménilmontant**. There on the hill, the grapevines blossomed while the wine flowed copiously in the *guinguettes*, or suburban pubs. The wine may not have been the

Above: To buy or not to buy? Above right: It is a tight squeeze in Rue de la Duée! Right: A beautiful summer day in 1990.

most select, but to compensate, it was dirt cheap, and for a special reason: Until Paris annexed it, the farmers' village of Ménilmontant was beyond the city's toll limits. What a luck for the Parisians!

The 20th Arrondissement was able to retain its rural character up until the beginning of this century. Edith Piaf, the "sparrow of Paris" (*piaf* means "sparrow" in French slang), who was born here, played with the free-ranging chickens and geese in the street-dust, singing for a couple of *sous* in peoples' backyards. Maurice Chevalier and Charles Trenet celebrated their first successes in the cabarets of Ménilmontant. Now, however, it has been a long time since the last curtain dropped here.

With a halfway decent nose for such things, on the stretch from Ménilmontant to Belleville one can become a traveler between the two worlds. Granted, an ambitious social housing project is devouring the neighborhood; nonetheless, you can still detect the old spirit of the quarter from some of the little passages and yellowed façades that once created a subdued backdrop for the glittering city of lights.

Village Life in the Big City

Our hike starts out from the Télégraphe métro station. By heading uphill along the **Rue du Télégraphe** a couple of strides, at nr. 49 you will discover two commemorative inscriptions placed right next to each other.

Congratulations, you have just made a successful ascent to the highest point in Paris, at 128.508 meters above sea level. In 1794, Claude Chappe erected a telegraph tower here – and thereby the first "optical telephone line" between Paris and Lille.

At the first intersection, veer right into the Rue de Borrego and walk downhill to reach Rue de la Duée.

On the right-hand side of the street, it's a few steps down into the long, narrow **Passage de la Duée**. Beware of oncoming traffic, which means that one must either put one's back up against the wall and suck in one's stomach – or else shift into reverse gear. At some points, the passage is just 80 cm wide. Follow the Rue de Pixérécourt downward to the left, then at the intersection with the Rue de Ménilmontant descend the latter. Go beyond the Rue des Pyrénées, continuing on to the Rue de l'Ermitage, which turns off to the right.

Then, in the Rue des Cascades, you will come upon the **Regard St.-Martin**, a decaying stone that once served as an aqueduct. Opposite it, the **Rue des Savies** plunges steeply down hill. The bumpy cobblestone pavement on this narrow street awakens a lot of reminiscences of days long gone....

In 1951, the film *Casque d'Or* (Golden Helmet) was shot here, featuring Simone Signoret in the leading role. The film dealt with the life of Amélie Mélie, whose magnificent reddish-golden hair

earned her the nickname *casque d'or*. For over 20 years, at the beginning of this century, Parisian society was kept on the edge of its seats by her numerous and adventurous love stories. The three little cottages on the **Rue des Cascades** (nrs. 64-68) are a memorial to those days. At the next intersection, head left down the Rue de la Mare.

Jules and Jim in the Backyard

On the opposite side of the street, a steep staircase leads into the **Passage de Plantin**, along which one-storied cottages with pointed, gabled roofs huddle up against each other.

The Rue de Transvaal runs at right angles to the passage. Just to the left, at nr. 16, a wrought-iron gate closes the entrance to the **Villa Castel**. With a bit of luck, one can open the gate and set foot in a world thought to have perished long ago. As in some narrow village alleyways, one house nestles right up to the next, flowers and bushes flourish in the

background, and cast-iron water-basins shimmer in a coat of green moss alongside the steps. François Truffaut shot scenes for *Jules et Jim* in this cul-de-sac.

You are standing at the upper entrance to the **Parc de Belleville**. This steeply inclined, public garden of some 47,000 sqm in area was opened at the close of the eighties. From this height, one can enjoy an overwhelming vista of Paris.

A long row of grapevines are a reminder of the area's bacchanalian past. The watercourse leading into the valley, which had a number of decorative fountains, has, unfortunatly, dried up. Soon after they were put into operation, the responsible authorities determined – to their great horror and dismay – that the subsurface was too porous, meaning that instead of flowing into the pool, the water was running right into the nearby Métro shaft.

Above: Belleville has become the new home for many who were once foreigners. Right: Black Africans belong to the cityscape.

The Rue Piat runs along the eastern edge of the park to the next cross-street, the **Rue de Belleville**. This was already a bustling main street in the days when Belleville was just a village outside the gates of the metropolis, and is still full of life and small shops today.

During the 18th and 19th centuries, the wildest and most notorious of the annual Mardi Gras parades romped down the Rue de Belleville. A convoy of more than 1000 floats moved down the steeply inclined route to the applause of an wildly costumed and thoroughly enthusiastic Paris. The parade, named *Descente de la Courtille*, took place for the last time on Shrove Tuesday, 1838.

In the Refugees' Promised Land

The first newcomers to this area came from the center of Paris. The *grands travaux*, the extensive urban renovations that took place at the close of the 19th century, forced large numbers of inner-city residents to seek housing in Bel-

leville. They were followed by the "economic refugees" from the southeastern province of Auvergne, one of France's poorest regions. The next arrivals were Jews from Russia and Poland escaping pogroms. Next came Armenians, who fled Turkey in 1915 to escape genocide, Greeks who came here for the same reasons in 1922, and then Jews, who hoped to escape the Nazi terror in the Third Reich. Belleville became a new home to all of them – as well as to the next wave, including Arabs from North Africa, followed by Yugoslavs, Portuguese and Slavs, all of whom started arriving in the fifties. Most recently, increasing numbers of Asians have also begun squeezing into the district.

Sadly, the city's redevelopment plans carry with them the prospect of throwing the fragile balance of this most international of its quarters awry and destroying its unique atmosphere forever.

Tuesday and Friday mornings are the best times to saunter down the **Boulevard de Belleville**, because the markets are open then. The market stands extend for over a kilometer until just short of the most famous of Paris' cemeteries, the Cimetière du Père-Lachaise.

The market is an exciting adventure for all the senses. Deep red, sweet pomegranates alongside juicy Chinese lychees vie for the buyers' favor. At the next stand, one faces the confusing challenge of settling on one of the varieties of potato on display, including African sweet potatoes. Around lunch time, an international throng rules the scene, while sellers and their customers haggle over prices in a Babylonian confusion of tongues – all at a deafening volume! This marketplace shouting-match has even been the subject of a socio-linguistic study.

A leisurely stroll from stand to stand amounts to a culinary voyage of discovery encircling the entire globe. Scents of fresh curry, freshly picked mint, Turkish mocca coffee, Antilles rum and sesame cookies waft through the air. At dark booths, second-hand clothes are sold off bazaar-style at dirt-cheap prices.

Jim Morrison. These are only a few of the multitude of celebrities who have found, under these shady old trees, their final (and now and then exceedingly ornate) resting places.

At the entrance to the cemetery is a map describing the way to the more prominent graves. Find out for yourself why the Cimetière du Père-Lachaise holds slot number six on the hit list of most-visited sights in Paris.

PLACE DE LA BASTILLE
11th Arrondissement

The Boulevard de Ménilmontant on the southwestern edge of the Père-Lachaise is the border of the 11th Arrondissement. The lodestone of the area, however, is on the other side; namely, the **Place de la Bastille**, a name that has penetrated to even the most remote corners of the western hemisphere.

Just about every Frenchman and non-Frenchman has heard of or read about the 1789 destruction of the fortress *Bastille* in their history lessons. In memory of the victims of the revolution of 1830, the **July Column** today rises up from the center of the Place de la Bastille. The column bears a gilded statue that has been dubbed *Le Génie de la Bastille* by the locals. The other great sight on the Place de la Bastille and subject of some controversy in musical circles – is the opera. It actually stands in the 12th Arrondissement and therefore its rightful place is a little further into this chapter.

Hidden in a little side street, located near the Ménilmontant métro station, is the **Edith Piaf Museum**. This memorial to the district's most famous daughter resembles a doll's house. In two rooms of a private apartment, the famed black dress the chanteuse used to wear on stage is displayed, in addition to all her trophies and photographs.

A high stone wall shields the **Cimetière du Père-Lachaise** from the intrusion of traffic noise. Opened in 1804, it can look back on a long history of interesting anecdotes. This burial ground has been transformed into a battlefield. In 1871 participants of the Commune rebellion were executed by firing squad against its walls. Today the peace here is disturbed only by the endless flood of visitors making pilgrimages to the graves of Honoré de Balzac, Frédéric Chopin, Molière, Edith Piaf and the rock singer

A tip: Don't head out on this foot tour on Sunday, when all of the businesses and workshops are closed. On weekdays this is a thoroughly bustling part of town. Over centuries, it has been the domain of many craftsmen, cabinet-makers, inlayers, wood carvers and stone cutters. For several years now, however, changes have been in the offing with quite another group of residents making inroads into the quarter. By and by, abandoned factory

Above: Chopin's grave in the cemetery of Père-Lachaise. Right: "Le Genie" on the July Column at Place de la Bastille.

buildings are being converted into lofts, attracting a pell-mell crew of artists, painters, sculptors, photographers, architects, ad agencies, dance studios and contemporary art galleries.

The entire district around the Rue de la Roquette and the Rue du Faubourg Saint-Antoine is pierced with passages, unusual gangways and secretive interior courtyards. If time allows you should take the opportunity to discover these concealed gems that show a delightful side of "old" Paris.

A Stroll on the Rue de la Roquette

From the Bastille Métro station, head onto **Rue de la Roquette**, the district's main artery. It begins at the Place de la Bastille and ends at the Cimetière du Père-Lachaise.

The street is hemmed by innumerable little shops in which Tunesians sell groceries and Africans stock Vietnamese products. In the last few years, the street has been developing a new "look" due to the arrival of designers' clothing boutiques. In nr. 9, an abandoned fitting factory, the shop *L'Usine* sells contemporary furniture, tableware and carpets.

Afterwards, saunter down the **Rue de Lappe** as well, opening up the door to nr. 34. The trees and green of the interior courtyard transport one to the countryside for a few moments.

Returning back then to the Rue de la Roquette, the more hard-boiled among us might take along a durable souvenir from the tattooist *Etienne* (nr. 40). A few steps further on, you can recover from the shock in the **Passage de la Main d'Or** (nr. 10). A good place to take a break and breathe the atmosphere of long-gone days is in *À l'Ami du Pierre*, a saloon out of the last century.

Afterwards, followers of the avant-garde theater can check on the schedule of performances at the **Théâtre de la Main d'Or Belle de Mai** (nr. 15). At nr.

70, modern-day city slickers seek a bit of refuge by the 19th-century **Fontaine l'Abreuvoir**. The **Théâtre de la Bastille** (76, Rue de la Roquette) keeps its audiences entertained with theater, dance and musical performances, and also with an avant-garde orientation.

Past the synagogue, the **Charles Dallery** and **Bafroi Passages** branch off the Rue de la Roquette. The decaying exterior walls, cobblestoned streets, and dark courtyards here bring to mind the Paris of bygone days so vividly described in the writings of Victor Hugo.

The Rue de la Roquette remains quite lively until far into the night, when the tireless among us swarm into the coffeehouses *L'Iguana* (nr. 15) and *La Rotonde* (nr. 17), as well as the countless Thai, Japanese, South American and Russian restaurants and "in" spots such as the *Goûts et Couleurs* (nr. 22).

And in the Rue de Lappe one can dance until dawn, perhaps in the *Balajo,* where night for night the young (and the young at heart) swing their bodies to

rhythms thought long forgotten, like the cha-cha, old-fashioned rock and roll, and hits from the sixties. Inquire ahead of time, though, as the musical program changes each evening. Tropical rhythms and jazz resound in the **Chapelle des Lombards**. Devotees of hearty, down-to-earth French cuisine will meet up with regulars from the quarter in the pleasing atmosphere of the restaurant **La Galoche d'Aurillac** (Rue du Lappe nr. 41).

Through Rue Keller and Rue de Charonne

From the Passage Charles Dallery you can make your way via the Passage Bullourde into the **Rue Keller**. Some 20 galleries featuring contemporary art have set up shop next to each other. Nearly every facet of the movement is represented, from video and photography to the latest in minimalism, and figurative painting

Above and above right: Street life in the east of Paris.

following examples set around the turn of the century. Now and then, less experienced viewers may find themselves a bit overstrained by the degree of stamina and tolerance exacted of them. On the other hand, the truly interested should inquire about the available catalogue providing precise information about each and every one of the district's galleries.

Next, the tour brings you to the **Rue de Charonne.** Towards the Charonne Métro station, the "women's house" opens its gates at nr. 94. It was constructed in 1912 in a manner common to its day, with a combination of bricks and ceramic decor; it was acquired in 1926 by the Salvation Army. Today, it provides shelter to low-income women. The interior with its wood and ceramic ornamentation is well worth a look.

After the exertions of your journey, you can recover for a while in the coffee-house *La Palette,* at the intersection of Rue de Charonne and Avenue Ledru Rollin. It possesses a façade dating from 1900. Underneath its wrought-iron balcony, a gilded inscription catches the eye: *Au vrai Saumur, café à 10 centimes la tasse, billard.* Nowadays one can no longer play billiards here, unfortunately, and the coffee costs a bit more than 10 centimes a cup as well....

The Rue de Charonne is also home to galleries of contemporary art. Among the best-known of these are the galleries *Lavigne-Bastille* and *Nane Stern* in the **Passage de l'Homme**.

You might also take a look inside the antique dealerships, which have specialized primarily in furniture and other articles from the fifties and sixties. It's not always easy, of course, but the persistent collector can now and then find a thoroughly good deal there.

The "Furniture Street"

The nearby **Rue du Faubourg Saint-Antoine** is the backbone of this quarter, which is prominent for its crafts and small enterprises. Long ago, Louis XI granted the woodworkers' guilds in this settlement complete freedom. They established themselves in a labyrinth of courtyards and passageways.

Some of these have a curiously romantic appearance, such as the **Passage du Cheval Blanc**, which consists, in turn, of an inextricable tangle of little courtyards bearing the names of each month of the year.

The **Passage du Chantier** has preserved its 19th-century appearance particularly well, with large cobblestoned pavements and narrow sidewalks bordered by old furniture warehouses and the workshops of stone cutters and lacquerers. As a workers' district, this neighborhood has supplied the various revolutions with comrades-in-arms, supporting the storming of the Bastille, the revolutions of 1830 and 1848 and the Paris Commune.

On a stroll down the Rue du Faubourg Saint-Antoine, the window displays and furniture shops are particularly impressive. Beware, however, of the salesmen along the sidewalks who use all their powers of eloquence to try to get passers-by to pull out their billfolds. At nr. 71, the artists' association *Le Génie de la Bastille* provides comprehensive information on the quarter's art offerings. Every year (usually towards the end of October) they organize an open-house day, during which visitors can make personal contact and hold discussions with the artists in about one hundred studios.

Around Place Léon Blum

Having arrived at the intersection of the Rue du Faubourg Saint-Antoine and Avenue Ledru Rollin, continue along the latter in the direction of the Cimetière du Père-Lachaise.

Once you have crossed the **Place Léon Blum**, a large public park is visible to the left. The Prison de la Roquette (the entry hall of which has been preserved) once stood on this site. The five unusual, large stones opposite it at the intersection of the Rue de la Croix-Faubin once served as a pedestal for the guillotine. Numerous public executions took place on the Rue de la Roquette until the beginning of the 20th century.

At this point, head down the Rue Merlin and turn to the left onto the Rue Duranti. At nr. 7, the architecture of the **Charles Munch Conservatory** will surely arouse the visitor's sense of awe. Its ceramic-covered, cubist contours endow it with all the characteristics of a building of the post-modern era.

If you head a bit off the most heavily-trodden paths, you will come upon the **Eglise Sainte-Marguerite** at nr. 36, Rue Saint-Bernard. It is situated amidst cabinet-makers' and laquerers' workshops.

The church's architect, Victor Louis, enlisted the assistance of Italian artist Brunetti for the creative work. As backdrop painter for the Comédie Française,

Brunetti was a true master in the art of illusion. Indeed, he succeeded in the execution of a most unusual decor. All around the chapel, Brunetti simulated an Ionian columned hall; rising above it are various symbolic statues.

To the left of the church is a graveyard, supposedly Louis XVII's burial place. Other voices claim that the son of Louis XVI, who died at the age of ten, is buried elsewhere. An exhumation of the corpse did indeed reveal that it belonged to a considerably older youth. The mystery of where the *dauphin* is buried has yet to be solved and, if nothing else, it encouraged a host of false Louis' each calling himself the XIX.

12th Arrondissement

The first known mention of this area dates from the early 12th century: *Insula Bercilis* is what the people of the time

Above: The new Opéra de la Bastille symbolizes Paris at the turn of the century.

called this rural parcel on the right banks of the Seine. Of course, the Romans had explored the terrain long before. In AD 52, when they attacked *Lutetia*, they advanced by way of the *Via Carentonis*, which is known today by the name Rue de Charenton.

The abbey of **Saint-Antoine des Champs** was founded in 1198. Once a country lane, the latter-day Rue du Faubourg Saint-Antoine connected it to Paris. Numerous cabinetmakers, carpenters and furniture craftsmen settled in the vicinity to work for the monastery. The countless furniture stores and workshops established around the street are still full of evidence of this past.

The Seine has always been an important transportation route for every imaginable sort of freight. During the 18th century, Bercy developed into a reshipment point for wines, liqueurs and other sorts of *eau de vie*. In 1806 the first warehouse for wines and spirits was opened up. At that time, it was still located outside the toll-limits of Paris.

A People's Opera in the Workers' Quarter

Before plunging into the 12th Arrondissement from the Place de la Bastille, take one more sniff of the scent of the wide world at the **Bassin de l'Arsenal**, the yacht harbor of Paris, which extends along the Boulevard de la Bastille. Between 200 and 300 small boats can dock here. The green park on its left bank is an attractive place to take a stroll.

Next destination is the new **Opéra de la Bastille**. The gigantic proportions of this edifice now dominate the site where the Bastille railroad station once stood.

President Mitterand planned this great auditorium as an opera for the common man. In a symbolically significant ceremony, it was opened on the eve of July 14th, 1989, for the 200th anniversary of the French Revolution. Like most mod-

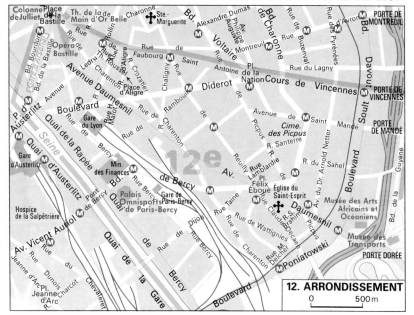

ern buildings in Paris, this one, too, has caused its share of controversy.

From this point onward, you should follow the Rue du Faubourg Saint-Antoine. One gets the feeling of being in a *souk*, an Oriental bazaar, in the **Passage du Chantier** nr. 66.

After passing by the **Square Armand Trousseau**, a park grounds with a small public music pavilion, turn at the second intersection onto the Rue Crozatier, and shortly thereafter take a right into the **Rue d'Aligre.**

The Haymarket – a Shoppers' Paradise

A colorful, bustling market dominates the scene here in the morning hours (except on Mondays). Africans wearing their traditional varicolored, batik garb, veiled Arabic women and retired Frenchmen with their customary berets do their shopping in perfect harmony.

As early as 1778, there was a market at the adjacent **Place d'Aligre**. At that time

the main commodities for sale were mainly straw and oats. Now, in addition to fruits, vegetables, flowers and cheese, the *Marché d'Aligre* also features a flea market, although one should not set one's hopes too high for discovering a thrilling treasure there.

If you're in the mood for a rest at this point, a hearty reception awaits you at the **Baron Rouge** (Rue Théophile Roussel). When visiting the Red Baron, it doesn't take long to get into the spirit of things. At this wine dealer (with tasting room) the precious liquid is tapped fresh from the barrel. The atmosphere is accordingly buoyant.

The Rue Héctor Malot leads to the Boulevard Diderot and in the process to the **Gare de Lyon**, the grand gateway to the Mediterranean – all trains headed towards the Mediterranean begin their journeys here.

The station was enlarged in 1889, following the artistic spirit of the epoch, and promptly reopened in time for the world exposition of 1900. Not only is the Art-

Nouveau façade of interest – so is the restaurant **Le Train Bleu** on the second floor. The *belle époque* glows in full splendor within; ceiling and walls are graced with 41 paintings by the most renowned artists of the era, colorfully illustrating the train stops along its southbound journey. The interior of the Train Bleu is a protected historical monument, and its cuisine has reaped an impressive four stars.

BERCY

Upon departing the Gare de Lyon, turn around the corner to the left and follow the pedestrian passage of the **Rue de Bercy**. After years of dogged resistance, the Minister of Finance and his staff finally cleared out of their former headquarters (in a side wing of the Louvre) and, in 1989, moved into their present, futuristic palace.

Above: Insiders meet at the 11th Arrondissement. Right: A huge hall staging sports and music events is located in Bercy.

Located across from it, is the **Palais Omnisports de Bercy**. There is room for an audience of 17,000 in this gigantic, multi-purpose hall with exposed blue steel girders and grass roof. The programming ranges from rock concerts clear to surfing competitions. On a walk around the building you will come across a graduated terrace-style fountain. Its pool alone covers a surface of some 1600 sqm.

The Rue de Bercy, once the main street of the community for which it was named, leads to the remains of the historical wine-making village. Along the way, you will spot a memorial plaque on a building wall at the corner of **Rue Corbineau**. It indicates the water level that was reached during a flood in 1910, in the course of which kegs of wine went floating through the streets.

The End of a World

"At the age of 17, I started out here as a messenger boy at a cognac merchant's. In those days, the work week still lasted

from Monday morning until Saturday night. Oh well, to be a wine merchant – that was always a profession of the *bon vivants,* people who have no great ambition, but love life above all. The people sang while they worked."

René C. started out in the wine village of Bercy in 1930. In those days, the business was in full bloom. Some 380 dealers had established themselves in the low wooden shacks and long cellars. Deliveries were done by horse-drawn carriage. It would happen now and then that the horses took their overtired drivers, who had fallen asleep on the driver's seat, back to the stalls in the evening on their own. On the weekends there were barbecues in front of the storehouses. The workers played *boules* beneath the towering old chestnut trees if there weren't musicians on hand to strike up a dance.

"Inherent to our profession back then was a certain *noblesse,* perhaps also because we only dealt with tools made of wood and copper. Those are materials that age unhurriedly, with dignity," remi-

nisces Réné C. After long years of training, the former messenger boy took over the cognac firm along with its old delivery logbook from 1880, which still registers the likes of Maxim's and purchasers from South America – and weighs so much that it takes two men to carry it.

In the meantime, the elderly man has sold his business. However, as he has now been doing for some 60 years, he comes to the office every day, and regularly inspects the expansive, antiquated cellar areas, in which tools of the trade from days long past and some bottles from the middle of the last century have stayed right where they are.

Soon, though, Monsieur C. will have to vacate his cognac house and leave the site permanently. The bulldozers have already completed their preliminary work in the neighborhood, and have left nothing more of the former rows of dreamy and ivy-covered buildings than a huge churned-up construction site. The "new Bercy" is planned as an extensive resi-

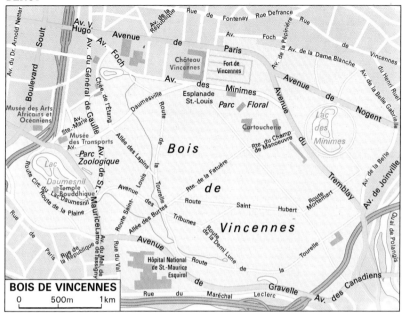

BOIS DE VINCENNES

0   500m   1km

dential complex amidst ample greenery, with a trade center for wine, spirits and foodstuffs of the luxury class. Only two of the old building complexes, which have been declared historical monuments, are to be preserved, as well as a portion of the stand of old trees.

In addition to a 700-bed hotel, the **American Center** (a gigantic United States cultural center), a conference center, some smaller restaurants and an exhibition complex with a museum annex are foreseen.

By that time, Réné C. will certainly have brought the treasures out of his cellar: "The past belongs to us – after all, we shaped it. People must be encouraged to keep its memory alive."

The Church from the Orient and the Cemetery of the Nobility

By way of the Rue Proudhon, one arrives at the Rue Taine and the **Place Daumesnil.** The center of the broad plaza is dominated by a fountain boasting eight water-spewing lions. As you continue your walk, pay attention to the façades. Their Art-Nouveau features have been preserved here virtually in their original condition.

On the Avenue Daumesnil one should leave sufficient time for exploring the **Église du Saint-Esprit.** This astonishing edifice, the construction of which was executed by Paul Tournon between 1928 and 1935, is an emulation of the venerable Hagia Sophia in Istanbul. The ground plan was realized with the most modern construction methods available at the beginning of this century.

The **Rue Sidi Brahim** begins opposite the church's entrance. It runs into the **Rue de Picpus**, on which you take a left turn. At the corner of Rue Lamblardie, you will come upon a section of the "green promenade." Upon its completion, it will connect the Place de la Bastille with the Bois de Vincennes, following along the former railroad route for 4.5 km.

The high walls at nr. 35, Rue de Picpus conceal the **Cimetière de Picpus,** also sometimes referred to as the "Nobility's Graveyard." 1306 victims from the period of the Revolution are interred there. During June and July 1794, the guillotine stood on the Place du Trône – present-day **Place de la Nation** – decapitating a total of 2765 people within a period of only six weeks.

Those who select the Cimetière de Picpus as their final resting place must fulfill the strict regulations of the private cemetery management: One of his or her ancestors must have been among the victims of the Place du Trône.

BOIS DE VINCENNES

The **Bois de Vincennes** had been a royal hunting-grounds since time immemorial. Or at least since the days of kings and queens.

Events of the post-revolutionary period resulted in the park's transformation into a military exercise area until Napoléon III concluded a contract with the city. He consequently turned over the administration of the park to the municipal authorities – on the condition that it was to be accessible to the public in the future.

As soon as the weather permitted, the Parisians stormed their "urban forest." No square inch of grass was spared, and that even though the Bois de Vincennes comprises 995 hectares.

The Métro transports the visitor to the main entrance (Porte Dorée station). On the left-hand side rises the **National Museum of African and Oceanian Art.** In addition to woodcarvings, masks and ceremonial garments from Black Africa and elaborately worked pieces of jewelry from the continent's northern coast, the museum also features the remarkable crocodile pit.

If your visit should happen to be in April or May, the **Foire du Trône,** a folk festival of superlatives with an annual attendance of five million, could properly finish off your liquid assets. The origin of

this "gingerbread fair" extends back over 1000 years: During a serious famine, the monks of the nearby monastery Saint-Antoine-des-Champs distributed small loaves of rye and honey to the starving. This became a tradition maintained each year during the Easter week until 1719, when this springtime festival was established with snack booths, showmen, games and clowns.

Now your path continues on into the park. The **zoo** is situated on the left, next to the **Lac Daumesnil**, where rowboats and bicycles are available for rent. The zoological gardens were France's first, established under the Hagenbeck administration in 1931.

One can see the 70-meter-high monkey-rock from quite some distance. Its state of dilapidation has been a source of considerable worry for the municipal administration for some time now. Demolition would be the most cost-effective solution – but the possible destruction of their "Eiffel Tower of the 12th Arrondissement" has met with embittered resistance from the local residents.

The **Parc Floral** guides the visitor into a resplendent world of fauna and flora, including vales of flowers, an aquatic plant installation and a garden of the four seasons. An exploratory tour here is pure adventure, especially for children.

The massive complex of the **Cartoucherie**, a former weapons arsenal with a powder factory, has now been taken over several theater troupes. Beneath its high ceilings are the "headquarters" of Ariane Mnouchkine's *Théâtre du Soleil,* among other theater groups.

The **Château de Vincennes** has a turbulent history behind it. Constructed in the 10th century as a hunting lodge, it was later expanded into a fortified castle, and has even drawn comparisons with the King of England's royal palaces. Its fortunes have played out as follows: Henry V, ruler of England and occupant of the Vincennes palace, succumbed to a bout

of dysentry within these walls in 1422. Up into the 17th century, Vincennes served as residence of the French kings – not least due to its good air – until they finally switched their preference to Versailles. As of that point, the dungeons were used for the detention of prominent captives – for example, in 1777, the Marquis de Sade and Mirabeau were held in neighboring cells.

Beginning in 1840, the Château de Vincennes was armed as a military fortress; in 1871, under martial law, nine participants in the Commune were executed there by a firing squad. During the Second World War, Vincennes was occupied by the Germans. On August 20th, 1944, 30 hostages were murdered; four days later, the occupying forces blasted the historic casemates and a fire destroyed one of the pavilions. The reconstruction work went on for decades.

Above: Until our presentdays the Château de Vincennes defyingly presents itself to the visitor.

3rd ARRONDISSEMENT
Accommodation
MODERATE: **Hôtel du Plat d'Etain**, 69, rue Meslay, Tel: 42 78 04 04, Métro République. **Hôtel Bellevue et Chariot d'Or,** 39, rue de Turbigo, Tel: 48 87 45 60, Métro Étienne Marcel. *BUDGET:* **Hôtel de Bretagne**, 87, rue des Archives, Tel: 48 87 83 14, Métro Fille du Calvaire.
Museums
Musée Carnavalet, history of Paris, 23, rue de Sévigné, Tel: 42 72 21 13, open 10.00 a.m.-5.40 p.m., closed Mon. **Musée Cognacq-Jay,** rococo collection, 8, rue Elzévir, Tel: 40 27 07 21, open 10.00 a.m.-5.40 p.m., closed Mon. **Musée de la Chasse et de la Nature,** 60, rue des Archives, Tel: 42 72 86 42, daily 10.00 a.m.-12.30 p.m. and 1.30-5.30 p.m., closed Mon. **Musée de l'Histoire de France,** 60, rue des Francs-Bourgeois, Tel: 40 27 60 00, daily 1.45-5.45 p.m., closed Mon. **Musée National des Techniques**, 292, rue Saint-Martin, Tel: 42 71 24 14, Tue–Sat 1.00-5.30 p.m., Sun 10.00 a.m.-5.00 p.m., closed Mon. **Musée Picasso**, Hôtel Salé, 5, rue de Thorigny, Tel: 42 71 25 21, daily 9.15 a.m.-5.15 p.m., Wed until 10.00 p.m., closed Tue.
Restaurants / Nightlife
Marais Cage, 8, rue de Beauce, Métro Arts et Métiers, Tel: 48 87 31 20, specialities of the Antilles. **Taxi Jaune**, 13, rue Chapon, Métro Rambuteau, Tel: 42 78 92 24, moderate prices. **Les Bains-Douches**, 7, rue du Bourg-l'Abbé, Métro Étienne-Marcel. Disco and restaurant in a former public bath, one of the trendiest inplaces, Tue–Sun 11.30 until dawn. **Le Tango**, 11, rue Au-Maire, Métro Arts-et-Métiers, disco, afro-sound, Wed, Thur, Fri, Sat 11.00 p.m. until dawn. **L'Hélium**, 3, rue des Haudriettes, crazy scene-bar, 8.00 p.m.-1.00 a.m., closed Mon.
Market
Marché du Carreau du Temple, rue Perrée – rue Dupetit-Thouars, daily from 9.00 a.m.-1.00 p.m., closed Mon. Lively market selling cheap clothing, bargaining is possible.
Post
Post Office: 67, rue des Archives, 8.00 a.m.-7.00 p.m., Sat 8.00 a.m.-12.00 noon, closed Sun.

10th ARRONDISSEMENT
Accommodation
MODERATE: **Hôtel Flora**, 1-3, cours de la Ferme Saint-Lazare, Tel: 48 24 84 84, Métro Trinité. **Hôtel Albouy**, 4, rue Lucien Sampaix, Tel: 42 08 20 09, Métro Jacques Bonsergent. *BUDGET*: **Hôtel d'Alsace**, 85, boulevard de Strasbourg, Tel: 40 37 75 41, Métro Gare de l'Est, near the rail terminal.

Museums

Musée Baccarat, 30 bis, rue de Paradis, Tel: 47 70 64 30, daily 9.00 a.m.-6.00 p.m., Sat 10.00 a.m.-12.00 noon and 2.00-5.00 p.m., closed Sun. **Musée Hoguet**, 2, bd. de Strasbourg, Tel: 42 08 19 89, by appointment 9.00 a.m.-12.00 noon and 2.00-6.00 p.m., closed Sat, Sun and in August.

Post

158, rue du Faubourg Saint-Martin, at the rail terminal Gare de l'Est, Mon–Fri 8.00 a.m.-7.00 p.m., Sat 8.00 a.m.-12.00 noon, closed Sun.

11th ARRONDISSEMENT
Accommodation

MODERATE: **Hôtel de la Tour d'Auvergne**, 81, rue de Charonne, Tel: 43 71 33 15, Métro Charonne. **Hôtel Arcade**, 15, rue Bréguet, Tel: 43 38 65 65, Métro Bastille.
BUDGET: **Hotel de l'Europe**, 74, rue Sedaine, Tel: 47 00 54 38, Métro Voltaire.

Restaurant / Nightlife

Le 26, 26, rue de Lappe, Tel: 48 06 08 90, Métro Bastille, restaurant in a former carpenter's studio. **Tapas Nocturne**, 17, rue de Lappe, Bodega bar. **Le Balajo**, 9, rue de Lappe, Tel: 47 00 07 87, discotheque. **La Chapelle des Lombards**, 19, rue de Lappe, Thur–Sat from 10.30 until dawn, disco with Salsa music.

Post

21, rue Bréguet, Mon–Fri 8.00 a.m.-7.00 p.m., Sat 8.00 a.m.-12.00 noon, closed Sun.

12th ARRONDISSEMENT
Accommodation

MODERATE: **Novotel de Bercy**, 85, rue de Bercy, Tel: 43 42 30 00. **Amadeus Nation**, 39, rue Claude Tillier, Tel: 43 48 53 48.

Restaurants

Le Trou Gascou, 40, rue Taine, Tel: 43 44 34 26, impressive selection of Armagnac-liqueurs. **Le Train Bleu**, Gare de Lyon, bd. Diderot, Tel: 43 43 09 06, elegant, expensive. **Wattignies**, 6, rue de Wattignies, Tel: 46 28 43 78, inexpensive.

Museums / Sightseeing

Women's Gallery **Le Septième Continent**, 43, rue de Charenton, Tel: 43 44 88 41. **Musée National des Arts Africains et Océaniens,** 293, av. Daumesnil, Tel: 43 43 14 54, Mon–Sun 10.00 a.m.-5.00 p.m., closed Tue. **Opéra de Paris-Bastille**, 120, rue de Lyon, Tel: 40 01 17 89. **Château de Vincennes** with **Musée Historique du Donjon**, Tel: 43 28 15 48, in summer 10.00 a.m.-6.00 p.m., in winter 10.00 a.m.-5.00 p.m.

Shopping

Le Baron Rouge, wine seller, 1, rue Théophile Roussel. **Marché d'Aligre**, Rue d'Aligre, daily except Mon. **Printemps**, department store, 21, cour de Vincennes. **J-L Scherrer,** elegant couture, 29, av. Ledru-Rollin, Tel: 43 43 58 34.

Tourist Information / Post

Town Hall, 130, av. Daumesnil, Tel: 43 46 06 03. **Post Office,** 30, rue de Reuilly.

19th ARRONDISSEMENT
Accommodation

MODERATE: **Forest Hill Paris La Villette**, 28 ter., av. Corentin Cariou, Tel: 44 72 15 30. **Arcade de la Villette**, 31-35, quai de l'Oise, Tel: 40 38 04 04. *BUDGET:* **Atlas**, 12, rue de l'Atlas, Tel: 42 08 50 12.

Museums / Sightseeing

Cité des Sciences et de l'Industrie, 30, av. Corentin Cariou, Parc de la Villette, Métro Porte de la Villette, Tel: 40 05 70 00, open 10.00 a.m.-6.00 p.m., closed Mon. Science and technology center. In the Cité: **La Géode**, 3-D-film theater inside a giant aluminum globe. **Zénith**, 211, Boulevard Jean Jaurès, Tel: 42 00 22 24, Métro Porte de Pantin, large tent-covered arena for pop concerts. **Parc des Buttes-Chaumont**, Métro Buttes-Chaumont and Botzaris, in summer 6.30 a.m.-11.00 p.m., in winter 7.00 a.m.-9.00 p.m.

20th ARRONDISSEMENT
Accommodation

MODERATE: **Europark-Hôtel**, 60, rue des Frères Flavien, Tel: 48 97 92 92. **Super Hôtel**, 208, rue des Pyrenées, Tel: 46 36 97 48. *BUDGET:* **Ermitage**, 42 bis, rue de l'Ermitage, Tel: 46 36 23 44.

Restaurants

Chez Vincent, 60 bd. de Ménilmontant, Tel: 46 36 07 67, Mon–Sat 12.00 noon-3.00 p.m., Fri, Sat until 9.45 p.m., closed in August, hearty fare from Brittany. **Le Viet-Nam,** Rue de Belleville, Tel: 46 36 67 33.

Museum / Sightseeing

Musée Edith-Piaf, 5-7, rue Crespin-du-Gast, Tel: 43 55 52 72. Open in the afternoon by prior appointment. **Cimetière du Père-Lachaise**, Métro Père-Lachaise, Tel: 43 70 70 33, Mon–Fri 8.00 a.m.-5.00 p.m., Sat, Sun 9.00 a.m.-5.00 p.m. Last resting place of celebrities such as Edith Piaf, Jim Morrison and Yves Montand.

Theaters

Théâtre de l'Est Parisien: 159, av. Gambetta, Tel: 43 63 20 96. **Théâtre National de la Colline,** Tel: 43 66 43 60.

Markets

Marché de Belleville, bd. Belleville/Ménilmontant, Tue and Fri mornings. **Flea Market Montreuil**, Métro Porte de Montreuil, Sat and Sun.

EXCURSIONS

The greater metropolitan area of Paris, known as the Île-de-France, is symbolized on its coat of arms as a white flower on a blue background. The flower does not correspond to the royal *fleur-de-lis*, rather it symbolizes the "self-limiting crown" – the rings of delightful, pastoral landscape around Paris. These *petites et grandes couronnes* allow visitors to explore the vicinity of the city and move on out to expansive fields and forests in excursions of one-half to one whole day by Métro or RER.

Basilique Saint-Denis

One of these destinations, to the north of the city, can be reached with a ride on the Métro: **Basilique Saint-Denis**. Those with an interest in French history will be fascinated with this basilica, a stone edifice jutting ruggedly above the proliferating, surrounding urban environs. This monument of masterful Gothic architecture, crowded in by profane buildings and eaten away by air pollution, looms over the scene with grim dignity. For a long period, the church was a burial place for kings; the medieval and Renaissance sculptures on their graves are among the finest artworks of their kind.

Pont des Sèvres

One can be assured of an entirely different experience after taking the métro to **Pont de Sèvres**, the southern terminus.

Once there, as you make your way across the bridge, you will experience a river bordered by broad, earthen banks instead of being wedged into the stony encasements of the city. The Seine here brings to mind a woman who sighs as she frees herself from a corset.

After crossing the bridge, the **Musée de la Céramique** is visible to the right,

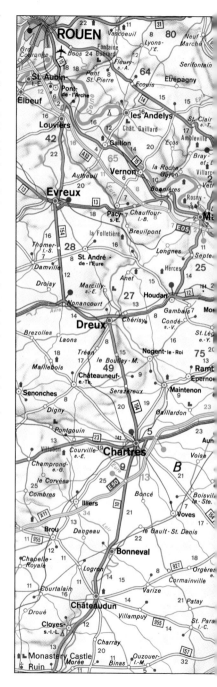

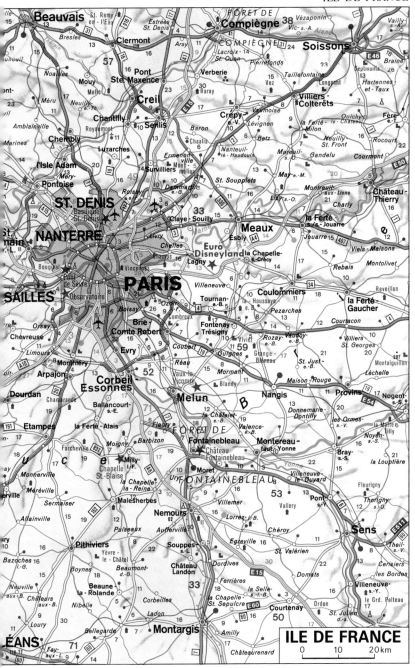

ILE DE FRANCE

0   10   20km

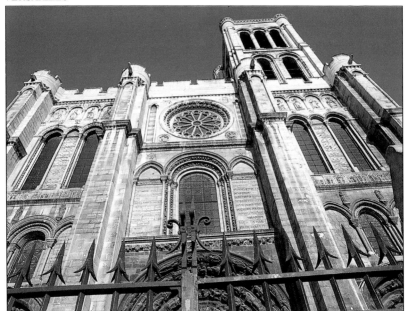

for 200 years the home of the highly-regarded Sèvres porcelain. Behind the graceful castle on the river-bank, a forested hill ascends to the **Terrace de Meudon** (follow the Rue du Château some 11 kilometers). The **National Observatory** is situated up on top; on its grounds one can enjoy a relaxing stroll through soft breezes under the shade of trees by day, added to which is a splendid view over Paris' scintillating lights by night.

Another elevation, swathed in cooling breezes during the summer, is the "chic" city district of **Saint-Germaine-en-Laye**. Since the 12th century, the buildings have clung to the hillside like so many swallows' nests. The castle, once a royal haunt, now shelters a collection of prehistoric art and articles for daily use. The town can be reached on a short trip with the RER A-line.

Previous pages: A kind of magnificence that seeks its equal – Versailles. Above: The basilica of Saint-Denis is the final resting place of the French kings.

Versailles

In virtually no time at all one can reach **Versailles**, the site of Louis XIV's majestic *spleen* to the south of Paris, by way of the RER Line C. This town is, however, equally connected in French history with the Revolution and its aftermath.

After 200 years, the palace has regained much of its pre-Republican splendor. In order to do justice to its importance as a tourist magnet, a new subway access is planned, in addition to a museum hall. It is unclear if this will reduce the crowding and pushing tourists, especially in the renowned **Gallerie des Glaces** (Hall of Mirrors), where mirrors are aligned to reflect the high windows, opening up a broad vista over gently rolling lawns and and clusters of trees.

The **park** of Versailles was designed by André Le Nôtre, the landscape architect to whom posterity owes the artistic conception of the garden *à la française*.

The **Grand Canal**, laid out in the form of a royal lily (*fleur-de-lis*) divides the broad park into two halves. The immense sea of green is sprinkled with groves and glades, flowerbeds, fish ponds, statues and fountains. Again and again, when one leaves the shadows of the trees and returns to the broad, sun-flooded path along the canal, the shimmering image of the palace appears abruptly, like a mirage.

If you're not quite exhausted from exploring the Palace of Versailles alone, then why not push on to Paris' second "corona"? Trains of the SNCF run regularly from the Gare du Nord to **Chantilly**. In the middle of a dusky forest region, the gentle contours of the park clearing open up around the castle, with its dreamlike moat and slate-blue roof.

Its interior houses the remarkable **Condé Museum,** which features exhibits of magnificent paintings by Botticelli, Raffael, Giotto and Holbein.

The Forest of Compiègne

The forests around the capital city are like jewels in the "outer crown." The importance of their tasks as climate regulators and oxygen producers can hardly be valued highly enough. Also a mere hour removed from the Gare du Nord towards the northeast, arising from the surrounding wheatfields is the most stately one of the region: the **Forest of Compiègne**. Starting out from the railway station, you cross the River Oise, arriving in the center of town with its Gothic **Hôtel de Ville** (town hall). It houses a well-organized tourist information office capable of providing brochures or assisting in the arrangement of bus tours and bicycle rentals (among other things).

The town hall is of refined, ornate architectural design and boasts what is allegedly the oldest bell in France. It is regularly set in motion by some curious little figures, the *picantins*, who have themselves become symbols of the city. Maps available from the tourist information office describe various walks around this area, including the route to the **Abbey Saint-Corneille** and to the **Château,** which contains the largest automobile museum in France.

In order to appreciate the forest itself, one should set out (with good footwear!) on the path to the nearby heights, named **Les Beaux Monts.** After covering the final steep section of the path, the hiker is rewarded with a view over the "Royal Way", a light-green breach in the dark forest that leads up to a castle.

Those visitors who are either not so light on their feet or thirsty for more knowledge can opt for the SNCF bus tour through the forest, which makes its first stop in the **Clearing of the Cease-Fire Accord**. At this location in 1918, the German capitulation was signed in a railroad car – which later found its way back to the site. Wax figures in the car's interior re-enact the event, though the collection of photographs in its side-compartment is far more riveting, to be sure. Through a stereoscope, the visitor can contemplate photos with titles such as *Life in the Trenches* and *The Battle on the Marne*.

If you're traveling by automobile, you ought to push on through to the forest village of **Vieux Moulins** and have dinner in a cosy *auberge*. Since the days of Empress Eugénie (wife of Napoléon III), who discovered it, this town has been a fisherman's paradise. Back then, the imperial couple took their vacations at **Pierrefonds Castle**, which is situated above another charming village on a lake fed by the River Berne.

Around 1400, a castle – or, more precisely, a mighty fortress – was erected at this site. It was later abandoned and used as a quarry for other construction activities following the Revolution. During the (historical) restoration, the structure itself was also (literally) restored, and by the architect Violet le Duc at that, to whom most of the more-or-less successful reconstructions of Gothic monuments in this area can be accredited. In this case,

the result was an unreal idealization of a medieval edifice. It looks like some kind of fairy-tale castle from a children's book, reminiscent of the runaway escapism of Germany's Neuschwanstein.

Vaux-le-Vicomte

To the south of Paris, about an hour away from the Gare de Lyon by train lies the town of **Melun**: Another 7 km along the way is the castle **Vaux-le-Vicomte**. This aged complex provided the basic blueprints for Versailles (an enlargement!). It was also planned by the same architects and landscape designers. Nicholas Fouquet, Louis XIV's treasurer, commissioned its construction. The grandeur of this edifice, however, brought about the downfall of its master.

As a patron of the arts, Fouquet supported the dramatist Molière and the

Above: The splendor of the 17th century appears unmatched. Right: Fontainebleau in the days of Napoléon I.

fabulist La Fontaine. He was also known as a rather important socialite, who threw extravagant parties. When he constructed his modest residence, the best at their craft was (just) good enough for him – the architect Le Vau and the landscape designer Le Nôtre.

With its park, Le Nôtre set a new standard. The symmetry of the French Garden reflected the ground plan of the castle. In 1661, for the completion of the grounds, Fouquet planned a sumptuous festival, which was to serve simultaneously as the Sun King's birthday celebration. The fountains gushed forth and sparkled, champagne flowed, musicians made merry by torchlight. For the edification of the king, dancing horses took to the "stage" (indeed, several of them drowned in the castle's moat). But there was considerable evidence to support the charge that Fouquet's power and wealth were being acquired at the king's expense. That same evening, before the last torch was extinguished, Fouquet was arrested and brought to the prison of Pignerol (today in Italy).

With his still-wounded pride, Louis began the construction of Versailles, while Fouquet languished away in the dungeon until his death. Since then, his castle has passed through the hands of numerous owners, always seeming to bring with it a curse. The current owner, however, seems to have managed to keep his and the castle's fate in check – by opening its gates to tourists.

The furnishings and kitchen equipment in this castle are particularly interesting. In addition, a diverse collection of coaches awaits the visitor in its spacious horse stables.

The Vaux-le-Vicomte offers its guests an exceptional experience on Saturday evenings in the months from June through September: Candles illuminate the paths amid surroundings creating an atmosphere that Master Fouquet would have liked to experience himself.

Fontainebleau

Fontainebleau is located somewhat further away, though it's also accessible via the Gare de Lyon. The 20,000-hectare, forested region surrounding it, with a fine stand of oaks, beeches, birches and pines, is a key backdrop of French history. It is also considered an El Dorado for mushroom hunters, animal watchers and even climbers – no joke, since in certain parts of the forest there are bizarre rock-towers at every turn of the trail that boast every degree of alpine difficulty *en miniature.*

Astonishing as it may seem, the train stops right in the middle of the forest. In order to reach the **Château Fontainebleau**, however, you can also hop on a bus in the city. As early as the 12th century, French kings liked to ride out to the lodge to stay after their day's boar-hunting expedition.

The castle building is so spread out and tortuously intricate that Kafka could have drawn inspiration for his literary pursuits here. Each successive ruler tried to put his own personal stamp on the royal holiday resort by means of architectural "enrichment." Francis I particularly distinguished himself in this regard. The rambling, airy ballroom and light-permeated gallery are attributed to him.

Napoléon I left behind his signature with the construction of an imposing throne room, cleverly entitled *Cour des Adieus.* This is where he took his leave from his Imperial Guard after he had departed from a Paris in rebellion.

A monument of much less grandiose proportions is located not far away in the quiet village of **Milly la Forêt**. The **Chapelle Saint-Blaise** is a permanent testimonial to the memory of Jean Cocteau, who was laid to rest there. He personally decorated the walls of this 12th-century chapel, which once served as a lepers' ward. His flower garden twines around the outer walls. When the sunlight is strong, the blossoms glow through the little, bull's-eye panes into the cool, dusky interior. A stone cat rests above the

219

holy-water font. Over the altar, Cocteau attempted a portrayal of the Resurrection in clear lines and tender hues.

The town was once home to some monks who were active as healers. They picked the herbs that were known as *simples*. Several shops sell these, in particular a local variety of mint, the *menthe de Milly*. The roofed **marketplace** forms the core of the village; its huge roof of rough-hewn chestnut has provided merchants with shelter since 1497. A glimpse into the shop windows of the antique dealers and real-estate agencies reveals the development of Milly from a refuge for lepers to an "asylum" for well-to-do Parisians in flight from the turbulence of urban life.

Chartres

Chartres is among the most rewarding destinations around Paris for a day's outing. From the Montparnasse railway station, the town can be reached in about an hour by train (runs at regular intervals).

This medieval city rises up over a broad expanse of wheat fields, crowned by the spires of its **cathedral**, which have served over the centuries as signposts for approaching pilgrims. The cathedral is one of the earliest buildings in pure Gothic style. It was constructed between the 11th and 13th century. The basilica has three naves and a choir with five naves. The space of the Gothic interior is well ordered according to height and depth. Each separate element can be examined by the visitor. Its stained-glass windows are considered one of the world's great cultural treasures. A **museum** here is devoted to this art, dealing particularly with the production and preservation of *chartreuse bleu*. When the sun breaks through these blue panes, it generates an unforgettable play of light and color.

Right: Standing in the colossal nave of Chartres cathedral.

Among the church's many admirable details is the **labyrinth path** of inlaid paving stones. By way of this tortuous path, pilgrims skid forward towards the altar on their knees. Portions of the crypt date from as early as the 9th century. The main facade, the *Portail Royal*, displays the highest degree of refinement. It is obviously a very appealing motif for painters and draughtsmen; there are constantly a number of them taking pains to render this stony storybook of Catholic Christianity.

The city's old center is today protected as a historical monument. Its pedestrian zones, shops and attractive eating establishments easily seduce one to take a stroll. Leading along the River Eure is a promenade with old *lavoirs*, where aristocratic linen was once beaten, wrung and rinsed. The charming **Église Saint-Pierre** is a little sister to the cathedral, situated on the edge of the old town near its former defensive wall.

Euro Disney Resort

A trip by car or with the RER out to **Marne-la-Vallée**, some 32 km from Paris, can replace an expenisve flight to Florida or California. Since April 12, 1992, another Disneyworld, the **Euro Disney Resort** has been unleashed on the public. It's open year round, and certainly one of the latest and greatest European tourist attractions.

Although construction has not yet been completeted, this one already measures 2000 hectares, one fifth the size of the heart of Paris. For the moment it boasts 30 Disney-style attractions from five countries, including *Big Thunder Mountain, Adventure Isle, Alice's Labyrinth,* and *Snow-white and the Seven Dwarfs*. The entertainment center *Festival Disney* is 18,000 sqm in size, and golfers have an 18-hole, imaginatively landscaped course at their disposal. Accommodations are available at *Camp Davy Crockett* (181 tent spots, 414 cabins), or in 5200 beds spread out over six hotels.

THE PARISIANS

The deliberate Parisian, who could never possibly live beneath another sky, does not have the same pedigree as the other people of France.

The members of this unusual species of humanity are simply different, more independent and fancy-free, more enterprising, but also more stressed out. They're quicker, more experienced, but lead more anonymous lives, since the city they inhabit is a hurly-burly whirl.

The Parisian always seems to come from one extreme or another. Either he is so poor that he sleeps under bridges as a *clochard*, or else he poses as being so unconscionably rich that people think he must be a *mega-in*.

In addition, he is also more cultivated, multicultural, articulate and versed in the ways of the world....

Above: Paris demonstrations often turn into public festivals. Right: A woman selling flowers behind her colorful stand.

This man or woman of the "enhanced" species has made of Paris a city of constant changes, the machinations of which are rather reminiscent of an ant hill.

This Parisian industriousness has always been the subject of more than the occasional wisecrack in the provinces, particularly in Southern France.

However, rather than allow themselves to be "buried in the provinces," these "fools for Paris" accept the commotion in the métro, constant traffic jams, waiting in lines, alienation, air pollution, high noise levels and so on, as part of the bargain. Indeed! To live in Paris is considered quite a privilege by its inhabitants...

Do the Parisians conduct themselves in a blasé manner when visiting the provinces? It certainly appears that way. The restaurant owners and hotel operators rub their hands with glee when the hordes of urban tourists from Paris pull up with bleached-out complexions.

It must be admitted that their smugness and their particular brand of manner of

conquering the soil everywhere they set foot has generated a bad reputation for the Parisians, which hurries on ahead of them wherever they go.

On home soil they behave completely differently. Thrilled with the opportunity to show their cousin from Auvergne or their foreign friend *their* city, they spice up a sightseeing tour with the inevitable excursion into that "great restaurant around the corner."

Yes, but...for this sort of graciousness, the Parisian unfortunately finds precious little time. He is running hard the whole day, squeezing in some sports between two appointments – after all, he is quite aware of his oxygen shortage.

The "favorite sport" of the Parisian, by the way, is called "taking fido for a walk." They can be observed, accompanied by their four-leggers, dressed in their jogging suits with walkmen glued to their ears as they criss-cross the plazas and parks with tiny steps.

The Parisians' love of animals, dogs in particular (of which there are 900,000 in the city) necessitates special patrols equipped with an astonishing new invention, the *filth-sucker,* to remove the dog feces. (Certainly residents of other major cities worldwide would also value this new service industry.)

Do the Parisians love animals more than their fellow man? It has been determined, at any rate, that inhabitants of the capital are less family-oriented than other French people, and if unmarried or divorced, they often reside alone in their apartments.

Is the Parisian In and Fashionable?

Whether skinhead or punker, cutie pie or blazing intellectual, according to the popular singer Renaud, the Parisians love only one thing – the *look!*

To get it, they invest quite a large proportion of their income, and are thoroughly skilled at sprucing up their appearance. From the mountain of their excellent education in the subject of "how to dress oneself," they peer down at

Beyond all of this "cultural" coquetry, *culture*, especially the cinema, actually does occupy an important place in the daily life of the Parisian.

On Wednesday, for example, the inviolable day of new cinema releases, long lines can be seen on the sidewalks before the cinemas. Few, apparently, are prepared to wait the crush out for a week before viewing the latest Lelouche, Godard or – even better – Kurosawa film. It is considered a question of honor to become familiar with the latest cinematic novelty before the rest of the world.

The Reverse Side of the Coin

The *jeunesse dorée,* active, dynamic women in their mid-forties who are equally skilled at handling both family and profession – all these positive illusions mustn't allow us to forget that there is a multitude of "stepchildren" here (in numbers increasing each year) for whom the only remaining place to live is the subway station. Reeling off a little tune or delivering a monotone recitation of their beggar's plea, their hopes ride on the kindness of the passengers. They exist in the lowest third of the so-called "two-thirds society" and, if they chance to roam these wordly streets, they are little more than cruelly blinded by the neon lights of stylish Paris.

Are the Parisians Friendly?

In the face of – and at the same time because of – the city's housing density, which forces upon its inhabitants an inescapable coexistence, relations among neighbors are not always as friendly as one might wish.

Since fellow inhabitants are frequently morose and hardly in the mood to talk to anyone, it's hardly surprising that they manage to walk past each other for 20 years without feeling any desire to develop or express a sense of familiarity.

everybody and everything that is not "up to date." After all, if the Parisian is not following fashion, he is making it.

Leaving behind the absolute claim to knowledge of what fashion is, the *mega-in* crowd knows better than all the rest what one *must* have read, seen, heard, eaten and toured – in short, they are at the crest of the wave in every realm of culture and knowledge.

They are the worthy successors of the affected society populating the salons of Paris in the 18th century, whose members were of the opinion that it was *they* who dictated whether it rained or the sun shone. They animate their often vain, empty world with fancy words, judgements and biting criticisms, meeting together to trade their palaver at dress rehearsals and gallery openings.

Above: Paris is still the avantgarde city of fashionwear. Right: A multicultural encounter – an old French and Arab playing checkers at Centre Pompidou.

Hidden mistrust has an insidious manner of preventing people from forming interpersonal relationships. This behavior is further supported by the fact that only 80 percent of Parisian residences are equipped with a telephone.

Stress and Haste

In order to combat headaches, stomach complaints and other disorders of psychosomatic origin, the Parisians plunge into yoga, meditation, acupuncture and other unconventional therapies.

When the Parisian is not rushing through the subway, he works himself up behind the wheel. Like most of his contemporaries in Western Europe, when he is wedged into a traffic jam, he becomes enraged, even aggressive.

For this reason, it is advisable for outsiders to avoid engaging in competition with the roughly 550,000 automobiles bearing Paris license plates (all numbers beginning with 75) or with those from the Île-de-France bearing 92, 93, 94, 95.

Night Hawks

The nocturnal "moths" of Paris flutter along determined routes. First off, after they've landed for a bit in the *Acide Rendez-Vous, L'Usine Ephémère* and/or the *Viva Maria*, the ecstatic journey proceeds to the *Balajo, La Locomotive* and the *Power Station* – and then most certainly to the *Bains-Douches*.

In these temples of the night, an atmosphere of loose unreality, an uncertain nervous titillation and affected nonchalance predominate.

The city's bon-vivants can choose from countless restaurants, bars and discos that are open all through the night. These indefatigable figures lose track of both date and hour when they are looking for amusement.

By the way, the expensive discothèques organize even "insider evenings" during the week, in order to avoid blending the Parisian public with the suburbanites, who show up on Saturday nights in search of entertainment!

MINORITIES

Emperor Charles V noticed it long ago, full of admiration: "The other cities are cities – Paris is a world." For over 200 years, France has considered itself the land of liberty and human rights. These national values have had the effect – or so it would seem – of a magical magnet. The first immigration wave, between 1885 and 1895, brought about one million people from neighboring Italy into France. Without their help, the French wouldn't have had enough laborers to carry through their industrial revolution.

In 1920, the *Grande Nation* sent trains off to Poland, Hungary, Yugoslavia and other Balkan states in order to recruit still more manpower. During this period, Paris was a stylish refuge for the Russian nobility fleeing the Bolsheviks, as well as the quintessence of the muse for artists from all over the world.

Above: Arab women are at home in Paris.
Right: Black is beautiful, at least in Paris.

While Germany was in the hands of the Nazis, many Germans who where Jewish or otherwise considered "undesirable", found a tenuous hiding place here.

And in the sixties, a third wave of immigrants came rolling in: Arabs from the former French colonies in North Africa, altogether some four million people, of which the greater portion settled within the capital city's urban maze. In the mid-seventies, following the first oil crisis, France took steps to tighten up its borders, but the stream of illegal immigrants has not yet been fully stanched.

All the Colors of this World

The entire world is either at home in or on a visit to Paris. Every twelfth inhabitant of the capital is a foreigner. North Africans represent the largest group in this category. The multi-ethnic *mélange* is fascinating. However, thinly concealed behind the colorful social strata are specific job divisions – from the Moroccan street sweepers to the concierge from

Portugal, from the Brazilian transvestite to the Japanese business student and on to the Lebanese multi-millionaire, all aliens are assigned their station.

In short, without its foreigners, Paris wouldn't be Paris. And the fact that foreigners don't stay that way for all eternity is underlined by the familial history of every third Frenchman, since this third of the population is descended from immigrants who arrived within the past four generations.

The visitor to Paris wishing to explore other worlds needs no more than a city map. Whether you desire to relax in the oriental steam bath of the Grand Mosque, eat a bowl of *borscht* in an original Russian restaurant, or practice meditation exercises in the Buddhist temple – the métro will undoubtedly get you there. The city's culinary diversity is so great that one restaurant critic with some imagination even expressed the opinion that if there was a tradition of fine dining on the moon, then Paris would have a locale with "lunar specialties."

Jangling through the Parisian ether is an incomparable multiplicity of tones: A virtually Babylonian snarl of languages and music rules the scene. International press is displayed at most newsstands, alongside of which appear newspapers published by several of the city's ethnic minorities.

The foreigners have also left a clear trail behind them in "high" culture, contributing to a broadening of the Parisian horizon in their wake. In this spirit, renowned conductor Pierre Boulez has expressed the opinion that artists the likes of Karajan, Solti and Barenboim have furnished the French music scene with new quality. Impetus – if not a downright rebirth of the theater culture – has come from such directors as Peter Brook, Claus Peyman and others in the Seine metropolis. And their relationship with Paris has always been a mutually profitable contract, each contributing to the

fame and the artistic career (and pocket book) of the other. That the cultures of this world should be at home in Paris corresponds to the wishes (and policies) of Minister of Culture Jack Lang. So it goes without saying, that at the highly official celebration for the Declaration of Human Right's 200th anniversary, artists of every ethnic and national background were present – a successful sprucing-up of the dream of the *Grande Nation.*

Of course, this multicultural coexistence doesn't always run a peaceful and harmonious course. The lofty, national ideals of liberty, equality and fraternity apply primarily to the "more equal" among the equal. The simple foreign laborers inevitably stand at the lower end of the social ladder. The satellite settlements in the vicinity of Paris are threatening to deteriorate into ghettos. Northern and Central Africans comprise the largest groups of foreigners here. In these "problem zones," it is no rarity that in one single classroom children of up to 29 nationalities may be seated together.

PARISIAN ART HISTORY

From the Gallo-Roman Epoch to Romanesque Style

There is little information remaining to us from the Gallo-Roman period about the cultural and artistic life of ancient Paris with the exception of a very few, still extant Roman structures. However, we can advance the theory that the Parisians of this period indulged in the same pleasures as their Roman contemporaries. They loved the games and battles that were held in the arenas, but also prized theater and the fine arts, including poetry, music and painting. From the end of the third on through to the sixth century, a period influenced most notably by the barbarian invasions, a considerable number of religious foundations were established that maintained schools for the scribes; of these, only some texts remain from those somewhat dark days – otherwise they left no visible trace behind.

It took until into the 11th century before a style evolved that would exert an influence on medieval art: the Romanesque. Monumental pieces of architecture were created, among them the Saint-Denis Basilica, which became the final resting place of French kings centuries later; the church of Saint-Germain-des-Prés; and the Notre-Dame Cathedral.

The Gothic Style of the 12th and 13th Centuries

In the second half of the 12th century, Paris became an artistic focal point. The city had established itself as capital at a time when the Capetians were expanding their monarchy and thus strengthening their influence.

Paris and the Île-de-France played a predominant role in the development of a

Right: "La Dame à la Licorne" in Cluny Museum (end of 15th century).

new artistic style, the Gothic, which then replaced the Romanesque. In 1144, the abbot Suger consecrated the chancel of the Saint-Denis Basilica. From 1163 on, the Parisian community of architects was engaged in the construction of Notre-Dame Cathedral, in which the first vaulted arch appeared in 1185. This and the flying buttress were the architectural elements that would enable the Gothic master builders to erect structures into which large windows could be inserted (the Sainte-Chapelle, for example) due to the supports having been reduced to a mere skeleton. By the beginning of the 13th century, the influence of Notre-Dame began to be visible not only in Paris, but in other regions as well, as can be seen from the Bourges Cathedral.

Courtly Arts and Royal Patrons

From the mid-13th century on, Paris developed both economically (with the driving force of maritime trade) and intellectually. In 1215, its first university was founded, followed in 1253 by La Sorbonne. The city became an educational center influencing the development of styles in architecture, sculpture, and the so-called "minor" schools of art (painting, woodcarving, gold smithery, etc.).

A sort of rivalry developed between Louis IX (St Louis) and the city's Catholic prelates, the *Grand Seigneurs*. This brought about the development of court art during the 14th century. Its main expression was found in many drawings – such as the pictures of Mahaut d'Artois and Jeanne d'Evreux – and in miniatures with religious motifs. The ivory carvers were gathered mostly in the quarter surrounding the church Saint-Germain l'Auxerrois.

Simultaneously, a new phenomenon appeared, which would last through the entire century and would play a significant role in the city's artistic and cultural expression. The royal (or aristocratic) pa-

tron, sustained by a societal evolution that brought with it a new notion of humanity's relative importance. Charles V's patronage should be mentioned in this regard. With his outgoing personality, Charles V had a masterful grasp of how to harmonize the work of artists from various disciplines (sculpture, architecture, glass painting, icon painting and gold smithery). The stylistic expression of this harmony exerted a decisive influence on the whole of French art for almost a hundred years.

Henry IV

In the 16th century, Francis I relocated the court society to the Île-de-France, to Fontainebleau and Saint-Germain en Laye. Paris was neglected by the succeeding kings for almost a century.

At the end of the 16th century, Henry IV came back to a Paris that had been destroyed in the course of the religious wars. The "good king" took an interest in urbanization and ordered far-reaching changes in the districts of Paris. In order to renovate the medieval city, he created open squares, of which the most famous was the Place Royale, the present-day Place des Vosges. Henry IV also pressed forward with the construction of the Louvre and the Galérie du Bord de l'Eau, and came up with the idea of reserving the ground floor for the court artists. To have lodging in the Louvre.... for the artist this was, of course, a very significant official acknowledgement of success, but it was also accompanied by not insignificant financial advantages.

The Further Evolution of Architecture and the Arts

Under Louis XIII, the construction plans Henri IV had supported were once again privatized. New city districts came into being: Île Saint-Louis, Le Quartier du Marais, Le Quartier du Temple. The streets became hemmed with distinctive pieces of architecture (among them the Hôtel de Sully and Hôtel de Carnavalet).

In the course of the 17th century, a change in taste and general mentality took place. The interior accouterments of a building were accorded increasing importance. This trend is demonstrated with particular clarity by the Hôtel Lambert and the Palais Mazarin, the present-day National Library. These buildings, surrounded by splendid gardens, were constructed in the 18th century and consist of a great number of rooms, including many reception areas: vestibules, anterooms and salons. The greatest artists of this epoch, Boucher and Natoire, created an interior decor consisting largely of genre pictures and pastoral scenes, following a general tendency towards frivolity current at the time.

The first art salons were established. In the reception areas of the mansions of the major financiers in the suburb of Saint-Honoré, philosophers, authors, scientists and artists met with one another, together launching the Enlightenment, which was to bring fundamental changes to the European mentality. Though Paris had been considered a center of the arts for centuries, this reputation would be further strengthened during the 19th century. A great many artists came to the capital city to live there, express their *joie de vivre* and participate in the salon society. The most famous of these institutions was that of Madame Récamier, which was held in the former Bois abbey. It was attended daily by prime minister Chateaubriand, who would read aloud a few pages of his *Mémoires d'outre-tombe* (Remembrances from beyond the Grave).

The Impressionists

As a result of Baron Haussmann's urbanization measures, Paris rapidly assumed the visage of a modern city.

This modern character now drew the Impressionist painters into Haussmann's rejuvenated boulevards. A considerable

Above: Here along the quay of the Seine, a piece of Parisian art history is reflected.

number of them, including Monet, Renoir, Pissarro and Degas, brought the city the immortality Napoléon III had wished for. They recorded impressions of Paris for eternity: the gawking crowds, scenes from concerts, theaters, and coffee houses. The coffee houses became the place for meetings, an exchange of thoughts and discussions for artists not associated with the Academy. They were all obsessed with the same desire – to fight against "established" art. Between 1866 and 1874, the artists who would later be counted among the Impressionists – Manet, Monet, Cézanne, Pissarro, Degas and Bazille – met together in the Café Guerbois.

In 1874 the *Salon of the Rejected* came together in the Atelier Nadar. Its participants were those artists from the Café Guerbois whose paintings had been rejected that year by the official Art Exhibition because they contradicted the criteria of the Academy. Viewed with 20/20 hindsight and in light of the ensuing developments in art appreciation, it's certainly difficult for us to conceive how such masters could have been repudiated. However, in that epoch, the Impressionist seemed intent upon stirring up trouble in the conventional world of painting by bringing their easels out of the atelier to paint nature and things transitory. Other art "scandals" were to follow the Impressionists in the course of the 20th century.

The Bateau Lavoir and the Quartier Montparnasse

At the beginning of this century, a dirty and comfortless shack went into the annals of art history: the *Bateau Lavoir* ("wash boat") in which numerous artists lived and worked. The best-known of its residents were Picasso, Juan Gris, Van Dongen, Herbin, Braque, Reverdy and Apollinaire. Among other works, Picasso created *Les Demoiselles d'Avignon* there, which is considered to be the manifesto

of Cubism. With the Bateau Lavoir, the district Montparnasse became a melting pot of modern art before World War I and during the twenties. Artists from around the world (including Brancusi, Chagall, Fougita, Matisse, Max Jacob, Modigliani and Picasso) ate, drank and discussed their ideas in Le Carrefour Vavin, at the Dôme and the Rotonde. At the close of the 20's, La Coupole was added to this group of intellectual restaurants.

Paris and the International Art Scene

During the first half of the 20th century, Paris was *the* arts center – the place where avant-garde movements had their origins. The flush of artistic activity kept Paris in a creative fever that only recovered partially from the interruption following World War II. Since then, the greater part of the international arts scene has relocated to New York City. Of course, among artists Paris is still a place of choice for a sojourn, but it has lost its "Olympian" superiority. The Montparnasse has had to suffer the ravages of urban renewal; many of its older buildings have been demolished. One can still view some of the artists' ateliers that existed at the beginning of the century in the 13th and 14th arrondissements (for example, La Butte-aux-Cailles, Rue Campagne-Première, Villa Seurat). However, in the last 15 years, artists have been settling predominantly in the 11th and 19th arrondissements. The galleries of contemporary art followed in their trail and are located, for the most part, on the Rue Keller and the Rue de Charonne. Many galleries moved from the Seine's Left Bank over to the Right Bank when the Centre Georges Pompidou was constructed in the seventies on the Plateau Beaubourg. The population of Paris has been provided the opportunity to become more familiar with French and especially foreign artists through the efforts of the gallery operators.

MUSIC LIFE

Paris brings to mind a song, a strain which fills the air with a thousand ringing notes.... Taking Paul Verlaine's concept literally – he envisioned "music above all else" – Paris has inspired a truly impressive number of musicians and lyricists. So, just as it is claimed that music makes life easier, your stroll through the streets of the capital may also be brightened by the tones of some ingratiating, little melody wafting out of an open window.

Paris has drawn the best ot its rugged shores, from Rameau and Couperin in the age of Louis XIV, to Liszt, Chopin, Berlioz (19th-century) and the great school of Nadia Boulanger, the Conservatoire Americain, in the 20th century. Edith Piaf, Yves Montand, Georges Brassens, Jacques Brel – in his or her way, each of

Above: University fanfare provides a lively street atmosphere of its own. Right: The Parisian violin-makers on Rue de Rome know their trade.

them has contributed to the City of Light's pride and distinction, as have, though a bit more modestly, the street singers, who have now been supplanted by the musicians in the métro stations. For music lovers, life in Paris is a true delight. Countless concert halls are set vibrating each evening by classical, jazz, rock, reggae and folk music from all over the world. No matter what your tastes may be, you are sure to find a nightspot where you can trip the light fantastic. To get a quick overview of the available options, a glimpse at the music pages of the events magazines (among them *Pariscope* and *Officiel du Spectacle*, published daily) is quite sufficient. These can be obtained at all magazine shops.

Did You Say Classical?

Well then! Head out onto the town and discover – if you enjoy gala performances – the perfect acoustics of the Pleyel concert hall, the wood-panelled walls of the Théâtre des Champs-Élysées, and the

contemporary style of the Opéra de la Bastille (not to forget the concerts, recorded by Radio France). Far removed from the pompous atmosphere of these music palaces are the concerts of chamber music and lieder recitals put on each evening in churches and small auditoriums. A long list of them can be found in the daily events publications. In this manner, one can combine a cultural evening with a nocturnal foray through the Île de la Cité, the Place de la Madeleine or the Quartier des Halles.

Inspired by the dream of revivifying the musical ambience of the former-day Viennese concert-cafés, *L'Opus* has outstanding acoustics for chamber music and *bel canto* – and offers the audience a menu with excellent fare on the side. It is housed in the renovated portion of an abandoned printing shop.

"When the jazz comes, the Java goes," sings Claude Nougaro in his warm southern accent. It's true that in Paris, jazz pushed Java to the side. The city now attracts the best of the world's jazz artists

each year. The stars meet and jam in the *New Morning*, the *Petit Journal* or the *Méridien*, where one can enjoy select pieces while sitting in a comfortable *fauteuil* and sipping at a cocktail.

Pop Music – Advice for Fans

For variety shows, rock, pop and reggae one should take time for a closer study of the events magazines to discover the true range of choices available. Paris has several beautiful, large concert halls like *Le Zénith, Le Casino de Paris, L'Olympia* and *Le Palais des Sports,* whose walls continue to reverberate with the greatest of musical events.

On a somewhat more modest level, one can go out on a small-scale musical excursion in one of the many smaller halls and piano bars; these are situated primarily along the Rue des Lombards and the Rue Mouffetard. It remains to be noted that rock concerts are often put on in nightclubs. A sizzling atmosphere in these places is virtually guaranteed!

WHERE THE CAMERAS WHIR
WITHOUT CEASE

If there was an Oscar awarded for the town seen most often on the silver screen, beyond any doubt the city of Paris would have a long-term subscription to the distinction. Year in, year out, the city is overrun by an immense host of camera teams, who use it as a stage backdrop for feature and television film productions, videos and advertising spots. On any given day, there is an average of ten cameras rolling at various locations around the metropolitan area.

Since the invention of the cinema, Paris has always been close to the heart of screenplay authors. (The first public showing was given by Parisian inventor Louis Lumière in December 1895). After all, whether the script deals with a political or criminal game of intrigue, whether a spy-thriller or a heart-rending love story, the "city of lights" always has the right backdrop at the ready. The ad agencies think similarly; in fact, Paris seems to half-way guarantee the success of an advertising spot.

Another contributing factor is that studio filming has become somewhat taboo in recent years. Natural decor is *de rigueur*, and in this respect, Paris has advantages that other shooting locations can only envy. A city that has different characteristics from quarter to quarter, enjoying a mild climate well-suited for filming and much-lauded light conditions, it can fulfill even the most particular of a director's whims and inspirations. In the city hall, applications for filming permits consistently pile up sky-high.

However, filming in Paris is neither simple nor without its price. Even the smallest project necessitates a good dozen of different permits and day-long rounds to various governmental agencies.

Right: New and old movie hits are always among the favorite Parisian topics.

The afflicted in this matter can lay the blame on Napoléon III, who decreed in 1862 – and thereby decades before the first blossoming of the film industry – a law which continues to be in force: "It is forbidden to operate any sort of enterprise on public land without having obtained prior permission from the competent agency."

On the other hand, the administrative authorities are thoroughly amenable to the film producers. After all, we're dealing here with the best imaginable free advertising for the metropolis as well as considerable additional revenues for the city's coffers. Expense allowances, rental payments, permit and user fees add up often enough to a tidy sum.

The city hall could write an anthology of some directors' thoroughly eccentric wishes. For the shooting work on a James Bond film, the production company wanted to monopolize one of the city's main arteries (cutting right through the city center along the Seine) for several days (!), catapult the hero's automobile onto a barge and finally rescue the unruffled secret agent from his precarious situation by helicopter. The scenes were actually done – in a moment when the artery happened to be closed for repairs.

Almost anything can be arranged. For the director who wanted to put up flags emblazoned with the swastika along the Champs-Élysées for the shooting of a documentary film on the German occupation, the fashionable Avenue Foch was made available to his team on a low-traffic August day at six o'clock in the morning. Takes of a spectacular, giant, chain-reaction traffic accident on the inner-city freeway were done at night, under the illumination of blinding searchlights, when a section of the eight-lane "race course" had been closed for maintenance purposes.

Some of the good citizens of Paris can recount the horror which gripped them when those film people were let off their

leashes right in their very own street! Neither simulated chase scenes with shrieking car tires and breathtaking stunts culminating in junkheaps, nor stage-bullet gun battles between the gangsters and the *flics* are among the sort of sonic backdrops that the poor, unsuspecting resident has in mind as he settles down at the table to sip his morning coffee – let alone when he comes home from a day at the office.

It would, of course, be false to assume that a director in Paris can simply do whatever he or she pleases. Filming work in the city hall or under the nose of the president in the splendid Élysée Palace are just as decidedly out of the question as projects stepping too far over the borders of good taste. Just a short while back, for example, the municipal administration refused to allow an advertising spot for the latest swimsuit fashions to be filmed at the Cimetière Père-Lachaise. A production company was also sent packing with its idea of filming a Roman-style orgy in the catacombs beneath Paris. And the ad agency which needed shots of

the "city of lights" cloaked in darkness and demanded that the electricity be shut off for an entire district without further ado was similarly out of luck.

Of course, for generations of cineasts, the great majority of applications has requested access to the widely-recognized, all-time optical "hits." The Eiffel Tower is the most frequently filmed construction. Other classics of film history include Notre-Dame, the Champs-Élysées, the Louvre, the Place de la Concorde, the Île Saint-Louis and the Bois de Boulogne.

Most recently, the Centre Pompidou, the skyscraper district La Défense, as well as the museum and recreation park La Villette have been enjoying the cineast's attentions ever more frequently.

At the Arche de la Défense (Mitterand's gigantic triumphal arch) and the glass pyramid in the Louvre, filming teams from around the world were already waiting, cameras at hand, when the construction fences around the sites were still standing.

DINING IN PARIS

A trip to the "gourmet capital" Paris without a thoroughgoing study of the gustatory delights it has to offer would be an educational gap that should most certainly be filled – and pleasurably, at that. After all, this rambling metropolis is a gastronomic melting pot, in which both conservative and adventurous, well-to-do and more modest diners and drinkers find just what they're looking for – although it must be noted that those who really want top quality must usually slaughter their piggy banks, since at the cheaper price levels not everything which sounds delicious always is.

What is described as "French cuisine" derives its multitudinous variety from the country's numerous provincial, rural cooking styles, which have been blended with a pinch of Parisian "cosmopolitan

Above: Every city district has its own street market. Right: With more than 400 cheeses to choose from, decisions can be difficult.

spice." *Pot-au-feu* (a meat and vegetable stew), *bœuf bourgignon* (Burgundian beef ragout), Provençal *bouillabaise* (fish stew), southwestern French *cassoulet* (stew of white beans and meat) and Alsatian *choucroute* (sauerkraut generously laced with smoked pork, liver dumplings and sausages from Strasbourg, which look the same as frankfurters) are among the most widely known of the typical dishes served in the brasseries. Brasserie, by the way, means brewery and usually denotes a place serving a particular beer or associated with a specific brewery. These are standard fare in many bistros now as well. The renowned French onion soup (the perfect dish for night hawks after one-too-many glasses of wine) can still be had at several bistros in the Halles district.

The run-of-the-mill bistros generally offer (at digestible prices) down-to-earth, simpler fare such as *coq au vin* (rooster in wine sauce), *raie au buerre* noir (ray with melted butter and capers), and *quiche lorraine*. For dessert there's *crème caramel*

(egg custard with caramel sauce), chocolate *mousse, tarte tatin* (heated apple tart), fresh fruit or *fromage blanc* (curd cheese with sugar)

The basic food of the bistro devotee, however, is and will remain *steak frites* with green salad, and *wiener schnitzel* (veal cutlet) with fries and a salad garnish. Usually about the consistency of shoe leather, accompanied by some limp French fries and a couple of tired lettuce leaves in *vinaigrette* (consisting in France of oil, vinegar and sharp mustard) the *steak frites* is usually edible only in dire emergencies.

Those preferring a snack might select a *croque monsieur* (toast with ham and grilled cheese), a *croque madame* (the same with a fried egg) or a half baguette with butter and cheese, ham or *rillettes* (pork paté with lard). This is usually consumed with a little pitcher of red wine (1/4 liter) – the standard wine in bistros is the *Côtes-du-Rhône* – or *un demi* from the tap (not a half-liter of beer, as one might think, but rather one-third at most).

The noise sensitive should be forewarned of the racket in the bistros and brasseries as well as their usual crowdedness. They are not suitable for an intimate *tête-à-tête*.

In the populous arrondissements there are still a few genuine local taverns where the neighbors stop in *en famille* any time of day to chat and have a drink at the counter.

Certain of the bistros and brasseries are renowned for their decor, originating from the thirties and further back. Naturally, this ambience costs a bit more, which is not to say that you should refrain from spending an evening in such outstanding atmosphere. The usual bistro, with its fluorescent lighting, artificial leather seats, pressboard furniture and pre-prepared dishes warmed up in microwave ovens is not especially conducive to lingering, that is unless it has a street terrace not too close to the traffic, where it is possible to sit outside in good weather and watch the bustle of Paris at a respectful distance from the lead-laden exhaust fumes. Be forwarned, however,

that it is much more expensive at a table than at a bar.

In addition to a growing number of cosy, tranquil wine bars and tea rooms, in the last few years a trend has been observed among delicatessens (*traiteurs*), bakeries and patisseries: An ever increasing number of them are putting a few tables in the shops and on the sidewalks in front of them, where the goods on sale can be consumed right away at reasonable prices. Some bakeries have installed actual cafés serving freshly prepared plates and various salad combinations daily. These are a cherished alternative for the multitude of office employees who no longer find time for the two-hour-long, three-course, midday meal of yore.

Nowadays, only the evening is reserved for this lingering over a meal. With the gastronomy guide in hand, the ambitious culinary explorer is almost

Above: An opulent meal at the Place du Tertre. Right: Such a meal is ideally topped off with a strong cup of "Café Cognac".

scientifically prepared for the coming gustatory experimentation. The selection is huge at all price levels, and the choice more than difficult, since even the gastronomic literature can offer only subjective points of reference.

On a visit to Paris, one should by no means pass up the fresh seafood and fish from the Atlantic, the North Sea and the Mediterranean, which arrives at the table prepared in such a multitude of ways. Seafood is found primarily in the brasseries, although an increasing number of fish restaurants bears witness to its growing degree of popularity. Here, as elsewhere lighter and more healthful alternatives to meat are *en vogue*.

The traditional war being played out amongst the "gastrosophers" in gourmet literature concerning which cuisine is the "real" cuisine – traditional or modern, *nouvelle cuisine* or culinary orthodoxy – will most certainly continue, although it is not considered to be of much importance by the top chefs. At present, a trend can be detected in the direction cham-

pioned by tradition-bound, Lyon-born chef Paul Bocuse. Part of this includes the reintroduction of heartier portions. The rule "the more expensive the restaurant, the smaller the portions" doesn't even satisfy snobs anymore. What really counts today in the *haute cuisine* is creativity, fantasy and the quality of the ingredients. The "ninth art" draws equal inspiration from the traditional French and regional cuisines as well as the many international influences to which a modern chef is exposed – especially in a cosmopolitan metropolis like Paris.

Due to this multiculturalism, the individual tastes of visitors to Paris can also be indulged. There is hardly a national cuisine in the world that is not represented here. Whether one craves northern or southern European, Far Eastern or South American, Russian, Indian, Arabic or African food, the culinary adventures here know no boundaries!

On such gourmet expeditions, aficionados should certainly avoid obvious tourist traps the likes of Montmartre, the Rue Mouffetard or the pedestrian zone of the Quartier Latin. In these places, the unsuspecting visitor to Paris is fed – accompanied by music and at the highest attainable prices – "food" from the conveyorbelt: meats grilled to a char, deep-frozen pizza and chemical *Bordeaux*.

Don't be too much of a skinflint when it comes to choosing a wine if you lay any value on a decent one. In addition to the classics from the Alsace, Burgundy, Bordeaux and Champagne, there are numerous regional wines that have established themselves as respected competitors of the traditional varieties. These include wines labeled *Côtes-du-Rhône, Chinon, Vouvray, Bandol, Hermitage, Fitou....* Even the vintners of southern France have been putting a bit more effort into improving their cheaper table wines in recent years, employing more careful production methods instead of blending them with cheap Italian imports. Admittedly, a culinary tour in the Seine metropolis is nothing for poor students, but what a celebration for the taste buds!

Nelles Maps ...the maps, that get you going.

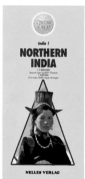

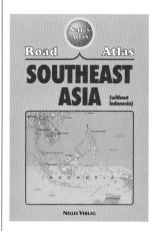

- Afghanistan
- Australia
- Bangkok
- Burma
- Caribbean Islands 1 / Bermuda, Bahamas, Greater Antilles
- Caribbean Islands 2 / Lesser Antilles
- China 1 / North-Eastern China
- China 2 / Northern China
- China 3 / Central China
- China 4 / Southern China
- Crete
- Egypt
- Hawaiian Islands
- Hawaiian Islands 1 / Kauai

Nelles Maps

- Hawaiian Islands 2 / Honolulu, Oahu
- Hawaiian Islands 3 / Maui, Molokai, Lanai
- Hawaiian Islands 4 / Hawaii
- Himalaya
- Hong Kong
- Indian Subcontinent
- India 1 / Northern India
- India 2 / Western India
- India 3 / Eastern India
- India 4 / Southern India
- India 5 / North-Eastern India
- Indonesia
- Indonesia 1 / Sumatra
- Indonesia 2 / Java + Nusa Tenggara
- Indonesia 3 / Bali
- Indonesia 4 / Kalimantan

- Indonesia 5 / Java + Bali
- Indonesia 6 / Sulawesi
- Indonesia 7 / Irian Jaya + Maluku
- Jakarta
- Japan
- Kenya
- Korea
- Malaysia
- West Malaysia
- Nepal
- New Zealand
- Pakistan
- Philippines
- Singapore
- South East Asia
- Sri Lanka
- Taiwan
- Thailand
- Vietnam, Laos Kampuchea

GUIDELINES

PREPARATIONS

Climate and Clothing

There is no doubt that Paris is at its most beautiful by fine weather, but unfortunately it rains more frequently than some travel brochures would lead one to believe. This should definitely be taken into account when packing your bags. Bring an umbrella, or plan to buy one in Paris. During the winter months, the thermometer usually hovers just above the freezing point, while an unpleasant, drizzling rain becomes a constant outdoors companion.

At night it might be warm enough for a light summer jacket or cold enough for your winter wardrobe. Furs, however, are usually exported rather than actually worn here (except for show, of course!). Also, heavy winter boots with treaded soles are almost never necessary in Paris, since snow is an event the city isn't blessed with every year.

In summer, however, one must figure on a period of dog days, when scarcely a breeze blows in the dusty streets, and it can become almost unbearably stifling and hot in this crowded, heavily trafficked metropolis.

Above all, the footwear you pack must be comfortable. There is so much to be seen everywhere that you will scarcely realize how many kilometers you cover daily on foot.

More attention is paid to outer appearances in Paris than most other places. One journalist received confirmation of this in a curiosity test: In some shops, she was simply derided when she appeared there as a potential customer – but not clothed in the "style of the house." In addition, the Parisians maintain the practice of ignoring whatever doesn't happen to be within their scope. This fact carries with it the advantage, that one can parade through the streets with blue hair, a bone in his ear or a red clown's nose and go just as unnoticed as if he were wearing a grey double-breasted suit.

Etiquette and French for Beginners

To the Parisian, foreigners are part of the urban scene, and in general tourists are fairly well-liked. Those making a lot of noise, pushing ahead of others in queues or snapping their fingers for the waiter, however, will be treated with icy rejection.

You can't count on much helpfulness when asking for advice on the street in your mother tongue or trying it in English before at least taking a shot at French. Frequently it takes nothing more than a completely desperate *où* ? (pronounced oo, meaning "where") in combination with an extended city map to open up a true wellspring of sympathy. If you then thank your rescuer with a heartfelt *merci* and add a *Madame, Monsieur* or *Mademoiselle*, you will be seen as well-bred and versed in the ways of the world. *Madame* and *Monsieur* belong after every *bon jour* ("hello") and *au revoir* ("goodbye"). *Pardon* is always handy, whether the goal is to address someone or merely to squeeze past people. It also serves as a question if you haven't understood something.

This is the basic vocabulary which at least secures an open ear. Even if it seems a bit ridiculous, be generous with the *monsieurs* and *madames*. At the beginning, one really doesn't need a lot more French than this. Everything else can simply be expressed with the hands. After all, the French themselves are enthusiastic gesticulators.

Even if you're not exactly in the mood to smile – that can happen now and then in this loud and hectic city – practice putting a friendly fold or two in your visage. This is one key to the heart of most French people.

These bits of advice apply to encounters with the "normal" Parisian. However, in a metropolis like Paris you can run into figures with intentions on your billfold, as well as people who you can't shake loose because your smile may have looked a bit too encouraging. Simply call out *Au secours!* (pronounced ohseckoor), which means "help!" In this way, you will at least draw the attention of passers-by – and thus almost certainly become free of the unwelcome "admirer."

GETTING THERE

Enquire at your travel agency concerning what sort of documentation is required for your entry into France. Traveling by car within the European Community, you'll find some border crossings to France to be unguarded. The visa imposed on US citizens in 1986 after several terrorist bombings has quietly been revoked.

Arrival

If not coming in by automobile, you will either arrive at the Charles de Gaulle Airport in Roissy-en-France, Orly International Airport or one of the city's six railroad stations. From the railroad stations the next leg can really only be managed by Métro or taxi. The airports have outstanding shuttle services – bus, train, even helicopter to La Défense – between each other and to downtown Paris.

PRACTICAL TIPS

Banks and Exchange

The banks have varying hours of business. The majority, though, close at 5 pm and on Saturdays. If you call up the *Office du Tourisme* (47 23 61 72) and name the district where you are, they will give you the address of the closest, open exchange bank.

Books and Magazines

Within Paris, especially at the tourist centers, there is international press available at virtually every kiosk. If the selection isn't sufficient, then try your luck in the *drugstores* (that is what they are called!), the train stations and the larger

papeteries (book and stationery stores). Books in many languages are available in the FNAC (Les Halles Forum), where one can also obtain information on where to find additional literature. A famous English-language outlet is Smith's bookshop at the corner of Rue de Rivoli and Rue Cambon (near Place de la Concorde).

Buses

Using the bus is a bit more complicated than riding the Métro since there are more than 50 lines, but a close study of the bus schedule will be of help. Bear in mind that one sees more of Paris from the bus.

Children in Paris

Contrary to general belief and despite the fears of their parents, children like Paris. They love the play of lights along the brilliantly illuminated streets, the activity, the display windows, the numerous playgrounds, the pony riding in the major parks (Luxembourg, Tuileries, Monceau) and the many carousels. And, not least, they like the French clowns, the *guignols*, whose green-painted, wooden huts, signifying a child's world, stand in many of the smaller and larger parks.

Children are welcome almost everywhere and enjoy special treatment as well. Many restaurants pamper the little ones with special meals. In others, even the finer establishments, they are quite prepared to cook up something that isn't on the menu. They are pleased to improvise for the dear little ones. In addition, a number of museums will transport your little angels into a world of enchantment.

The largest and most interesting playgrounds are, without a doubt, in the Cité des Sciences (19th Arrondissement) and in the two *bois* (forests), the Bois de Boulogne and Bois de Vincennes, though all of the parks have some kind of attraction for children. The Bois de Boulogne and Boid de Vincennes.

Other points of interest to families are located outside of Paris. In addition to the

Métro
RER
(Regional Express Network)

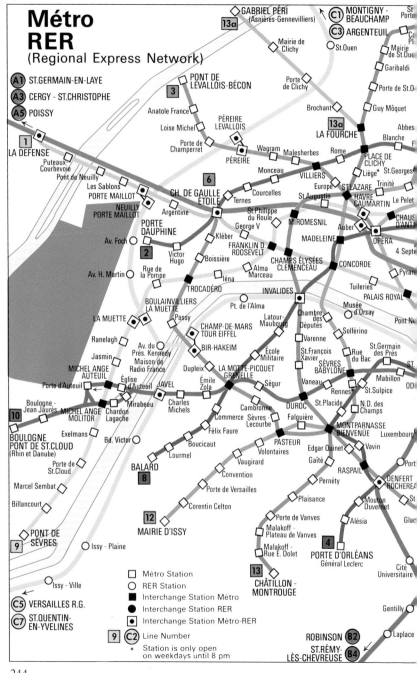

A1 ST.GERMAIN-EN-LAYE
A3 CERGY - ST.CHRISTOPHE
A5 POISSY

	Legend
□	Métro Station
○	RER Station
■	Interchange Station Métro
●	Interchange Station RER
◉	Interchange Station Métro-RER
9 C2	Line Number
*	Station is only open on weekdays until 8 pm

GABRIEL PÉRI
(Asnières-Gennevilliers)
13a
MONTIGNY - C1 BEAUCHAMP
C3 ARGENTEUIL
St Porte
Mairie de Clichy
St.Ouen
Mairie de St.Oue
Garibaldi
PONT DE LEVALLOIS-BÉCON
3
Porte de Clichy
Porte de St.O
Anatole France
Brochant
Guy Môquet
Loise Michel
PÉREIRE LEVALLOIS
Porte de Champerret
Abbes
Blanche
PÉREIRE
13a LA FOURCHE
Wagram
Malesherbes
Rome
PLACE DE CLICHY
1
LA DÉFENSE
Puteaux Courbevoie
Pont de Neuilly
Les Sablons
PORTE MAILLOT
NEUILLY PORTE MAILLOT
Argentine
6
CH. DE GAULLE ÉTOILE
PORTE DAUPHINE
Av. Foch
2
Victor Hugo
Rue de la Pompe
Av. H. Martin
Kléber
Boissière
Monceau
Courcelles
Ternes
St.Philippe du Roule
George V
FRANKLIN D. ROOSEVELT
Alma Marceau
Iéna
TROCADÉRO
INVALIDES
Pt. de l'Alma
Liège* St.Georges
VILLIERS
Europe
St.Lazare
ST.LAZARE
HAVRE CAUMARTIN
St.Augustin
MIROMESNIL
MADELEINE
CHAMPS ÉLYSÉES CLEMENCEAU
CONCORDE
Trinité
Le Pelet
Auber
OPÉRA
CHAUS D'ANTI
4 Septe
Pyran
Tuileries
PALAIS ROYAL
Pont Ne
BOULAINVILLIERS LA MUETTE
LA MUETTE
Passy
Ranelagh
Jasmin
Av. du Prés. Kennedy
Maison de Radio France
CHAMP-DE-MARS TOUR EIFFEL
BIR-HAKEIM
Dupleix
LA MOTTE-PICQUET GRENELLE
Émile Zola
Chambre des Députés
Latour-Maubourg
École Militaire
Ségur
Varenne
Solférino
Musée d'Orsay
St.François Xavier
SÈVRES BABYLONE
Rue du Bac
St.Germain des Prés
ST.
MICHEL ANGE AUTEUIL
Porte d'Auteuil
Boulogne-Jean Jaurès
MICHEL ANGE MOLITOR
Chardon Lagache
Église d'Auteuil
Mirabeau
JAVEL
Charles Michels
Commerce
Cambronne
Sèvres Lecourbe
DUROC
Falguière
Vaneau
Rennes
St.Sulpice
St.Placide
Mabillon
OD
N.D. des Champs
10
BOULOGNE PONT DE ST.CLOUD
(Rhin et Danube)
Exelmans
Porte de St.Cloud
Marcel Sembat
Billancourt
Bd. Victor
BALARD
8
Boucicaut
Lourmel
Félix Faure
Convention
Porte de Versailles
Corentin Celton
Vaugirard
Volontaires
PASTEUR
Edgar Quinet
Gaîté
RASPAIL
Pernéty
Plaisance
MONTPARNASSE BIENVENÜE
Luxembourg
Vavin
Port
DENFERT ROCHEREA
St
Glac
9
PONT DE SÈVRES
Issy - Plaine
12
MAIRIE D'ISSY
Issy - Ville
C5 VERSAILLES R.G.
C7 ST.QUENTIN-EN-YVELINES
Porte de Vanves
Malakoff - Plateau de Vanves
Malakoff - Rue E. Dolet
Mouton Duvernet
Alésia
4
PORTE D'ORLÉANS
Général Leclerc
13
CHÂTILLON-MONTROUGE
Cité Universitaire
Gentilly
Laplace
ROBINSON B2
ST.RÉMY-LÈS-CHEVREUSE B4

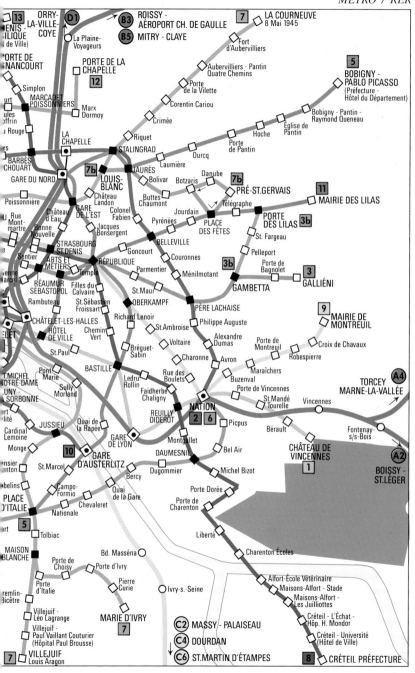

city's two zoos (Vincennes and Jardin des Plantes), day outings to the Thoiry and Saint Vran wildlife preserves are worthwhile. More information can be obtained from the *Office de Tourisme.*

Cinema

It goes without saying that a city as cosmopolitan as Paris also has a thoroughly international cinema schedule. The *Pariscope* can be obtained at any kiosk; it provides (among other things) a complete listing of the week's film schedule, which begins on Wednesdays. On that list, the abbreviation *VO* indicates the the film is being presented in its original language with French subtitles. *VF* is the abbreviation for films dubbed into French. This small-format weekly is inexpensive and also provides the schedules of theaters and concert halls, and information on the hours of the major museums as well as their special exhibits, in addition to listing numerous restaurant, cabaret and other useful addresses which can make a stay in Paris even more enjoyable.

Consulates / Embassies

Great Britain, 9 Av. Hoche, 75008 Paris, Tel. 42 66 38 10. *Australia,* 131 rue de la Pompe, 75016 Paris, Tel. 45 53 51 32. *Ireland,* 12 Av. Foch, 75016 Paris, Tel. 45 00 89 43. *Canada,* 35 Av. Montaigne, 75008 Paris, Tel. 47 23 01 01. *New Zealand,* 7 ter rue Léonard de Vinci, 75016 Paris, Tel. 45 00 24 11. *Netherlands,* 7 rue Eblé, 75007 Paris, Tel. 43 06 61 88. *USA,* 2 Av. Gabriel, 75008 Paris, Tel. 42 96 12 02.

Dining

Upon entering a restaurant, the first thing to do is wait quietly by the door until the *maître d'hôtel* shows you to your table. This is common even in the smallest of restaurants.

Meat is ordered: *cuit* = well done, *saignant* = rare, *à point* = medium, *bleu* = seared (very rare).

Entrées, Hors d'œuvres are appetizers; *Plats* are main courses, frequently subdivided into *Poisson*: fish, *Crustacés*: seafood, *Viande: meats, Volaille*: fowl, *Fromage:* cheese, *Dessert:* same, *Boissons*: beverages.

A la provençale . with plenty of garlic!
Agneau . . . . lamb
Ail . . . . garlic
Aloyau . . . . beefsteak
Andouille . . . . . . type of sausage
Assiette de... . . . . . combination of...
Assortiment de... . . . assortment of...
Baignet . . . . . French-style doughnut
Bar . . . . perch
Batavia . . . . . variety of green lettuce
Bavarois . . . . whipped cream torte
Bavette . . . . beefsteak
Blanquette . . . . ragout
Bœuf . . . . beef
Bouchée . . . . tidbit
Braisé . . . . braised
Brochette . . . . skewer
Cailles . . . . quail
Campagnard . . . . . . with cold cuts
Canard (Caneton) . . . . duck
Carré . . . . . . pork or lamb cutlet
Cassolette . . . . baked in a small
          casserole pot, au gratin style
Cassoulet . . . white beans with pork,
          bacon and sausage
Chantilly . . . . whipped cream
Charcuterie . . . . sausage and
          similar products
Chavignol . . . . goat cheese
Chou . . . . cabbage
Civet . . . . ragout
Cochonailles . . . . cold cuts
Confit . . . . conserves (jam)
Consommé . . . . soup
Contrefilet . . . . beef fillet
Coq, coquelet . . . . chicken
Côte . . . . ribs
Coupe . . . . cup or bowl
Crème . . . . . . soup or creamy dish
Crudités . . . . raw vegetables
Daurade . . . . bream (fish)
Dinde, Dindonneau . . . . turkey

Emincé . . . . stroganoff-style	*Morue* . . . . stockfish
Endives . . . . . . chicory (not endives)	*Moules* . . . . mussels
Entrecôte . . . . beef rib steak	*Mousse* . . . . mousse
Escalope . . . . cutlet	*Mouton* . . . . mutton
Estouffade . . . . . stewed or braised	*Museau* . . . . snout (aspic)
Esturgeon . . . . sturgeon	*Navarin* . . . . ragout
Farci . . . . stuffed	*Noisette* . . . . nuggets (meat)
Faux-filet . . . . beefsteak	*Noix* . . . . . chunks or cubes (meat)
Feuilleté . . . . in a pastry crust	*Oeufs* . . . . eggs
Flageolets . . . . broad beans	*Oignons* . . . . onions
Flan . . . . egg custard	*Onglet* . . . . beefsteak
Foie . . . . liver	*Panaché* . . . . mixed...
Fourré . . . . filled or stuffed	*Pâté* . . . . pie
Frisée . . . . green salad	*Pâtisserie* . . . . pastries
Frites . . . . French fries	*Paupiette* . . . . rolled meat
Friture . . . . fried in oil	*Pavé* . . . . thick beefsteak
Fruit . . . . same	*Pêche* . . . . peach
Fromage de tête . . . . . head cheese	*Petit Salé* . . . . . smoked pork chop
Fumé . . . . smoked	*Pied* . . . . leg/knuckle
Garniture . . . . . . garnish/side dish	*Pintade* . . . . guinea hen
Gâteau . . . . cake	*Poire* . . . . pear
Gigot . . . . leg (of mutton)	*Pommes* . . . . apples
Glace . . . . ice cream	*Pommes...* . . . . potatoes
Gratin . . . . au gratin	*à l'huile* . . . .in oil (cold)
Haché . . . . chopped	*à la vapeur* . . . . steamed...
Hachis . . . . ground beef	*au four* . . . .baked
Haricots . . . . green beans	*robe des champs* . . . boiled, unpeeled
Herbes . . . . herbs	*sautées* . . . . . . fried, hash browns
Huîtres . . . . oysters	Porc . . . . pork
Hure . . . . aspic/ jellied meats	*Porcelet* . . . . piglet
Jambon . . . . ham	Potage . . . . soup
Jarret . . . . knuckles/ leg	Poulet . . . . chicken
Julienne . . . . . . mixed vegetables	Profiterolles . . ice cream in puff pastry
Laitue . . . . green salad/ lettuce	*Quiche* . . . . quiche
Langue . . . . tongue	*Rillettes* . . . . paté with pork and lard
Lapin/Lapereau . . . . rabbit	*Ris de veau* . . . . . veal sweetbreads
Lardons . . . . bacon/lard	*Rognons* . . . . kidneys
Légumes . . . . vegetables	*Rôti* . . . . roast(ed)
Lentilles . . . . lentils	*Romaine* . . . . lettuce
Lieu . . . . pollack	*Rouget* . . . . barbel (fish)
Limande . . . . dab	*Salade de saison* . . . . . seasonal salad
Loup . . . . bass	*Saucisse* . . . type of sausage (heated)
Macédoine . . . . mixed...	*Saucisson* . . . . sausage as cold cut
Magret . . . . breast (cut of meat)	*Saumon* . . . . salmon
Mache . . . . lamb's lettuce	*Sauté de...* . . . . ragout of...
Maquereau . . . . mackerel	*Scarolle* . . . green lettuce (escarole)
Mélé . . . . mixed...	*Semoule* . . . . semolina
Meringue . . . . meringue	*Sole* . . . . sole
Montbéliard . type of sausage (heated)	*Sorbet,* . . . . sherbet

Suprême . . . with cream-based sauce
Tartare . . . . raw, chopped meat (beef)
Tarte . . . . pie
Tarte tatin . apple tart (heated or cold)
Terrine . . . . type of paté
Tournedos . . . . rumpsteak
Truite . . . . trout
Tranche . . . . slice
Tripes . . . . tripes
Vacherin (glacé) . . . . . meringue pie
Veau . . . . veal
Velouté . . . . soup

To request the check: *L'addition s'il vous plaît.*

Tips are given when the service is satisfactory (even if it says *service compris* – service included – on the menu). It is simply left on the table when you stand up and amounts to a rounding off of the total.

Driving

If you dare to visit Paris by automobile, first off some good advice. Don't park your car just anywhere. Of course, this is the favorite sport of the indigenous population, but it's also quite expensive. You should know that cars here are swiftly towed away, and that a ticket for illegal parking in the city costs at least 150 francs (if the sum isn't paid up within two weeks, it doubles). The days when foreigners were still treated accommodatingly are over. *Parkings,* as the Parisians call parking garages, are available; usually spaces in them as well. They are not too expensive – in comparison with the risked parking tickets. It's also good to know that one may be able to move about in Paris *independently* with a car – but not quickly. Newspaper reading at the wheel is no rarity. Neither are dents. Passing on the right, cutting others off, disregarding rights-of-way, and driving through red lights – this is the driving-style of the genuine Parisian. You'll have to decide for yourself if this venture is worth it. If you think you're capable,

don't forget your *complete* set of insurance documents.

Health

Find out from your health insurance company/group which documents you should take along for France. In France, it is usual to pay for the physicians and medications, later filing for a reimbursement. In hospitals patients are treated for "free" if they present their international insurance card.

Hotels

Paris is well stocked with hotels of all categories. In case you haven't booked a hotel room in advance, then you should go to the *Office de Tourisme* for help in finding accommodation. During the main travel season try to get a hotel room before traveling to the city. Carry along the address of your hotel with you, since it happens quite frequently that tourists can't find their hotels again.

When a room is reserved for two people, then as a rule it will be equipped with one large bed (standard width 1.4 meters). If this is something you are unaccustomed to, then request a room with two beds *(deux lits).*

Information

The *Office de Tourisme de Paris* (Tourist Information Office) can offer further assistance if yon need additional information.

Office de Tourisme: 127, Champs Élysées (8th Arrondissement); Métro Étoile; business hours: daily, 9:00 am to 10 pm (summer), 9:00 am to 8:00 pm (winter); Tel. 47236172.

Office de Tourisme and SNCF (French national railway): lobby of the Gare d' Austerlitz, entrance 25; Métro Gare d'Austerlitz; business hours: 8:00 am to 10:00 pm; open every day.

Office de Tourisme: Gare de 1 Ést (opposite track 26/7); Métro Gare de l'Est; business hours: Monday-Saturday 8:00

am to 1:00 pm and 5:00 to 8:00 pm. *Office de Tourisme*: Gare de Lyon (main hall); métro Gare de Lyon; business hours: same as Gare de l'Est.

Office de Tourisme: Gare du Nord (across from track 19); Métro Gare du Nord (Tourist Information Office), business hours: Monday to Saturday 8:00 am to 8:00 pm.

There are also tourist information offices in each of the city's airports.

The *Offices de Tourisme* have a real bonanza of brochures at the ready. The visitor can obtain much more than just a couple of brochures with information on hotel rooms, one example being tips in a variety of languages on such practical matters as the reclaiming of sales tax.

So much material is available at these offices that you will probably not even know what to ask for. For this reason, here is a selection of what information sheets can be obtained free of charge:

Hotel lists with additional suggestions for campers and addresses of the youth hostels *(auberges de jeunesse)*. Restaurant lists. Pamphlet on the Parisian nightlife (bars and discothèques). Calendars of events (concerts, conferences, exhibits, theater, etc). A listing of all museums. Brochures with a selection of excursions within the Ile-de-France as well as to the nearby seashores. Selections of sightseeing tours. Lists of the primary interesting sights. Brochures for handicapped tourists. Information on the major institutions (and summer universities) offering French courses for foreigners. Address lists of mediators for au-pair positions. A Paris Journal in several languages, with good suggestions and useful addresses. And not least, of course, good maps.

As a result, there is a constant crush in the tourist offices. If the personnel is overloaded when you drop in, it's a good idea to write a little list containing the things that you are particularly interested in and simply hand it to the representative behind the counter.

Loss of Documents

The first thing to do is have the nearest police station fill out a declaration of loss. Once in possession of this form, go to your consulate.

Métro

Paris' outstanding public transportation network is a good alternative to its chaotic, street-traffic conditions. If you don't like being squeezed in shoulder-to-shoulder, then travel first class (at twice the fare). At these times, the Métro and bus lines may run nearly minute-by-minute, but they are packed to the gills nonetheless. Firm departure and arrival times exist only for the suburban trains and the RER (Express Métro).

There are information counters in the major transfer stations, where one can obtain maps and information sheets on special tickets for tourists. The simplest thing to do is pick up a *carnet* at the counter of any Métro station or tobacco shop (ten fares; one-third cheaper than when individually purchased), which can then be used for both the bus *and* the Métro. Within the Métro system, passengers may ride as long and far as desired.

In buses, the routes are divided into sections; two fare zones = one ticket. With each transfer, a new ticket is required. Some of the bus lines travel nothing short of "sightseeing tours," though with the zone system they can get rather expensive in a hurry.

If you want to explore Paris by bus, it's a better idea to obtain a special tourist's ticket. Information on them is available in the major Métro transfer stations and the *Office de Tourism*.

Some things you must know: The Métro stations have signs with a large *M* on a red background; the Express Métros, an *RER* on a blue background. Within Paris, the same tickets are used for both systems.

Money

Banks, post offices and change bu–
reaus can and will change money or cash
a Eurocheck with varying fees. Credit
cards are used even in supermarkets,
which is handy. But keep track of your
expenditures: France, and Paris in particular, is not cheap.

Museums

Paris can boast of some 50 state-run
museums in addition to countless private
ones. The state museums are open daily
except Tuesdays, private museums set
their own opening hours, and some can
only be viewed by prior arrangement. For
these reasons, it's definitely advisable to
stop by the *Office de Tourisme*.

Outings

Every travel guide rightfully en-
courages the visitor to undertake excursions to Versailles, Fontainebleau and
other renowned sites of interest. Here's
one tip that may save you considerable
disappointment: Even if you're a dyed-
in-the-wool individualist, it's better to
book a guided tour at a reputable travel
agency than to head off for, say, Versailles on your own. During the summer
months, in particular, the throngs of tourists are so overwhelming that upon arrival you must first go through an endless
waiting line just to get tickets.

If you survive this torture, you will be
shoved through passage and salon sar-
dine-style, without even knowing where
you are – unless you're a head taller than
the knowledge-hungry masses. In contrast, on a guided tour you will be fun-
neled in rapidly and not only learn something about the interesting sights, but
even *see* some of them, since some spac-
ing is maintained between the groups.

Postal Service

If you need postage stamps or want to
make a telephone call, it's a good idea to
visit a *Bar-Tabac* (sign features a red
rhombus), since at the post office one
must put up with long waiting lines. If,
however, a visit to the post office is unavoidable, go there as early as possible –
with a bottle of patience pills.

In a *Bar-Tabac* it is possible to obtain
(besides tobacco) postcards, stamps, tickets for the Métro and cards for coinless
telephones. They also have public telephones and lavatories.

Taxis

Parisian taxis are affordable and, in
normal situations, there are enough to
meet the demand. In figures: They transport 100 million people annually, though
at an average speed of 14 kilometers per
hour – a further indication of the traffic
density in Paris. In rush-hour periods,
they're hard to nail down, and police-su-
pervised waiting lines (necessitated by a
lack of customer discipline) at the railroad stations and airports are no rarity. As
a rule, the taxi drivers are considered
honest, even though a few of them take
"detour" routes (often to get around traffic jams). It is not out of line if additional
fare is exacted for large pieces of luggage
and/or trips to the railroad stations or airports. In addition, the taxi driver is
authorized to refuse groups of more than
three passengers.

Telephoning

You are best off purchasing a telephone card at a *Bar-Tabac* or at the post-
office as soon as you arrive in Paris or
France. Telephone booths have operating
instructions in several languages, including international dialing: 19, wait for
tone, area code of the city (in Europe,
without the initial zero), and then the
main telephone number. Domestic calls:
first dial 16, wait for tone, then dial the
eight-digit number direct.

AUTHORS

Gabi Lefèvre: Once a widely (and enthusiastically) traveling interpreter and translator, this Parisian-by-choice from northern Germany now continues her profession at her own desk. She was project editor of this book.

Olivier Soufflet: This dyed-in-the-wool Parisian started with his career in journalism right after completing his studies at a recognized Parisian school of journalism. His travel reports have been published in *Le Monde* (among others).

Myriam Blitz: This French journalist has been living in Paris for more than twelve years.

Grace Moran: Grace has lived in Paris for an "eternity" with her husband and child. When Paris gets too cramped and smoggy, your lungs will be grateful for her hints on the outings to be made in the surroundings of Paris.

Eliane Hagedorn: Married to a Parisian southern-Frenchman-by-choice (with one foot in Germany), she lives with one foot in Munich and the other in France! A graduate in German language and political science, she wrote the history section for us.

Renaud Lefèvre: Renaud was employed at the Parisian daily *Libération* until he settled on freelance journalism.

Eleonore Baumann was born in southern Germany, though she feels at home in Paris. This successful translator has specialized in cuisine.

Veronika Hass / Darrell Delamaide: This American-German couple has been living, traveling and working together for 15 years. After spending ten years in Paris, they took their leave with the co-written article on *The Brain of Paris*.

Barbara Böhm comes from a small French town and describes, in addition to the district where she now resides (the 11th Arrondissement), two adjacent ones: the 10th and 13th. The art-historical out-

line in the latter portion of the book flowed from her pen as well.

Peter Heusch studied in Aachen, Germany, before he transferred to the Sorbonne in 1982, there completing his studies in Romance languages and literature. Since 1985 he has been a freelance correspondent for German newspapers and a publicity agent.

Suzanne Krause is a German-born broadcast journalist, who lives in Paris and focuses on socio-political themes.

PHOTOGRAPHERS

Archiv für Kunst und Geschichte,
  Berlin   20, 24L, 24R, 27, 29, 31, 32, 33, 34, 149, 212/213, 218, 219, 229
Beck, Josef   108, 132, 165
Bondzio, Bodo   2, 38, 154, 162, 166, 194, 224, 238
Gaudeaux, Bernhard   cover, 1, 9, 14, 17, 21, 23, 26, 39, 49, 54/55, 58, 59, 62, 66, 67, 70, 73, 74, 75, 80, 82/83, 84, 88, 89, 96, 98, 99, 100, 101, 102, 104, 105, 106, 110/111, 114L, 116, 117, 122, 130, 138, 142, 143, 147, 158R, 163, 164, 168, 171, 172L, 175L, 175R, 176, 178/179, 186, 187, 192, 193, 195, 196L, 196R, 197, 198, 199, 201, 202L, 202R, 204, 206, 207, 210, 216, 222, 223, 225, 226, 232, 233, 236, 237
Kunert, Rainer E.   10/11, 16, 44, 48, 68, 121, 150, 221
Larose, Hugues   146
Liese, Knut   18, 45, 50, 65L, 65R, 71, 79, 91, 114R, 128/129, 140, 158L, 159, 174, 180, 183, 227
Radkai, Marton   12/13, 22, 30, 35, 37, 51, 52/53, 64, 76, 78, 90, 92, 93L, 93R, 94, 95, 97, 125, 126, 134, 135, 137, 152/153, 170, 172R, 173, 184, 188, 200, 230, 235, 239
Vestner, Heinz   42, 47, 112, 120, 123

Passage de Plantin 197
Passage des Panoramas 158
Passage des Princes 159
Passage du Caire 157
Passage du Chantier 203
Passage du Cheval Blanc 203
Passage Jouffroy 158
Passage Reilhard 190
Passage Verdeau 159
Pepin, the Short 20
Père Tranquille 64
Perrault, Charles 57
Perrault, Claude 59
Petit Palais 47, 137
Philippe Auguste 21, 44, 56, 58, 64
Philippe Egalité 61
Philippe II 27, 30
Piaf, Edith 232
Picasso, Pablo 113, 114, 165, 168
Pierrefonds Castle 217
Pigalle 155, **171-173**
Place Blanche 162
Place Charles de Gaulle 138
Place Charles Dullin 165
Place Clichy 162
Place d'Aligre 205
Place Daumesnil 208
Place de Grève 72
Place de la Bastille **200-206**, 200
Place de la Bourse 157
Place de la Concorde 134
Place de l'Alma 139
Place de la Madeleine 132
Place de la Victoire 45
Place de l'Étoile 46, **138-140**
Place de Martyrium 165
Place des Abbesses 165
Place des Châtelet 71
Place des Fêtes 196
Place des Innocents 67
Place des Vosges 74, 75, 229
Place du Caire 156
Place du Tertre 163, 166
Place du Thorigny 183
Place du Trocadéro 139
Place Émile Goudeau 165
Place Furstemberg 94
Place Igor Stravinsky 56, 69
Place Jean-Baptise Clément 166
Place Léon Blum 203
Place Louis Lépine 78
Place Marcel Aymé 169
Place Pigalle 162, 171
Place Saint-George 161
Place Saint-Gervais 72
Place Saint-Sulpice 89
Place Vendôme 45, 63, 64
Pleyel, concert hall 232
Poitiers, Diana of 26
Pompadour, Madame de 31, 67
Pompidou, Georges 39, 69

Pont d'Arcole 76
Pont de Bir-Hakeim 117
Pont-Neuf 80
Pont de Sèvres 214
Pont Saint-Louis 80
Pop Music 232
Porte de Clignancourt 174
Porte Maillot 147
Pré Catalan 144
Prefecture 30
Printemps, department store 161
Procope 97
Proust, Marcel 57

Q

Quai de la Tournelle 99
Quai de Mégisserie 71
Quai de Montebello 99
Quai d'Orsay 124
Quai Malaquais 94
Quartier Latin 38, 91, 162

R

Rabelais, François 26
Racine, Jean Baptiste 29, 95, 98
Rameau, Jean-Philippe 67
Rebellion of the Maillotins 23
Regency 143
Religious Wars 25
Renaissance 25, 45, 88, 102, 214
Renoir, Auguste 126, 167, 168
Résistance 37
Richelieu, cardinal 28, 61, 88, 133
Rive droite 45
Rive gauche 98
Robert, Hubert 150
Robespierre, Maximilien de 33, 72, 89
Rock Music **172-173**
Rodin, Auguste 102, 123
Rodin Museum 122
Roi des Coquillages 171
Romanesque style 92, 228
Romans 19, 228
Ronsard, Pierre 26
Rotonde 192
Rousseau, Jean-Jacques 30, 86
Rue Aubry 68
Rue Bonaparte 94
Rue Castiglione 63
Rue Champagne-Première 114
Rue Chaptal 161
Rue Charlot 185
Rue Crimée 194
Rue Crozatier 205
Rue d'Aligre 205
Rue d'Ankara 140
Rue de Belleville 198
Rue de Bercy 206
Rue de Buci 97

Rue de Charonne 202, 231
Rue de l'Abreuvoir 168
Rue de la Goutte d'Or 169
Rue de la Mare 197
Rue de la Parchemenerie 92
Rue de la Perle 184
Rue de l'Arbalète 102
Rue de la Roquette 201
Rue de l'Ermitage 197
Rue de Ménilmontant 197
Rue de Montorgueil 156
Rue de Pixérécourt 197
Rue de Rivoli 62
Rue des Archives 184
Rue des Blancs-Manteaux 185
Rue des Bons-Enfants 64
Rue des Eaux 140
Rue de Seine 97
Rue des Gravilliers 185
Rue des Lombards 70
Rue des Petits-Careaux 156
Rue des Picpus 208
Rue des Pyrénées 197
Rue des Saules 167
Rue des Vertus 186
Rue de Vaugirard 90
Rue du Faubourg Saint-Denis 189
Rue du Faubourg St.-Honoré 133
Rue du Mont Cenis 167
Rue du Parc Royal 183
Rue du Steinkerque 164
Rue du Télegraphie 197
Rue du Vieux Colombier 89
Rue Ferdinand Duval 73
Rue Flamel 70
Rue Jean-Henri Fabre 175
Rue Jules-Vallès 175
Rue Keller 202, 231
Rue Lepic 169
Rue Merlin 203
Rue Miguel Hilbage 195
Rue Mouffetard 102
Rue Myrha 169
Rue Paul-Bert 175
Rue Pernelle 70
Rue Piat 198
Rue Poulbot 166
Rue Ravignan 165
Rue Réaumur 157
Rue Royale 133
Rue Saint-André-des-Arts 97
Rue Saint-Antoine 73
Rue Saint-Denis 68, 157
Rue Saint-Martin 69
Rue Saint-Rustique 166
Rue Sidi Brahim 208
Rue Soufflot 87
Rue Tardieu 165
Rue Tronchet 132
Rue Vavin 114